Negotiating Age
Aging and Ageism in Contemporary
Literature and Theatre

Edited by Mária Kurdi

10.2478/9788367405423-toc

Table of Contents

Books by Mária Kurdi:

Nemzeti önszemlélet a mai ír drámában (1960-1990) [National Self-Portrait in Contemporary Irish Drama (1960-1990)]

Codes and Masks: Aspects of Identity in Contemporary Irish Plays in an Intercultural Context

Otthonkeresés a színpadon: Beszélgetések ír drámaírókkal [Searching for Home on the Stage: Talks with Irish Playwrights]

Representations of Gender and Female Subjectivity in Contemporary Irish Drama by Women

Kultúrák között. Magyar és más közép- és kelet-európai emigránsok a kortárs ír prózában és színpadon [Between Cultures: Hungarian and Other Central- and Eastern European Immigrants in Contemporary Irish Prose and on the Stage]

Approaches to Irish Theatre through a Hungarian's Lens

John Millington Synge: Az ír modernség drámaírója [John Millington Synge: Playwright of Irish Modernism]

Edited and Co-edited Books by Mária Kurdi:

HUSSE 3 Papers 1997 with József Horváth

Critical Anthology for the Study of Modern Irish Literature

Brian Friel's Dramatic Artistry "The Work Has Value" with Donald E. Morse and Csilla Bertha

Literary and Cultural Relations: Ireland, Hungary, and Central and Eastern Europe

The Binding Strength of Irish Studies. Festschrift in Honour of Csilla Bertha and Donald E. Morse with Marianna Gula and István D. Rácz

A színpadtól a színpadig. Válogatás Marvin Carlson színházi írásaiból [From the Stage to the Stage: Selections from the Theatre Writings of Marvin Carlson]

Radical Contemporary Theatre Practices by Women in Ireland with Miriam Haughton

Arthur Miller öröksége: centenáriumi írások műveiről [The Heritage of Arthur Miller: Centenary Writings about His Works]

"I love craft, I love the word": The Theatre of Deirdre Kinahan with Lisa Fitzpatrick

10.2478/9788367405423-fm

Praise for Maria Kurdi's *Negotiating Age*

"A fascinating collection of essays on one of the most important questions facing individuals, families, and communities: how to negotiate the aging process and to resist the harmful cultural stereotypes and discrimination against those entering the third age. The essays interweave recent theories of gerontology with thoughtful and engaging readings of the work of playwrights, theatre makers, and fiction writers, offering new insights into writers from Shakespeare to Irish and American dramatists and the novelists J. M. Coetzee and David Mitchell."

—Anna McMullan, author of *Samuel Beckett's Intermedial Ecosystems: Closed Space Environments across the Stage, Prose and Media Works* (2021) and *Performing Embodiment in Samuel Beckett's Drama* (2010).

"As aging is also social and performative, imaginative literature can provide an empathetic engagement with the experience of others, enhancing understanding and reducing stigma. With an impressive international range of subjects and contributors this collection addresses aging and ageism through a variety of texts distinguished by their courageous attempts to shed light on a condition too often shadowed by silence and marginalized through prejudice."

—Shaun Richards, co-author of *Mapping Ireland: Theories of Place and Space* (2013) and editor of *The Cambridge Companion of Twentieth-century Drama* (2004).

"Aging is a lifelong process. These essays explore multiple views of aging in several works giving us valuable insights as we engage in this lifelong process. This remarkable collection by an impressive group of scholars is a strong addition to age-related studies."

—Charlotte J. Headrick, co-editor of *Irish Women Dramatists 1908-2001* (2014).

NEGOTIATING AGE

Funding for this book has been provided by the Faculty of the Humanities, the Institute of English and American Studies, and the University of Debrecen

T·U·D·A

UNIVERSITY OF DEBRECEN
FACULTY OF HUMANITIES
SCHOLARLY FUND

ISBN 978-83-67405-42-3

Co-published by Debrecen University Press and Sciendo https://sciendo.com/book/9788367405423

10.2478/9788367405423-001

Preface

Mária Kurdi

As editor of the volume I am especially indebted to the authors, who have contributed essays which manage to bring fresh insights and relevant theoretical ideas to the scholarly discussion of literary works concerned with age, aging, and ageism as well as age-related clichés and stereotypes. Each of the essays follows arguments which open up new vistas for further research on aspects of the targeted subject in its complex ramifications. Equally, I am grateful to those members of the advisory board of the journal *HJEAS* who became involved in the peer-reviewing process of the papers, helping the authors by providing suggestions and recommendations for revising and improving their writings. Besides them, I owe thanks for the same reasons to fellow scholars Péter Dolmányos (Eszterházy Károly University, Eger), Judit Friedrich (Eötvös Loránd University, Budapest), Nicholas Grene (Trinity College Dublin), Csaba Maczelka (University of Pécs), Judit Molnár (University of Debrecen), Péter P. Müller (University of Pécs), Richard Rankin Russell (Baylor University, Texas), László B. Sári (University of Pécs), and Veronika Schandl (Pázmány Péter Catholic University, Budapest), who kindly complied with my request and participated in the work of peer-reviewing both conscientiously and effectively. I am also grateful to my one-time fellow university classmate Ferenc Kanyó, who generously offered a photo he had taken for the cover of the book. Last but not least, also on behalf of the authors of the included essays, my strongly expressed thanks go to Donald E. Morse, editor-in-chief of the New *HJEAS* Books Series, and István Rácz, editor of this collection, for the series, as well as

NEGOTIATING AGE

the University of Debrecen Press for the encouragement and help they gave me in the process of editing and publication.

10.2478/9788367405423-002

Acknowledgments

Five of the essays, "'No country, this, for old men': A View of the Aging Artist through Intertexts in J. M. Coetzee's *Disgrace*" by Angelika Reichmann; Noémi Albert's "'Life Is a Terminal Illness' The War against Time and Aging in David Mitchell's *The Bone Clocks*"; "Aging and Death in Edward Albee's *The Sandbox* and Tennessee Williams's *The Milktrain Doesn't Stop Here Anymore*" by Réka M. Cristian; "Old Age and Aging: Presence and Absence in the Plays of Brian Friel" by Giovanna Tallone and Ambika Singh's "'No Country for Old Men': A Poignant Portrayal of Aging and Ageism in Arthur Miller's *Mr. Peters' Connections*" have been published as a themed block in the Spring 2020 issue of the *Hungarian Journal of English and American Studies*. They are reprinted in this *HJEAS Book, Negotiating Age: Aging and Ageism in Contemporary Literature and Theatre* with the kind permission of Donald E. Morse, editor-in-chief of the journal *HJEAS* and the five authors themselves.

Christopher Murray's "Beckett and the Representation of Age on Stage" is an essay first published in the autumn 2006-winter 2007 issue of the *Princeton University Library Chronicle*, reprinted here in a slightly edited form with the kind permission of the author and the editors.

Special thanks to Jane Brennan, Alexandra Cann, and the Tom Murphy Literary Trust for their gracious permission for using the quotations from Tom Murphy's *Bailegangaire* in Csilla Bertha's "Tom Murphy's *Bailegangaire:* Transcending Despair in Old Age." All extracts written by Tom Murphy are copyright to the Tom Murphy Literary Trust.

Every effort has been made to trace the owners of copyright materials in this book, but in some instances this has proven impossible. The author and publisher will be glad to receive   information   leading   to   more   complete acknowledgments in subsequent printings of the book and in the meantime extend their apologies for any omissions.

Funding for this book has been provided by the Faculty of the Humanities, the Institute of English and American Studies, and the University of Debrecen.

10.2478/9788367405423-003

Introduction

Mária Kurdi

"Indeed, where once Freud suggested that sexuality lay at the heart of all our neuroses, and Erik Erikson later suggested that for the twentieth century our key problems, at a cultural and personal level, revolved around issues of identity, today it seems that our defining existential crisis is our fear of ageing and old age," a sociologist claims (Pickard 3). The majority of societies in the world today are challenged by the rapidly escalating phenomenon of an aging population with its unique problems and needs that tend to emerge after people have reached about seventy or more and call for being addressed both in daily life and in the realm of scientific research. From the end of the last century onward, age studies has developed as a comparatively new discourse within the humanities which, necessarily, is prone to explore crosscurrents between aging, feminism, gender, intersectionality, postcolonialism, class, dis/ability, and so on. Its widespread development has been supported by the realization that "of all body characteristics that have been employed to justify inequality—such as gender and race—age alone remains a 'fact' in both the popular and much of the intellectual imagination, and thus is all the more powerful for that" (Pickard 17). In 2010 the European Network in Aging Studies was founded to be closely followed by the launching of the North American Network in Aging Studies in 2013. Continuing the line, the Women and Ageing Research Network (WARN) became established after a major conference on the theme of Women and Ageing: New Cultural and Critical Perspectives, which took place at the University of Limerick in May 2015.

Among the prominent forums in the field, *The Journal of Women and Aging, The Journal of Aging Studies,* and *International Journal of Ageing and Later Life* came into being within the last few decades. Since their inception, they have been publishing articles that inquire into a considerable variety of issues pertaining to aging mainly from sociological and psychological angles. Following them, *Age, Culture, Humanities: An Interdisciplinary Journal* (2014-) begins its very first issue with the editors' column using the confident title "Age Studies Comes of Age." Here Cynthia Port and Aagje Swinnen introduce the ambitions of the new journal: "Our goal is to support a growing intellectual community that is developing humanities-based approaches to the study of age and employing them to help recalibrate cultural perceptions, generate new interpretive models, enrich the understanding of age, and, as a consequence, ultimately help enhance the lived process of aging across the lifespan." Also, the authors emphasize that work within the realm of Age Studies can lead to a potential intervention in the perpetuation of outdated views and cultural practices based on traditionally narrow ideas about aging and what it means and involves for individuals and societies: "Age is a facet of human experience that many—particularly in youth-centered Western cultures of the twenty-first century—are keen to resist, repress, or ignore. But failing to integrate age into our efforts to understand and interpret human experience leads to a distorted view that risks perpetuating ageist perspectives and policies and contributes to the widespread dread of getting older" (Port and Swinnen).

"Exploring the Boundaries of Literary Age Studies," an article by three scholars, reports about the results of "a roundtable at the MLA Convention in Philadelphia in January

INTRODUCTION

2017" (Swinnen et al. 19). Drawing on Sarah Falcus's relevant overview in the *Routledge Handbook of Cultural Gerontology*, they identify "a shift from the study of literary representations to more contextualized interpretations of aging in literature that, for example, question power dynamics in and surrounding literature as cultural practice or experiment with reader responses; a change from a focus on age as a particular crucial difference to an intersectional approach," stressing also that "literary age studies develops in tandem with cultural age studies, which is based on 'text' in the broadest sense" (23-24). Complementing this basis, analysts of representations of age, aging, and ageism in literature and the theatre agree that age is not merely a biological fact signaling the objective passage of time and the changes it eventuates but is also socially constructed and performative by nature, which undergirds the assumption that age is as significant a marker as gender, class, race, ethnicity, sexuality, and dis/ability for the understanding of patterns and shifts in both communal and personal identity.

In literary and theatre criticism, recently published monographs, essay collections, and special journal issues demonstrate the scholarly engagement with the ways in which age, aging, and ageism are portrayed while their ideological implications may become undermined. One of the pioneer critical volumes in the field, edited by Anne M. Wyatt-Brown and Janice Rossen under the title *Aging and Gender in Literature: Studies in Creativity* (1993), examines how the experience of growing older affects the career of writers and their aesthetic choices. Other aspects of the subject area are discussed by books such as *Adventures of the Spirit: The Older Woman in the Works of Doris Lessing, Margaret Atwood, and Other Contemporary Women Writers* (2007) edited by Phyllis Sternberg Perrakis, *Performing Age in Modern Drama* by Valerie Barnes

Lipscomb (2016), and Heather Ingman's *Ageing in Irish Writing: Strangers to Themselves* (2018), to mention just a few significant examples. Notably, the editors and authors of the above books and essay collections are women, suggesting that aging and its corollary might count as a gendered subject in both society and the world of letters or the performing arts.

The present collection of essays was conceived as a HJEAS Book after the successful debut of a themed block of five essays on age and aging in literature I had edited for the *Hungarian Journal of English and American Studies* in 2020, in which all the pieces were authored by women (from Hungary, Italy, and India). Interestingly, the works these scholars addressed came from male writers, while the aging protagonists constructed in them are both men and women. Indeed, aging does not always refer to characters being fairly advanced in years but can appear as an experience of any age group, underscoring, again, the culturally constructed and inculcated nature of experiencing one's age and the discourses which influence and contextualize it. To develop a book from the themed section of *HJEAS*, I included six new essays and a note about a recent and very timely theatre event in Ireland. This time the circle of authors contains some men, while among the literary or dramatic protagonists they investigate there are aging or age-conscious women, too, thus creating a more balanced and realistic structure as well as enhancing the variety of themes and approaches displayed by this collection. The essays are informed by selected up-to-date reference literature, theoretical and/or author-focused, and by observations of critical gerontology and international age studies. Also, the analyses demonstrate the importance of the subject area for writers, readers, and theatre audiences alike because of its conspicuously manifold relations to the actualities of their respective cultures, influenced and complicated by a network of fast-changing global tendencies. The volume opens with two essays that address ways of appropriating Shakespeare for the contemporary British stage. Kevin De Ornellas and Dónall Mac Cathmhaoill deal with the subject under the title "'You'll Get Old Sitting There': Contempt for Aged Males in Three 'Shakespearean' Works by Edward Bond." The authors posit the thesis that three plays by Edward Bond should be regarded as a loose trilogy, united because they all use the legacy of Shakespeare to provoke uncomfortable reflections on aging and ageism. So far, two Bond plays have been held by critics as attempts to engage with Shakespeare: *Lear* (1971), an appropriation of *King Lear*, and *Bingo* (1973), a bitter reflection of the dying Shakespeare on the worthlessness of his art. Beside these two, the authors of the essay consider the less well-known drama *The Worlds* (1979), an adaptation of *Timon of Athens*, thus completing the trilogy. Through this trio of plays the authors take a fresh look at Bond's inclination to address social concerns and show that here he cares specifically about those people who are marginalized and cast aside for the irrational reason of their age alone. In her "Moving Back from the Limelight: Aging and Ageism as the Shakespearean Actor's Tragedy in Ronald Harwood's *The Dresser*" (1980) Kinga Földváry argues that by its self-reflexivity of performance this play, although a comedy, is closely connected to Shakespeare's *King Lear* both as a textual heritage and because it evokes aspects of performance tradition. Harwood's aged and dying actor character, Sir's, nostalgic reminiscences of his theatrical past revolve around Shakespeare. The other protagonist, the titular "dresser" called Norman, is considered as a liminal figure, a mediator between illusion and reality, who always takes a pragmatic view and survives the symbiotic relationship with his master. Földváry also makes account of the variety of recent interpretational contexts to Harwood's play inspired by Shakespeare and briefly discusses a recent film adaptation of *The Dresser* directed by Richard Eyre and starring Anthony Hopkins in 2015.

Next there follow a group of essays which inquire into age-related issues in Irish drama from Beckett to Conor McPherson. As noted by many, the great majority of Beckett's stage characters are old, and if not actually old such as Lucky in *Godot* (1953) or Clov in *Endgame* (1957), they seem to have lost youth before enjoying any of it. Christopher Murray's "Beckett and the Representation of Age on Stage" confirms that his work is a point of reference for most of the Irish playwrights coming after him also in the field of depicting age and the relentless passage of time. In this essay, Murray presents the argument that Beckett's drama is for a "new age" because it defies the conventions of realistic playwriting while it weaves age into its thematic strands in new ways. As always in his eminent scholarship, Murray builds up a broad dramatic context to focus on Beckett's innovations. The critic offers a panorama of Irish playwrights and their concern with age, among whom he makes references also to Shaw's increasingly complex engagement with age, to *Back to Methuselah* (1921) in particular, and justifiably so. In this marathon drama, Shaw sarcastically posits that Englishmen should live much longer than they do because they are still boys when they die and would need more time to reach maturity. Surveying Beckett's aged characters, Murray reveals the great variety of ways in which the author undermines, ironizes, even ridicules the conventionally realistic or sentimental portrayals of old people, while occasional lyricism is not missing from the playwright's treatment of the theme either. On the whole, the essay takes a fresh look even at the much analyzed Beckettian plays, mobilized by Murray's enormous knowledge of the Irish and international theatre scenes, past and present, which he elaborates on in a both elegant and enjoyable style. The pivotal nature of this piece is also confirmed by the omnipresence of Beckett in the collection not excepting the chapter on fiction where J. M. Coetzee's use of Beckettian intertexts (among other modernist ones) becomes highlighted.

Csilla Bertha in her essay focuses on one play, *Bailegangaire* (1985) by Tom Murphy, whose old and bedridden central female character is often compared by scholars of Irish drama to Beckett's old and senile women or associated with the many different versions of Mother Ireland figures on the Irish stage. Titled "Tom Murphy's *Bailegangaire*: Transcending Despair in Old Age," Bertha's work has chosen a new angle for her in-depth analysis: from theories of aging she borrows the term "gerotranscendence" to approach Mommo's fragmented and staggering reminiscences of a life full of hardships and losses but at rare times also enlivened by flashes of joy and humor. Bertha observes a pattern of circularity in the old woman's story which is about a homeward journey from decades before, taken physically yet proving to be also metaphorical as the author's perceptive elaboration on the details confirms. Basically, in her broken narration Mommo is struggling with herself, as Bertha argues, and the nowhere-going circularity is changed into forward-looking linearity with the help of the old woman's granddaughters. This allows Mommo to achieve gerotranscendence in the form of moral and spiritual liberation from her depressing psychic burdens by the end of her life whereas, Bertha reminds us, transforming power is also the essence of theatre. Flanking Bertha's paper "Old Age and Aging: Presence and Absence in the Plays of Brian Friel" by

Giovanna Tallone considers the role of portraying age or only the subjective feeling of it as well as the fate of the older characters in some of Friel's plays, from *The Enemy Within* (1962) to *Dancing at Lughnasa* (1990), including *Aristocrats* (1979) among others, all of which are grounded in the historical changes of Ireland at the time when the action takes place. Tallone argues that the dramatist exploits the interaction of presence and absence as an important ingredient of his stagecraft in exposing the various conditions of aging and old age in relation to the Irish socio-cultural problems and constraints which admittedly shape the characters' temperament and behavior.

The closing two essays on age-related themes in Irish theatre focus on younger playwrights Martin McDonagh's and Conor McPherson's works, which introduce new forms of writing yet borrow from traditions especially when probing into the implications of age matters on stage. In "The Tyranny of the Old: Destructive Generational Relations in Brian Friel's *Lovers* and Martin McDonagh's *The Beauty Queen of Leenane*," David Clare and Mária Kurdi argue that *The Beauty Queen* (1996) stands apart from the author's other works set in Ireland as it blends different modes, embracing the tragic among them. The essay departs from the observation that McDonagh takes on and twists traditional postcolonial themes like parental dominance and continues to explore affinities between Friel's *Lovers* (1967) and *The Beauty Queen*. It is demonstrated that the plays critique the inherent destructiveness of the strict moral rules that the respective old mother figures embody by sticking to the surviving rigid ideals and expectations of the past. McDonagh uses a dual timeline with the 1990s superimposed over the 1950s, which the authors of the essay interpret as signaling the fact that the hyper-Catholic false piety and hypocrisy presented in *Lovers* through the aged characters have lived on into postmodern Ireland leading to family violence and tragedy. The other younger playwright, Conor McPherson, features in the last essay on representation of age in the contemporary Irish theatre. In "Perspectives on Lifespan and Regeneration in the Plays of Conor McPherson," Maha Alatawi and Eamonn Jordan consider a range of plays by McPherson from across his career, deliberating how characters negotiate and navigate through the issues of ageing and age-related stereotypes. Alatawi and Jordan express the view that while the Irish playwriting tradition is predominantly past-orientated, McPherson's dramaturgy re-imagines that positioning more towards the present, as well as the future. The essay argues that aging in McPherson is dramatized not as vulnerability, decline, debilitation, mourning over the loss of youth, or degeneration but as the achievement of a state comfortable with death resulting from a recuperative, celebratory, and consolidating consciousness, prompted by acceptance and generosity.

In the next section, devoted to American drama, "Aging and Death in Edward Albee's *The Sandbox* and Tennessee Williams's *The Milktrain Doesn't Stop Here Anymore*" by Réka M. Cristian compares aging women characters in the respective shorter plays of these major American playwrights. Cristian identifies differences in the dramatic construction of two selected women, yet she concludes that although different perspectives on aging and death are revealed through them, both plays offer transgressive images of aging and thus contribute to the ways and means of representing this complex and sensitive subject in the theatre and beyond. The title of Ambika Singh's essay, "'No Country for Old Men': A Poignant Portrayal of Aging and Ageism in Arthur Miller's *Mr. Peters'*

Connections," quotes Yeats in the title, the protagonist of the Miller play, Harry Peters, being really old, a retired pilot who, apparently, is no longer able to distinguish incoherent images criss-crossing his mind from reality. Considering the drama in the context of some earlier works of the playwright, the author of the essay argues that a lineage of protagonists of this kind is traceable across Miller's oeuvre, beginning with Willy Loman in *Death of a Salesman* (1949). Therefore, Singh notes, the thesis that playwrights place aged characters in the center of drama when they have already started to feel the weight of their own years does not hold true. Peters in *Mr. Peters' Connections* (1999) obsessively repeats the question what the "subject" is, until finally he realizes that perhaps "love" is the subject he has been searching for. In the concluding part of her essay, Singh opines that the combined articulation of both ambiguity and hope connects *Mr. Peters' Connections* also to Miller's other later plays such as *The Ride Down Mt. Morgan* (1991) and *Broken Glass* (1994).

In the section of essays investigating the main subject in fiction, "'No country, this, for old men': A View of the Aging Artist through Intertexts in J. M. Coetzee's *Disgrace*" by Angelika Reichmann deals with the age-related anxieties of David Lurie, a scholar of English Romanticism in *Disgrace* (1999). Reichmann's usage of the same Yeatsian intertext as Singh has chosen for the title of her essay serves to introduce not old-age dementia but the anxieties of the middle-aged intellectual protagonist. The author claims that aging and the evident approaching of death in the novel also function as images of the shared condition and fate of humans and animals, which is particularly relevant in the post-apartheid world of South Africa. Reichmann explores the ways in which intertextual references to modernist literary works, most poignantly borrowings from the poetry of W. B. Yeats and T. S. Eliot as well as the fiction of Dostoevsky, underpin and complicate, by highlighting negative stereotypes of aging, the representation of the joint crisis of the individual and the South African white community itself. Noémi Albert's essay, "'Life Is a Terminal Illness': The War against Time and Aging in David Mitchell's *The Bone Clocks*," analyzes how this novel, published in 2014, brings together by sophisticated fictional devices the personal level of aging as part of the protagonist, the writer Holly Sykes's, life course and the threateningly fast pace of humankind marching towards its self-extinction. The essay charts the structure of the narrative leading up to 2043 while it also explores the possibilities of the surreal in its narrative style, which enables Mitchell to distinguish and contrast two starkly opposed world-views, those of the Horologists and the Anchorites, revealed in their combat for dominating humankind's present-day attitudes and "future destinies," to borrow an expression from one of the titles of another contemporary writer of fiction, the Canadian Chris Turner.

In the "Coda" of the book, "'Who are you?': Notes on Aging and Dementia in Frank McGuinness's *The Visiting Hour* (2021)" by Donald E. Morse leads the reader to a very recent work, conceived and premiered during the COVID19 lockdown period. The play is emotionally gripping and prompts one to associate dementia with a kind of lockdown and lockdown with a kind of dementia, both damaging humankind in serious ways. Morse contextualizes this drama in McGuinness's oeuvre as one which focuses on the precarious emotional ties between the protagonists, a man living in a nursing home and his daughter visiting him during the pandemic when inmates and their relations could only meet separated by a window. These

"Notes" elaborate on the disjunctions of communication between father and daughter, for which mainly the chaotic and false memories of the old man were responsible, who, heartrendingly, is sometimes unable to recognize his own child. Singing can bring them together momentarily, which Morse places in the context of how much songs are loved and personalized in Ireland, illustrated by referring to Joyce's *A Portrait of the Artist as a Young Man* (1916). Although *The Visiting Hour* ends with the daughter's departure and the father's utter exhaustion, their using the same closing words may give some hope, Morse suggests. However, the author refers to Christopher Murray's idea that theater holds a "mirror up to nation" as applicable to this very personal play as well in that it calls attention to dementia and what it can do to family relationships, ultimately generating wide-scale social problems that demand public attention. Morse's "Notes" form an appropriate coda to a collection of essays which would like to be an eye-opener on the subject area it embraces, in addition to its contribution to literary and theatre criticism.

Works Cited

Murray, Christopher. *Twentieth-Century Irish Drama: Mirror up to Nation.* Manchester: Manchester University Press, 1997.

Pickard, Susan. *Age Studies: A Sociological Examination of How We Age and are Aged through the Life Course.* London: Sage, 2016.

Port, Cynthia, and Aagje Swinnen. "Editors' Column: Age Studies Comes of Age." *Age, Culture, Humanities: An Interdisciplinary Journal* 1 (2014). Web. 25 June 2022.

Swinnen, Aagje, Cynthia Port, and Valerie Barnes Lipscomb. "Exploring the Boundaries of Literary Age Studies."

INTRODUCTION

Frame 30.1 (May 2017): 19-30.

10.2478/9788367405423-004

Part I
Contemporary Adaptations of Shakespeare

"You'll Get Old Sitting There": Contempt for Aged Males in Three "Shakespearean" Works by Edward Bond
Kevin De Ornellas and Dónall Mac Cathmhaoill

> *"Time goes. I'm surprised how old I've got."*
> *Edward Bond,* Bingo

Introduction: Bond's "Shakespearean" trilogy about aged men

It is argued that three plays by Edward Bond, born in 1934, should be regarded as a loose trilogy—and that the plays are united because they use the legacy of Shakespeare to provoke uncomfortable reflections on aging and ageism. Two Bond plays are renowned for addressing the vexed legacy of Shakespeare head-on. *Lear* (1971) is an uncompromising appropriation of *King Lear* in which Bond "corrects" Shakespeare's too-casual treatment of the under-represented effects of the mad king's actions on the poor of the mismanaged kingdom of Britain; *Bingo* (1973) is a bitter depiction of a dying Shakespeare who realizes that his art has been worthless because it has done nothing to frustrate murderous inequalities in post-Tudor England. It is less well-known that *The Worlds* (1979) is also a Shakespearean adaptation—the story of an arrogant company director, Trench, who loses his position and degenerates into a rabid, destructive, tramp-like, terrorist-supporting misanthrope, is an adaptation of *Timon of Athens*. *Bingo* is a quasi-biographical conceit; the other two plays are radical appropriations.

CONTEMPORARY ADAPTATIONS OF SHAKESPEARE

Julie Sanders's definition of appropriation as opposed to mere adaptation is important here: "Appropriation frequently effects a more decisive journey away from the informing text into a wholly new cultural product and domain" (26). [1] In other words, appropriations, such as those by Bond, are new works in their own right—they are not adaptations of Shakespeare but radical new plays contrived to perpetuate Bond's theatrical, political, and moral vision. Many critics have written about Bond's engagement with Shakespeare—especially *Lear* and *Bingo*—but none have afforded *The Worlds* the same attention as the previous two. (*The Sea*, Bond's play from 1973, refers clearly to elements of *The Tempest*. However, that play cannot be said to be an overt appropriation of a Shakespeare work in the way that *Lear* and *The Worlds* both are.)

Crucially, critics have, understandably, concentrated on the quasi-Brechtian staging techniques in Bond's plays as well as the blistering, uncompromisingly leftist critiques of historical and contemporary economic and social inequalities, but none have addressed the arguably more humanistic issue of ageism. This is important because the lead characters in the three plays are all victims of ferocious ageism: despite his callousness, Bond's Lear is a man more sinned against than sinning because his aged impotence and alleged senescence are met with even more overt contempt than in Shakespeare's original; Shakespeare, in *Bingo*, is openly mocked for willful inactivity by his supposed friend, Ben Jonson, and by his shrewish daughter, Judith; and Trench, in *The Worlds*, is revered when fit to run his

---

1 Sara Munson Deats also usefully clarifies the differences between "adaptation" and "appropriation" in *The Faust Legend: From Marlowe and Goethe to Contemporary Drama and Film* (Cambridge: Cambridge University Press, 2020) 7-8. For some practical assistance in the production of this essay, we thank Anoush Simon.

company but ruthlessly marginalized and discarded when he is forcibly retired from his own executive board. The descent into psychological torment that all three lead characters endure is directly related to ageism. Aging is almost entirely presented as a cause for scorn and derision in these plays. Bond generally sidesteps any sense of aging well: in his plays, good aging cannot be bought. The three leading characters addressed in this essay do improve as people—but only within themselves and in a manner unnoticed and/or unappreciated by their contemporaries.

The plays are set variously in ancient Britain, in Jacobean England and in late-1970s Britain: it is widely acknowledged that Bond rightly or wrongly sees consistent economic discrimination across these vastly different eras—it should, we argue, also be apparent that Bond sees bigotry towards the aged as being another social malady that is consistent across centuries and even millennia. Shakespeare's plays are full of reflection on aging and on inter-generational conflict: characters in Shakespeare plays often "retire": King Lear relinquishes his kingship, Lady Macbeth skulks off and gives up on public life, and Prospero breaks his staff. Across his three plays, Bond appropriates Shakespearean meditations on aging and juxtaposes them with his own observations about society's disregard for those who are no longer economically productive.

Lear: From kingship to shovel—the decline of aged Lear

Lear, Bond's quasi-Brechtian, epic play of 1971, is framed by two contrasting events involving a wall. Lear is a despotic king, a man obsessed with enemies within and without. He is pursuing an unending building process: to build a giant wall around his kingdom. It is a monomaniacal pursuit, a depraved obsession that does nothing to add to the kingdom's security but does much to convey to us the closed nature of Lear's heart and mind. Building the wall uses up vast resources—Simon Trussler almost anthropomorphizes the wall when he describes its "insatiable demands for manpower" (22). The hopeless, Sisyphean job to build the complete wall recalls various, ultimately unsuccessful, efforts to build permanent walls in British history—Hadrian's Wall, Offa's Dyke, and various Saxon wall remains in East Anglia are obvious models—and Leslie Smith compares Lear's wall more specifically to certain East Anglian earthworks (73). Nonetheless, from a twenty-first-century perspective it is hard to look at Lear's meritless wall and not think about the "peace walls" that still scar Belfast, and it is especially hard to not think about Donald Trump's perpetually hyped but never realized border wall with Mexico.

Lear's role in the wall-building is determined, hands-on. And unforgiving. In the first scene, he personally shoots dead a supposed slacker—it is an unjust and counterproductive act that leads to the revelation that his daughters are plotting against him. Their shared contempt for the military uselessness of the wall and its ruinous impact upon the State's finances motivates them to do deals with the supposed enemies outside the wall. The fact that they in turn will become at least as murderous and totalitarian as their father is beside the point. The point is that building the wall has been a lifelong mania for Lear. "I started this wall when I was young," he asserts (3). The obvious implication is that he is not young now. He has aged with the wall—and it will outlast him: "My people will live behind this wall when I'm dead," he predicts, a little vaingloriously (3). So, the wall is at once a symbol of Lear's misguided life and a vanity project that will, he thinks, bring glory to him even in death. It is a wall contrived to defy aging—the wall can thwart aging and death and render him immortal. As Debra A. Castillo paraphrases Lear's glib thinking, the wall should facilitate "the continuance of polite society, of civilization, of a polished and perfect state that would be peaceful even if governed by fools" (80). Lear's two daughters, Bodice and Fontanelle, effectively stage a coup as soon as Lear shoots the supposed slacker.

Lear's fall is immediate; his intellectual decline is even more melodramatic and speedy than it is in Shakespeare's version of the story. He degenerates quickly into a sort of hobo character, an itinerant nobody who is haunted by regret and failure. His self-consciousness about aging is one of the few constants in his now-fractured existence. He is enduring a sort of living death. He claims that "I'm old and too weak to climb out of this grave again" (Bond, *Lear* 17). It is an almost Gothic image—a bleak meditation on a life ruined by familial treachery and defined by a realization that his rule was one of misguided authoritarianism that felt right to him when he was the one doing the terrorizing. Now, metaphorically, he is already in "my coffin" and his hate-filled daughters "tell me to die" (17). The monosyllabic language suggests the simplicity and constancy of Lear's thoughts: aging and death are the only things that he can think about.

This obsessive simplicity of fatalistic discourse is repeated in act 1, scene 6: a family that Lear has been staying with (he helps to manage their pigs) is attacked by a one-time lickspittle of Lear's—the now-deranged Warrington. Upon seeing this unholy reminder of the past, Lear says that "I'll die! I've seen a ghost. I'm going to die. That's why he came back. I'll die" (22). This formula of simple words expresses both a rational sense of mortality and an irrational sense of continued self-worth. Temporarily at least, Lear is over-looking his vexed legacy as an incompetent and tyrannical ruler. A local Boy gives Lear some updates about the wall: it is being pulled down, he asserts, quite triumphantly. He goes on to recall the horrors of building it—"living in a grave" (25). The squalor of working in the mud to advance the pointless wall will remind most audience members of the Great War malady of trench foot: "feet used to swell with the mud. The stick of it even when you were asleep," the Boy recalls, bitterly (25). Sleep offers no respite from the horrors of building the wall. There is substantial dramatic irony here: the Boy does not know that Lear is the former king. He believes that he is articulating the thoughts of one bruised, exploited nobody to a fellow nobody. In a sense he is, but what really matters is that the wall has had a nefarious effect on Lear's country—building it has caused people to live lives that feel like living deaths. Although the outcast Lear now has no responsibility, he is confronted with his abysmal legacy of counterproductive exploitation of men and resources. He has tried to somehow defy aging and mortality by building an ageless wall—but the wall subsequently becomes a symbol of his impotence and of the folly of one of his successor rulers, Cordelia, who commences work on the wall. (This Cordelia is not a relative of Lear—Bond's play is a truly radical appropriation of Shakespeare's).

Lear, who has survived various judicial and quasi-paramilitary attacks by rabid servants of his daughters and who has been brutally blinded, now only lives for a substantial period and even develops a cult following in the rural community that has adopted him. [2] Eventually, he has a meeting with the remorseless Cordelia. He tells her not to continue building the wall. She responds with the sort of

---

2 The technological nature of the cruelty inflicted on Lear is described and analysed effectively by Simon Shepherd, *The Cambridge Introduction to Modern British Theatre* (Cambridge: Cambridge University Press, 2009) 168.

monosyllabic, determined simple-mindedness that defined Lear's misrule: "We must" (84). It is a simplistic and brainless totalitarian response; as David L. Hirst reminds us, "Bond's condemnation of totalitarianism is unsparing" (135). Cordelia offers no real rational explanation for the necessity of the wall: as Lear himself states, she is continuing his legacy of irrational fear of putative enemies. Crucially, his late-life campaign against the wall has slowed down Lear's aging process. Indeed, he even fantasizes about holding off aging: "I have only one more wish—to live till I'm much older," he declares (85). He wants to impart wisdom, to teach—to make people realize the folly of material and metaphorical wall-building.

The climax recalls, with deep irony, the shooting incident at the start of the play, when Lear outrageously shot dead an alleged idler at the wall. The blinded, elderly Lear, armed with a shovel, decides to physically dismantle the wall and, with comic understatement, says: "I'm not as fit as I was" (88). It is gesture politics—and a fatal mistake because as soon as Lear breaks ground with his shovel, a hired hand of Cordelia summarily shoots him dead. The man who once shot people for not building the wall is killed quickly enough for trying to dismantle it.

The stage directions tell us that the shovel "*stays upright in the earth*" (88). Unlike Lear the shovel is erect, potent, but its symbolism might be more complex than is sometimes claimed. The symbolism of this scene has exercised Bond for half a century. As recently as April 2021, Bond, on his (excellent and substantial) website, railed against an academic who, Bond felt, had misrepresented the scene as being an absurdist symbol of futility and the pointlessness of confronting behemoths of injustice such as wage enslavement and prejudice ("Rough Notes"). The academic might regard the shovel as being an ironic symbol of potency—its strength and potential mocks Lear's aged impotence. But if one sees the shovel in less ironic terms we may align our thoughts more closely with Bond's. Bond insists that Lear's attempt to dismantle the wall is not futile because it offers hope, light, a pathway forward. The shovel may remind some audience members of the mid-seventeenth-century offshoot of the Levellers: the Diggers sect. [3] "The Diggers' Song" of *circa* 1649 proudly and repetitively suggests that spades and hoes are phallic symbols of a collective agrarian will to power—a proto-Communistic forerunner of the hammer and sickle that Bond might approve of (Woudhuysen 464-66). If we see Lear's shovel as being an extension of him rather than an ironic counterpart to him then we can think that Lear's agedness is not a useless agedness after all. Once psychologically encased within his wall and now physically aged and decrepit, Lear has managed to transcend decline to present to us an image of a better future—a future when genuine change can happen with wo/men using whatever tools they can to challenge the self-serving but destructive wall-building mania of tyrants. Once murderous and inept, Lear has aged surprisingly well: he dies not as an old fool but as an old hero.

Cast in this light, one can regard the contempt shown the elderly Lear as both the driver of his radical change and his redemption. The final shovel standing proud in the earth points to a more nuanced and politically charged reading of the final scene. The circumstances of Lear's death are rich in irony, but his legacy offers hope, the shovel representative of his

---

3 For one of several comprehensive studies of Gerard Winstanley's Diggers movement, see John Gurney, *Brave Community: The Digger Movement in the English Revolution* (Manchester: Manchester University Press, 2007).

conversion from authoritarian builder of walls to destroyer of walls.

Bingo: Shakespeare's willful catatonia and premature death
With its claustrophobic, small-town setting, its comparatively small number of characters, and its stress on the stifling gloom of life lived bitterly within a loveless family, *Bingo* seems like a chamber piece compared to the epic *Lear*. In *Bingo*, Bond effectively lifts some of the follies and aged vulnerabilities of Lear and projects them onto *King Lear*'s dramatist: William Shakespeare. The play, which was first performed at the Northcott Theatre, Devon, on November 13, 1973, depicts, unusually, a psychologically empty life and pitiful death of Shakespeare in 1616.

Fictional depictions of Shakespeare tend to be comic or rousing or at least affirmative in some way. For example, the American-made short film, *Master Will Shakespeare* (1936) presents Shakespeare as a sort of triumphant cowboy, an enterprising lone ranger who strolled into London town and took over the place. Similarly, *Will Shakespeare*, a John Mortimer-written television drama series from 1978, shows the dynamic upward trajectory of a supremely energetic man who is humbly holding horses for theatre patrons then swiftly replacing Christopher Marlowe as London's literary darling, seemingly within days. Many depictions are purely comic: G. B. Shaw's *Shakes versus Shav* (1949) is a puppet play that depicts a hysterically arrogant Shakespeare; in the *Doctor Who* story *The Shakespeare Code* (2007), Shakespeare is iconoclastically presented as a bad-breathed sex pest; and in the ongoing BBC sitcom, *Upstart Crow* (2016-present), Shakespeare is dramatized, reductively but amusingly, as an ordinary but vain man who is obsessed with trivialities such as baldness and poor public transport.

The film *All is True* (2018), directed by and starring Kenneth Branagh, is unusual in that it does dramatize the aging and ailing Shakespeare. *All is True*, however, is affirmative because Shakespeare uses the period of his decline to effectively remarry his hitherto embittered wife, to grow a garden, to fight accusations of slander against his daughter, Susanna, to make up with and inspire the writing career of his other daughter, Judith, to reflect proudly on the scale of his theatrical achievements, and to lay to rest the ghost of his son, Hamnet. It is an inverse version of the *Hamlet* narrative. The crucial point is that in *All is True*, Shakespeare is presented to us as someone we would like—a liberal and generous man, a man supportive of women's writing, a man untouched by the bigotry of his age, a loving father, and, ultimately, a loyal husband. It is an affirmative, Bardolatrous construction of a Shakespeare we can admire in the twenty-first century West. *Bingo* runs counter to all of those other depictions of Shakespeare: in *Bingo*, Bond delivers a bleak depiction of a Shakespeare who is defined by a sense of worthlessness that comes partly from community contempt for his lost powers. Simon Jones describes Bond's Shakespeare as "lonely and failed" (452). Simply, in *Bingo*, Shakespeare has, by and large, not aged well.

Bingo is a play that is contrived to move slowly in terms of narrative and in terms of its protagonist's slowness of thought and physical inactivity. Some melodramatic events occur in the play: an executed body (the Young Woman) is gibbeted, displayed; local people campaign vigorously against a land Enclosure that Shakespeare has passively facilitated; a mentally unhinged individual (the Old Man) is shot in a confused scuffle;

and Shakespeare kills himself in a sordid and anti-climactic scene. But with the exception of the deliberately underwhelming demise of Shakespeare, these events happen just offstage. As Michael Patterson writes, *Bingo*'s "overall mood is contemplative rather than theatrical" (415). Michael Billington characterizes Bond's Shakespeare as being "brooding, largely silent . . . Sitting wanly" (228). This is an unresponsive Shakespeare who is almost impervious to any stimulant. He responds only vaguely to traumatic events that do not directly concern him. Significantly, the stage directions tell us that Shakespeare sits *"facing away from the body"* of the displayed, dead Young Woman (Bond, *Plays: Three* 35). The point is that Shakespeare, to his moral and psychological detriment, just does not engage with the injustices of the Jacobean society that he has flourished in.

Shakespeare shows no emotion when the Old Man dies and barely notices the plight of the doomed Young Woman even when she begs at his very house. He is also blithely indifferent to the catastrophic consequences of the Enclosure act for the local poor—an act that he facilitates by blithely agreeing to legally allow the instigator, William Combe, to use Shakespeare's personal land as part of the Enclosed complex. Shakespeare is not an evil character as such; rather, he is massively disengaged from the suffering endured by the have-nots of his era. The play, slowly, progresses two thematic developments simultaneously: Shakespeare ages and declines with remarkable speed; at the same time, his insight into his own feckless apathy increases. A cliché of tragedy since the Greek era is that tragic heroes achieve more insight about their own follies and turpitude as their public standing plummets. This play, then, might be thought of as a tragedy in that Shakespeare's insights into his own failings increase in inverse proportion to the decline of his self-esteem and the increasingly hysterical revulsion for him by his own family. The fundamental tragedy is that Shakespeare realizes that he has done nothing to help others, only when it is too late—his literary powers, or at least, his motivation and drive to write, have burnt out.

Shakespeare already feels old at the start of the play, but his increasing sense of an irrevocable trajectory towards death is the only fast-moving force in the play. So *Bingo* is essentially a play about the deleterious effects of aging: effects that are almost parodically exaggerated. Shakespeare, after all, cannot be said to have been old during the period of the play's setting, 1614-16. This is not a history play, although the controversial Enclosure attempt referred to is historically documented. It is a play about the fictitious psychology of an individual who was fêted but who now feels impotent, useless, and who embraces physical and mental decline and literally has a distressing death wish—the suicide is, of course, entirely fictional. Early in the play, Shakespeare's shrewish daughter, Judith, slates Shakespeare for his lack of physical exertion: "You'll get old sitting there all day," she asserts excoriatingly (26). Shakespeare responds with pointed monosyllables: "I am old" (26). It is a simple exchange that will define the play: Shakespeare, barely fifty years old, has already retired from literary and public life. Bereft of ambition, he will do nothing in Stratford-upon-Avon except wither and expire. It is a self-fashioned, willful decline. As his decrepitude develops, his sense that his life's work failed to intervene in public wellbeing increases conterminously. It is an artistically contrived balance managed by Bond: Shakespeare's life force decreases as his insight into his work's pointlessness increases. The play never moves fast in terms of plot but Shakespeare's personal decline is rapid—indeed, the speed of Shakespeare's decline can be gauged by his self-pitying comments about aging, self-pitying comments that are articulated in each of the play's six scenes.

Shakespeare both embraces and fears aging. His world in Stratford-upon-Avon is, aside from the occasional, hysterical ejaculations of highly-strung characters such as the doomed Young Woman, the Puritan firebrand (the Son), and the mentally deranged Old Man, quiet, still, almost sterile in its lifelessness. Indeed, one of the first stage directions instructs directors to depict an atmosphere of *"Emptiness and silence"* (15). Shakespeare does very little—actors playing the role must exhibit great discipline by curtailing all unnecessary body movements; this is an almost parodically slowed-down Shakespeare. He tells Combe that "I weed a bit. I get tired" (18). His sense of economic impotence is expressed early on too: asserting that he cannot take any financial risks because he can no longer earn, he reflects on his father, who "went bankrupt when he was old" (21). Shakespeare is haunted by memories of his aged, irresponsible father. Perhaps it is because of his own contempt for his late father that Shakespeare tolerates the scolding of his daughter, Judith, who is perpetually frustrated by Shakespeare's emotional unavailability and his activity-dodging, supine disposition. Judith laments: "Why d'you make it necessary for a child to speak to its parents in this way?" (31) In abnegating his patriarchal rule, Shakespeare is almost becoming childish—the concept of Shakespeare's "second childhood" is, perhaps, one of the more pedestrian tropes of what is a disturbing play that so viciously attacks complacent assumptions about Shakespeare's supposed benevolence.

Scene 4 is crucial: Shakespeare has a drinking binge with Ben Jonson. In the reverent Branagh film, *All Is True*, the drinking scene with Jonson is affirmative and cozy because

Jonson praises and extols Shakespeare's genius. But in Bond's irreverent play, Jonson can express only contempt for Shakespeare's disengagement from creative life. Shakespeare repeatedly articulates negative words to Jonson such as "No" and "Nothing" and says bluntly that he has "Nothing to say" (43). Perennially conscious of mortality, Shakespeare tells the half-listening, intoxicated Jonson, "Time goes. I'm surprised how old I've got" (45). The latter clause is a trifle ambiguous. Does Shakespeare mean that he is surprised that it is 1616 already and that he is already fifty-two? Or is he surprised at how aged and decrepit he feels? Either way, it is clear that Shakespeare's bitterness is to an extent shared by Jonson, who complains about a range of matters including financial hardship and growing up fatherless. Jonson projects a sort of wisdom onto Shakespeare—a wisdom that Shakespeare does not have. Sarcastically, he applauds Shakespeare for knowing "when it is time to die" (48). "At least you're dying," he says to Shakespeare (48). It is important that this life-hating rhetoric is articulated by Jonson as well as by Shakespeare: when the two greatest playwrights of the era are so blatantly unsatisfied by their art and their lives it is apparent that this society is a broken and heartless one. The last two scenes depict Shakespeare's profoundly unheroic death. He catches a chill in the snow, observing meanwhile that this will be "perhaps the last snow I'll see" (56). He says that he "didn't want to die." The use of past tense is pointed: it means, of course, that now he does want to die.

In the last scene, we have a bedroom death scenario that is reminiscent of the death scenes in some of Shakespeare's plays: the sepulchral atmosphere brings to mind the tomb scene of *Romeo and Juliet*, and the catastrophic lack of communication between Shakespeare and his ignored wife reminds one of the non-meeting of minds between Othello and Desdemona. Shakespeare dies despising himself for not doing anything to help England's poor and abused. "I could have done so much," he mumbles to the Son, who expresses no interest in Shakespeare's words (62). Once England's greatest showman and impresario, Shakespeare has no audience at all now. And he has done nothing for that past audience rather than entertain them and reinforce the status quo of exploitation, division, and state-sanctioned murder of dissident thinkers. Shakespeare degenerates into a King Lear-like confusion about his status: "How long have I been dead?" he asks in soliloquy (65). Shakespeare literally dies with a whimper—as is made clear in the stage directions (66). Indeed, it is only in the stage directions that we learn that *Shakespeare has killed himself* (66); we don't even get to clearly see the once-great man take his own life. It is a massive, deliberate anti-climax. Shakespeare has petered out. He has accelerated his own aging process and eventually resorted to self-murder. Shakespeare's simultaneous contempt for his once-lucrative career and fatalistic response to aging manifests similarly in the character of the third of Bond's Shakespeare-related, aging-scarred male figures: Trench.

The Worlds: Trench's hysterical reaction to enforced retirement

Timon of Athens is, on one level, the simplest of Shakespearean narratives: a rich man is surrounded by fawning friends; he loses his money; his friends disappear; he spends the rest of the play cursing his one-time associates and railing against humanity in general; and he helps guerrillas attack his once-loved Athens. For *The Worlds*, a play that was initially performed by Bond-directed university students at Newcastle on March 8, 1979, Bond lifted this simple narrative and transplanted it into late 1970s, industrial strife-afflicted Britain. [4] Trench is the Timon figure: he begins the play as an apparently loved Chief Executive of his own company TCC; he soon loses that position; his friends ensure that he is properly marginalized; he loses his sense of reason; and he eventually helps terrorists to attack his old company and, by extension, capitalism in general. As well as the temporal and geographical change in setting there is one main innovation in Bond's handling of the Timon narrative: his character, Trench, is seen to be a victim of aging and, specifically, of society's prejudice against and contempt for those who are no longer economically useful.

Trench is an egoist. He begins the play festooned with vainglorious riches, self-praising his thirty-year rise from post-War obscurity to moneyed pomp. In the first four sentences of the play—all short sentences—he says "I" four times and "me" once: his world is the world he has self-fashioned (9). [5] It is his world, he thinks. His lackeys indulge him at this stage, even approving of his patronage of portrait painting and poetry—a callow, consumerist engagement with the arts that he shares with Shakespeare's Timon (11-12, 15). Trench is kidnapped by terrorists from the RRA, a thinly disguised version of the then-virulent Provisional Irish Republican Army, a left-wing group that had kidnapped high-profile businessmen during the 1970s. Trench is released and returns to the company: he beams with

---

4 For a full account of the Newcastle Playhouse production of *The Worlds*, see chapter 2 of Ian Stuart, *Politics in Performance: The Production Work of Edward Bond, 1978-1990* (New York: Peter Lang, 1996) 37-63.

5 All quotations from *The Worlds* are taken from Edward Bond, *Plays: Four*. London: Methuen, 1992.

pride as he reflects on the apparently warm welcome his staff gave him (33). But upstairs things have changed. He has been dumped from his own company: he is too old, he lacks dynamism, he has not paid board members well enough, he is yesterday's man.

Trench's intellectual and emotional decline is immediate: he rails and rails against his fair-weather friends; his ranting about "inane toadying" and "thirty pieces of silver" is a match for the dyspeptic ranting of Timon (42-43). And, like Timon in Shakespeare's play, Trench pretends to offer hospitality to his one-time colleagues but abuses them with insults and an elaborate but coarse practical joke. As Jenny S. Spencer put it, Trench shouts with "passionate outrage and increasingly sonorous monologues" (178). For all this bluster, Trench is a greatly diminished figure. Part 1 ends with Trench sitting alone on his floor and saying to himself that he is "afraid" (48). By the start of part 2, Trench is "dirty and unshaven" (51). He has gone to seed. He has now embraced economic dysfunctionality and rejects all superego appurtenances of presentation, hygiene, and politeness. He is helpless in his agedness; he has stopped trying to be productive or even presentable.

The play ends with Trench shooting another kidnap victim—an innocent chauffeur. The action is confused: it can only be assumed that Trench kills the man because he can see no reason for the man to want to live. By this stage, Trench has given up on humanity as a species: "The world's already ended except for the crying," he exclaims (73). Trench, at this stage, is wearing only a blanket: he looks less like the Chief Executive that he was and more like a political prisoner on a dirty protest. This is significant because the line between the man of commerce and the man of terror has become blurred. If anything, Trench is more nihilistic than any terrorist because at least the terrorist takes action to attempt to improve things. Trench despairs utterly; he has given up on "[m]ankind . . . A clown with a gun. An idiot with a stick . . . The human species. Homo mob" (74). It is language that recalls the hollow non-philosophy of Macbeth as much as Timon of Athens's misanthropy. [6] Indeed, Trench refers to the imprisoned chauffeur—repeatedly—as "it" (78). He surrenders to the police at the end of his play: now profoundly pathetic, he does not even have the sort of onstage death that is afforded to both Lear and Shakespeare in *Lear* and *Bingo*.

The *Worlds* is a complicated play that combines relative realism with a quasi-Brechtian epic structure; pathetic scenes of pity with burlesque and gratuitous scenes of obscenity and violence. Indeed, Bond is synonymous with stage violence: as William J. Free puts it succinctly and with agreeable understatement, certain scenes in various Bond plays "challenge the composure of their viewers" (87). Bond himself has said that his plays are not violent—they just have violent things in them and this is necessary because violence is "simply a fact of life" (Stoll 415). (The point is valid, of course, but the distinction is a fine one.) Complicated discussions about the corrupting powers of money are grafted onto the play and there is indeed a challenging debate about the nature of violence and the ersatz legitimacy of state-controlled repression of strikers and dissidents. But The *Worlds* can work on a much more basic, personalized level: simply, it can be read

---

6 *Macbeth* is alluded to specifically in Part Two, scene five, when two striking workers, Ray and Terry, say, fatalistically, that if the chauffeur "gets shot" then "He's shot"—it echoes almost word-for-word the dialogue in *Macbeth* when Lady Macbeth blithely says that if "we fail" to assassinate King Duncan then "we fail" (72).

as a man reacting hysterically to enforced retirement. In a capitalist system that fetishizes profit and casts aside the economically unproductive, the aged are marginalized and despised.

Trench has no hobbies or interests outside of his company; his interest in the arts is a mere pretense. Work is everything to him. When that is removed, he loses all sense of humanity and he loses all sense of proportion. *The Worlds* is not technically a tragedy, but it is a tragic depiction of contemporary society's detestation of aging and the aged. "My friends killed me," laments Trench (57). His oleaginous, self-serving colleagues did not kill him. They merely retired Trench, their one-time patriarch and meal ticket. In doing so they condemned him to a sort of living death—a paradoxical state of mental paralysis that Trench to some extent shares with both Lear and Shakespeare.

Conclusion: Pity for the aged
A more humane side of Bond's oeuvre

In the section on *Lear*, it was pointed out that in April 2021 Bond, aged eighty-six, castigated an academic for what he believed to be a misreading of Lear's effort to dismantle the wall. In his ninth decade, Bond remains belligerent, combatant, difficult. His depiction of the academic as typifying "the moral squalor, irresponsibility and indulgent triviality of our culture" may seem a little over-the-top, even ludicrous ("Rough Notes"). But Bond says some other things in that piece—important things. He takes time to refer to himself as a "socialist and a humanist." It would be easy to oversimplify Bond's understanding of what humanism is exactly. But the point is that Bond cares about humans and believes that they can do good things. They can even improve in age: Lear, blinded, humiliated, and despised in his aged infirmity can even show the way to a better future—his attack on the wall is not a futile gesture but a call for resistance, a start towards radical action. In *Bingo*, Shakespeare is a pathetic figure who acquiesces in an abusive Enclosure act and fails to even speak to his wife but he at least gains some insight into the uselessness of his art as he sees it through aged, jaded eyes. Insight into one's failings is at least better than self-delusional self-righteousness. And Trench in *The Worlds* is, like Lear, more sinned against than sinning because his forced retirement is done so swiftly and ruthlessly that it seems little less violent than the actions of kidnapping terrorists, white-collar fraudsters, and aggressive, greedy union leaders. All three leading characters do and say despicable things at times, but all three reflect on their aging processes and at least modify their hitherto selfish and simplistic assumptions about their sense of patriarchal and economic entitlement.

Aging means different things to different people in different places at different times. But aging is something of a leveller: suicide notwithstanding it is inescapable; it is a fundamental human experience and a fundamental human trauma. Delese Wear describes aging, aptly, as "one of the most mysterious and inevitable shared human experiences" (xvii-xviii). Bond's depictions of capitalist societies in various stages of development are invariably jaundiced, bleak and manically violent—but it seems clear that Bond does not see things only in terms of dialectics and material bases. He does care about people. And he cares specifically about those who are cast aside for the irrational reason of age alone.

Works Cited

Billington, Michael. *State of the Nation: British Theatre Since 1945*. London: Faber, 2007.

Bond, Edward. *Lear*. London: Methuen, 1995.

---. *Plays: Four*. London: Methuen, 1992.

---. *Plays: Three*. London: Methuen, 1994.

---. "Rough Notes on Reading an 'Ouch!' Book." *Edward Bond Drama*. April 2021. Web. 13 July 2021.

Castillo, Debra A. "Dehumanized or Inhuman: Doubles in Edward Bond." *South Central Review* 3.2 (1986): 78-89.

Free, William J. "Edward Bond." *British Playwrights, 1956-1995: A Research and Production Sourcebook*. Ed. William W. Demastes. Westport, CT: Greenwood, 1996. 80-93.

Gurney, John. *Brave Community: The Digger Movement in the English Revolution*. Manchester: Manchester University Press, 2007.

Hirst, David L. *Edward Bond*. Basingstoke: Macmillan, 1985.

Jones, Simon. "New Theatre for New Times: Decentralisation, Innovation and Pluralism, 1975-2000." *The Cambridge History of British Theatre, Volume 3: Since 1895*. Ed. Baz Kershaw. Cambridge: Cambridge University Press, 2015. 448-69.

Patterson, Michael. "Edward Bond: Maker of Myths." *A Companion to Modern British and Irish Drama, 1880-2005*. Ed. Mary Luckhurst. Oxford: Blackwell, 2006. 409-18.

Sanders, Julie. *Adaptation and Appropriation*. London: Routledge, 1996.

Shepherd, Simon. *The Cambridge Introduction to Modern British Theatre*. Cambridge: Cambridge University Press, 2009.

Smith, Leslie. "Edward Bond's *Lear*." *Comparative Drama* 13.1 (1979): 65-85.

Spencer, Jenny S. *Dramatic Strategies in the Plays of Edward*

Bond. Cambridge: Cambridge University Press, 1992.

Stoll, Karl-Heinz. "Interviews with Edward Bond and Arnold Wesker." *Twentieth-Century Literature* 22 (1976): 411-32.

Stuart, Ian. *Politics in Performance: The Production Work of Edward Bond, 1978-1990.* New York: Peter Lang, 1996.

Trussler, Simon. *Edward Bond.* Harlow: Longman, 1976.

Wear, Delese. "Editor's Statement." *Literature and Aging: An Anthology.* Ed. Martin Kohn, Carol Donley, and Delese Wear. Kent, OH: Kent State University Press, 1992. xvii-xviii.

Woudhuysen, H. R., and David Norbrook, eds. *The Penguin Book of Renaissance Verse, 1509-1659.* Harmondsworth: Penguin, 1993.

10.2478/9788367405423-005

Moving Back from the Limelight: Aging and Ageism as the Shakespearean Actor's Tragedy in Ronald Harwood's *The Dresser*

Kinga Földváry

The motif of aging and the plight of the aged, who struggle with their own failing bodies and minds while also suffering from the humiliation of having to give up their independence and control over their lives, have more than once been the focus of Ronald Harwood's dramatic work. At the same time, one could equally say that Harwood's main theme is the stage itself, and his long-standing love affair with the world of the theatre is what his plays regularly reflect on. Some of his best-known work, among them *The Dresser* (1980), combine the two themes, showing the way aging is itself a performance of sorts, a show that goes on in front of a dwindling and increasingly critical audience, which makes it an ideal case study for investigating forms of ageism in dramatic fiction. One of Harwood's later plays, *Quartet* (1999, adapted to film in 2012 as Dustin Hoffman's directorial debut), although sometimes dismissed by critics as "a flat-out crowd-pleaser" (*"Quartet"*), is even set in a retirement home and shows "the ravages of age on a profession which largely depends on staying young," as one reviewer summarizes the paradox of aging for performance artists (Morley). This is, of course, inherently tied to another paradox, rooted in the ruthlessness of contemporary society, which Harwood's theatre is also aware of, as pointed out by Sally Chivers:

> The cultural prescription to resist the apparently inevitable physical and mental decline that comes with age is accompanied by a competing cultural need to see older bodies

failing to reinforce the apparent strength of youth. This paradox is evident in *Quartet*'s combined portrayal of the physical changes that come with age along with the characters' apparent abilities to overcome them when they take the stage. (215-16)

Harwood's theatre is thus looking back nostalgically at what has been, and *The Dresser*, the play in the focus of this article, investigates the slowly but painfully fading past not only in terms of the personal life and achievements of individual performances, but also concerning the theatre as a medium. Partly relying on autobiographical elements and Harwood's personal recollections (discussed below), this nostalgically revisited theatrical past is embodied first and foremost by Shakespeare, both as a textual heritage and a performance tradition.

Shakespeare's oeuvre can be a natural choice for representations of age and aging, as it abounds in references to the controversial and often destructive power of time. We can find numerous examples all over his work, from the first group of the sonnets, which use various images to remind us of the inevitable passing of youth and beauty, to a wide range of dramatic characters and situations in which the source of the conflict is in some way related to human age. Yet the most iconic example of age demanding center stage is clearly *King Lear*, the tragedy of an octogenarian monarch and his similarly aged companions, the Earls of Kent and Gloucester. It is also fitting that this is the very play Harwood's protagonists, the aging actor and his dresser, are preparing to put on for what turns out to be the final time in the course of *The Dresser*.

If we look at the play not simply in search of age but also of ageism, Shakespeare's dramatic text proves just as much a treasure trove, as it includes plenty of lines that could be used as evidence for "discrimination based on age" (Gendron et al. 997). In fact, it is easy to argue—as several studies do—that the tragic denouement at least partly comes about as a direct result of this destructive attitude towards the elderly. Whether hearing Goneril's statement that "old fools are babes again and must be used with checks as flatteries" (1.3.20-21), or even the Fool's sympathetic and proverbial "thou should not have been old till thou hadst been wise" (1.5.41-42), one cannot but observe that in the play's world, old age is treated as a condition of decay and decline, which results in a complete loss of control over the characters' fate and the representation of their identity. *King Lear* is indeed such a perfect example of the problems of aging and ageism that it is often employed in medical, psychological, or sociological studies, to illustrate a variety of opinions of and about old people in critical situations (see, for example, Batch, Gullette, Krims, Ottilingam, Rapoport, and Truskinovsky). Some of the studies investigating ageism are somewhat reductive, reading textual symptoms in search of actual physiological conditions, but it is undeniable that this Shakespearean tragedy can easily be mined for proof that age can be used as an excuse for a discriminatory, or even downright cruel, treatment of the elderly.

At the same time, *King Lear* is not only a literary text and it does not exist in an abstract and isolated form, but in its stage or screen performances it also allows us to gauge contemporary artists' interpretations of the conflict between generations. What is more, it is also a prime example of the theatrical metaphor, seeing life as play-acting, and within this universal human spectacle, it presents the performance of old age, which can also be seen as a rehearsal for the greatest part of all: dying. In this respect, Margaret Morganroth Gullette observes an interesting tendency in the production history of the play, claiming that "ageism in *Lear* is a worsening trend" (62). She points out that "[l]ate 20th-century views and productions that find less fault with Goneril and Regan can do so because they are making Lear more arbitrary, and either arrogant or senilely 'cranky'" (62). She quotes a series of reviews from the past four decades that all refer to theatrical performances representing Lear in a manner that forces the audience to identify with the (traditionally "evil") daughters. Looking further back, she argues that "[i]n the history of the theater, productions of *King Lear* turn out to be a way to measure ageism—or its opposites" and concludes that "[w]hat horrified earlier centuries in Lear's fall derived from the play's inextricable and feverish combination of politico-religious beliefs in monarchical authority and deeply ingrained family duties toward fathers" (64). Nevertheless, Gullette admits that as a spectator, an arguably ageist contemporary performance of the play has made a deep impression on her, with its family dynamics that felt utterly realistic for the contemporary viewer.

What is, therefore, wrong with a performance that is able to engage its audiences with such elemental power? Gullette claims that the problem is identifying with the wrong side and taking the word of the evil daughters for granted, over the complaints of the aging fathers who have clearly never in their lives experienced a moment when the veracity of their statements would have been called into doubt. But how can we decide who is right or wrong in this debate, when the only evidence—the play's text—offers just as much support for one side as for the other? We do not actually see the riotous behavior of Lear's knights, only hear about it in potentially biased reports, but neither do we see the childhood of Lear's daughters, and without the "ocular proof," to use Othello's words (3.3.363), how can we decide which character is the one "more sinned against than sinning" (*King Lear* 3.2.59-60)? Yet some of these textual absences are—either by necessity or choice—embodied in performance, and performance is by its very nature self-reflexive: rooted in its present place and time. Therefore, it makes perfect sense that in our age, when popular culture tends to humanize monsters and audiences no longer accept an inherited viewpoint as the single interpretation, we need to see these trends in performances as a way towards a balance between representing either Lear or his daughters as victims of discriminative attitudes.

When casting actors for the role of Lear, the biological-biographical age of the actor is often relied on, to achieve a level of authenticity on the stage, even if this is not necessarily a requirement or a mark of value in a performance. This unity of actor and role can be seen as one of the keys to the play's power to engage audiences, and this self-reflexivity of performance is at the heart of Ronald Harwood's *The Dresser*, which is closely connected to Shakespeare's *King Lear*. In fact, *The Dresser* can be described as an adaptation or offshoot of Shakespeare's play (Nardo 105), as it offers a metadramatic look at the backstage drama of an aging actor and his equally aging companions, struggling through a final performance of *King Lear*. Interestingly, Milwaukee actor James Pickering refers to his age and life experience as an advantage in his representation of a whole series of old men, among them Lear, using a line almost verbatim from *The Dresser*: "I (was) practicing being old guys for a long time. . . . But I found year after year I'd have to put less makeup on my face" (Higgins).

In what follows, I intend to look at the ways the potentially ageist (or painfully realistic) experience of *King Lear* is transmitted through a peculiar chain of influences from

Shakespeare's tragedy to Harwood's *The Dresser*, looking at the variety of new interpretational contexts acquired along the way. Although the article focuses on the play itself, passing references will be made to a recent adaptation as well, directed by Richard Eyre in 2015. This BBC television adaptation of the play has been described by Joanna Norledge as "a theatrical story and dramatization which captures a vanished world. This world is brought to life in the screenplay and dramatic performances from the actors, both veterans of the theatrical world represented." The choice of veteran actors, both in their late seventies at the time of making the film—Anthony Hopkins as Sir, the dying Shakespearean actor, and Ian McKellen in the role of Norman, his dresser—distinguishes this adaptation from the 1984 film version, where Norman was played by 46-year-old Tom Courtenay, and Albert Finney, playing Sir, was only one year older, and as a result, the film's focus was elsewhere, less concerned with the plight of the aging and the aged.

It is undeniable that Harwood's play is a story primarily about the theatre, offering "a peep behind the curtain at a theatrical world that exists only in the memories of the oldest among us" (Berkowitz). Yet *The Dresser* is more than simply a backstage story, or a dramatization of a vanishing world, although naturally it is both. For one thing, not only does it capture more than one world in the process of their vanishing, but it also ends up questioning their significance—possibly even their existence—in the grand scheme of things. What is being lost here is theatre as a self-contained universe, in which Shakespeare is a language that everyone speaks and understands, and where the language learned from previous generations can be passed on effortlessly to the young equally eager to participate in the discussion. At the same time, the play, and particularly Eyre's film adaptation, also use the notion of aging as a metaphor, a mirror that reflects on the performative aspects of human life and the drama of aging.

In Harwood's play, we can find references to a variety of typical attitudes and stereotypes associated with old age, but the play offers no reference to the age of either of its protagonists, allowing various stage or screen productions to choose different paths in this respect. In contrast to *The Dresser*, the titular character in *King Lear* famously refers to himself as "a very foolish fond old man, / Fourscore and upward, not an hour more nor less" (4.7.60-61). This in itself is important, since Lear defines his age as a boundary beyond which one cannot and should not expect anything from life. Harwood's Sir, whose age is undefined, can be seen either as someone past his prime, or simply overwrought by a life of hardship in a repetitive professional life—Tzachi Zamir suggests that the play focuses "on how exhausting such a repetition can be for an actor" (241 n28), in itself a possible explanation for his decline. Whatever the cause, the "play's dramatic action centers on Sir's failing health and questionable mental capacity to perform Shakespeare's *King Lear*" (Essin 174)—ironically, the closer the actor to the actual age of the character, the harder it seems for him to present it on stage.

Yet the play is also a nostalgic contemplation of the past, and the looming specter of the journey's end. The nostalgia is directed at both personal and social losses, and the play can be perceived as a lament for a lost theatrical world, shown through the eyes of the most peculiar spectator, the liminal figure of the dresser, who inhabits the threshold between the stage and the outside world, between illusion and reality, trading in the secrets of both, being the star of neither. At the same time, we can also witness loss on a more universally human level: the loss of youth and what comes with it: a loss of control over one's mental and physical capacities, personal and professional choices, at times, even one's identity. This is in turn the aspect where the perspective of ageism becomes a useful tool to observe how Harwood's entertaining comedy hides painful and bitterly ironic truths about the world and how it sees old age.

To offer a brief summary of the plot: set on a single evening, before and after curtain up, *The Dresser* presents the last hours of Sir, a great Shakespearean actor-manager, performing *King Lear* somewhere in the provinces with his ragtag bunch of semi-amateur thespians. Apart from Sir, who is way past his prime, the play also focuses on his most faithful companion, Norman, the dresser, who has been assistant, confidante, nursemaid, even confessor, and thus witness—the ultimate spectator—to all the successes and failures of the past sixteen years. Outside of the theatre, the Second World War is raging: it is January 1942, bombs are falling on actor and civilian alike, and air raids are part of everyday life. On the inside, in the shabby dressing room of Sir, there are signs of decay, both physical and mental, both equally irreversible. The situation is almost a cliché, and the Learesque parallels between the two worlds—troubles inside and out—are clear, with the raging storm of the mind and the raging war in the world constantly reflecting on each other. Norman can also be seen as a version of Lear's Fool, the one who offers witty repartees and has a license to tell the truth, and whose existence is given meaning only through his service to his master. In the words of one reviewer, "Harwood's script, treating a touring Shakespearean troupe in the provinces of England during the Blitz, focuses on the symbiosis between Sir and his dresser Norman" (Grove 9). This symbiosis is only one of several—the two aging men are certainly two halves of one unit, unable to function without one another, but their whole existence would seem equally meaningless outside the world of the theatre and the tradition of Shakespearean acting in particular.

On the night when the play is set, Sir and his troupe are staging his 227th performance of *King Lear*, and it is evident that in this staging all motions, lines, technical details, and interpretive subtleties have been fine-tuned and honed by age and routine. Sir, however, is not exactly himself—he has not been well lately, and today he ended up in hospital after making a spectacle of himself in the street, discarding his clothes in a Lear-like manner, and then weeping by a lamppost. Yet, in spite of everyone's doubts whether he is well enough to go on stage at all, he refuses to cancel the performance, claiming that he "Can't. Mustn't. Won't" (Harwood 80). Norman, equally unwilling to admit defeat, uses all his tact and wit, coaching and coaxing, prompting and bullying Sir back to the old routine, to enable him to go through the process of divesting himself of throne and crown, sanity and life for the 227th time, not to mention carrying his no-longer-fragile Cordelia on stage.

Unsurprisingly, the atmosphere is melancholy and nostalgic; the old man's mind is clearly wandering towards his youth, his past fame and recognition. But, as already implied above, in Harwood's play it is not simply Sir's personal memories that are evoked, but a great tradition of Shakespearean acting which is seen to be vanishing with him, mostly because the world appears hell-bent on destruction and forgetting this noble past. Thus it is when his fears catch him in a more lucid moment that Sir tries to divide his kingdom and legacy, giving Madge, the faithful stage manager of twenty years, secretly in love with him, his press-cutting collection, spanning "a lifetime, an entire career," begging her to preserve his memory: "Talk of me sometimes. Speak well of me. Actors live on only in the memory of others. Speak well of me" (120). But Sir also offers her another symbolic object: "I want you to have this ring. If possessions can be dear then this ring is the dearest thing I own. This ring was worn by Edmund Kean in a play whose title is an apt inscription for what I feel: *A New Way to Pay Old Debts*. When you talk of it, say Edmund Kean and I wore it" (120). The reference to Kean is more than fitting, although subtly ironic as well; out of the long line of the great English performers of Lear, Edmund Kean's performance belonged to the "infirm tradition," together with David Garrick and Henry Irving, who represented the king as an "old man who is feeble (either hysterical or gentle) from the beginning" (Reuss, "Genesis"). But Edmund Kean's Lear was maybe even more memorable for the tragicomedy of the short actor struggling under the weight of his plump Cordelia (Reuss, *Shakespeare Londonban* 107, 112)—a plight Harwood's Sir could certainly sympathize with.

Through such references, the play expresses a longing for the past era of actor-managers who were no longer around, certainly not in 1980, when the play was written, but were in steady decline already by the 1940s, the time of the plot. Yet even the paratexts, most of all Harwood's Foreword, imply a more personal indebtedness: since he used to be the dresser of the great Shakespearean actor, Sir Donald Wolfit, the play inevitably pays homage to men like Wolfit, and "the tradition of actor-management," which defined British theatre "from the early eighteenth century until the late 1930s" (66). As the playwright claims, for all "their obsessions and single-mindedness . . . many of them were extraordinary and talented men; their gifts enhanced the art of acting; they nursed and kept alive a classical repertoire which is the envy of the world, and created a magnificent tradition which is the foundation of our present-day theatrical inheritance" (66-67). Yet in spite of this somewhat romanticizing view, using language colored by nostalgia, by the time we witness Sir and his entourage, his "compulsion to go on and on, bringing Shakespeare to every corner of Britain" (Berkowitz) seems doomed to fail, and he is fighting a losing battle that no one is able to believe in any longer.

The trouble is—who will remember Edmund Kean, let alone Sir, if the theatre as a physical reality is also in a state of collapse? The nostalgic longing of Sir is not only for the nineteenth-century theatrical tradition, but also for peacetime, when Lear's storm is not interrupted by air raid sirens and when acting in a Shakespearean company brought one glory and lasting fame. Now the memory of Sir's former glory no longer sheds any comforting light either on him or his fellow thespians, just coldness in every way, as Her Ladyship (Sir's Cordelia on stage, and not-quite-married partner off) bursts out:

> . . . I'm sick of cold railway trains, cold waiting rooms, cold Sundays on Crewe, and cold food late at night. I'm sick of packing and unpacking and of darning tights. I'm sick of the smell of rotting costumes and naphthalene. And most of all I'm sick of reading week after week that I'm barely adequate, too old, the best of a bad supporting cast, unequal to you, unworthy of your gifts, I'm sick of having to put on a brave face. (Harwood 117)

Yet Sir is unsympathetic to her complaints, because Sir's longing for the past cannot for a moment be mistaken for sympathy for the suffering of others. It would be natural for the aging and the aged to live in their memories, as Naomi Conn

Liebler refers to Italian philosopher Norberto Bobbio's thoughts to argue that "remembering is not only a kind of action but is the penultimate kind (just before dying), . . . it is in fact *the* important action of old age" (112). Yet there are instances when idealized memories are symptoms of the opposite: a lack of acceptance of one's identity and position in life. As the selfish figure of the old actor manifests, nostalgia is a self-centered sentiment, focusing on one's own losses, even if other, more momentous disasters attempt to blow these out of proportion.

Sir even takes the bombings as a deeply personal insult from the enemy, meant to undermine his work:

> SIR.   Do you know they bombed the Grand Theatre, Plymouth?
> NORMAN. And much else of the city besides.
> SIR.   I made my debut at the Grand Theatre, Plymouth.
> NORMAN. They weren't to know. (Harwood 86-87)

The German bombers, however, have not only launched an attack on Sir's personal memories, but they are constantly thwarting his artistic endeavors in other ways as well, leaving him with only a miserable skeleton cast. Norman, the dresser, takes the pragmatic view, as ever, having learned to make do with what is available, but for Sir, this will never do.

> SIR.   How then do we dispose our forces?
> NORMAN. Mr Thornton is standing by to play Fool.
> SIR.   And who as Oswald?
> NORMAN. Mr Browne, I'm afraid.
> SIR.   That leaves me a Knight short for 'reason not the need'.
> NORMAN. Ninety-eight short, actually, if you take the

text as gospel, so one more or less won't be
too upsetting.

SIR.   Thornton toothless as Fool. Browne lisping
as Oswald. Oxenby limping as Edmund.
What have I come to? I've never had a
company like this one. I'm reduced to old
men, cripples and nancy-boys. Herr Hitler
has made it very difficult for Shakespearean
companies. (Harwood 87)

If we look at Sir's "troubles" in the broader context of
ageism, we may in fact notice that it is not simply the elderly
who are seen as lacking in essential qualities. The play is set at
a time and place where being too old or too young (and too
damaged) to do a job perfectly is the norm rather than the
exception. And while *The Dresser* gives homage to all who have
struggled to keep up the good fight, while the more able-bodied
were doing the actual fighting on the battlefields, it also
acknowledges that a constant battle against prejudices and
stereotypes wears down the soul as well as the body. Everyone
in the troupe—on stage and off—knows what rejection and loss
feel like, and for that they deserve pity, even respect; at the same
time we can also see that the illusion they all struggle to
maintain is no longer tenable.

The physical buildings are crumbling in the same way as
the bodies of the players are, and it is not only Herr Hitler and
his bombs that are undermining the morale of the cast: the
harshest critic of the leftover would-bes and has-beens is Sir
himself. Everyone is pulling their weight as much as they can,
but nothing is quite good enough for him, as the storm is never
loud enough, yet in his self-centeredness, he never notices his
own failing capacities. As Her Ladyship complains: "You do

nothing without self-interest. And you drag everyone with you. Me. Chained. Not even by law" (115). She also takes the critics' ageist comments to heart, but then again, her tragedy is aggravated by the fact that as a female in a Shakespearean troupe, her professional lifespan is much shorter than that of the lead actor. When she is no longer young and light enough for the role of Cordelia, she will become expendable, and maybe young Irene, now map-carrier, will replace her like Her Ladyship replaced the previous Cordelia. Irene still thinks her youth is a virtue, but Norman soon disabuses her of these false notions:

> You're lighter than she is, ducky. . . . You're not the first to be placed on the scales. How do you think Her Ladyship got the job? Her Ladyship, when a slip of a girl, went from map-carrier to youngest daughter overnight. . . . It's not youth or talent or star quality that he's after, ducky, but a moderate eater. . . . So. Ducky. Keep well away. The old days are gone, the days of vim and vigour, what's to come is still unsure. (124-25)

It seems that the only character who sees clearly in this chaotic world of prejudice and destruction is someone who can understand the language of Shakespeare, someone who never leaves the closed world of backstage: the dresser. On the one hand, he is the primary spectator, and audiences are vital in reanimating the dying body of the actor and the theatre alike. It is only for the sake of the audience that Sir can get on the stage, since he believes that the theatre is the only way to heal wounds. As Norman says: "What'll happen to . . . the customers? There was a queue at the box office this afternoon, if four elderly spinsters constitute a queue. Pity to give them their money back, they've likely had enough disappointment in life as it is" (78). And the cue works, the vision of a full house gives Sir the strength to pull himself together one last time.

Yet the play's titular character is Norman, the dresser, the figure in the shadows, the one not meant for the stage, who is an equally aging character, having spent his active years in the service of Sir. He is no star, but his service is just as essential as that of the great actor, and his spectatorship—his constant watching over his master and his theatre—may be the key to the survival of this theatre. The play is set in the dressing room; even when we catch glimpses of the onstage action, our feet stay firmly planted in the wings, behind the scenes, in a position from which the onstage spectacle seems not much more than carefully constructed stagecraft. As Norman's slip of the tongue in the announcement manifests, his existence hovers on the threshold between illusion and reality. The halting announcement, meant to defy outer reality, claiming that in spite of the continuing air-raid warning the performance shall take place, makes it clear that for Norman the theatre is a question of life and death:

> NORMAN. (Softly) Ladies and gentlemen... (Louder) Ladies and gentlemen, the—the warning has just gone. An air-raid is in progress. We shall proceed with the performance. Will those—will those who wish to live—will those who wish to leave do so as quietly as possible? Thank you.
> (He stands rooted to the spot. Bombs.) (103)

Yet it would be wrong to think that his tongue slips on account of his fear of bombs—he is simply no actor and lacks the talent to tread the boards, and he is in his element only when he is backstage. He knows not only the routine of the performance, which costume and makeup is needed in which act, or how to operate the wind-machine and the thunder-sheet, but he can also prompt Sir when the play's first line eludes the great actor, and Norman appears to remember the whole repertory by heart. He and the dressing room are in fact the perfect *"lieux de mémoire* where memory crystallizes and secretes itself" (Nora 7), his "backstage perspective" (Essin 174) offering the intimately personal version of the mediated tradition that cultural memory is, passing a respectful attitude towards the monuments of the past down to the younger generations. Even though he can never watch the performance from the auditorium, only from the wings, his feedback is what counts the most to Sir, and in his feedback he once again relies on figures of cultural memory to reanimate the dressing room:

> NORMAN. . . . I've been mingling. You should hear what they think out there. I've never known an interval like it. Michelangelo, William Blake, God knows who else you reminded them of. One poor boy, an airman, head bandaged, was weeping in the stalls bar, comforted by an older man, once blond, now grey, parchment skin and dainty hands, who kept saying, "There, there, Evelyn, it's only a play," which seemed to me no comfort at all because if it wasn't a play "There-there-Evelyn" wouldn't be so upset.
> SIR.   Michelangelo, did they?
> NORMAN. And Blake. (118)

We are fully aware that some (or most) of this may be fiction—when he reports to Sir that Her Ladyship called his performance "mighty," she denies it right away: "I never said anything of the kind. He makes these things up" (114). Yet making things up is just as much a compulsory part of the routine, vital to keep up not only the pretense of success, but also necessary in order to put Sir back on his feet and enable him to give his all to his audience.

Norman may not work on stage, but his presence is vital—and by the end we realize that in this world of daily stage-pretense, his life is just as much at stake as anyone else's. In a painfully anti-climactic moment, after 227 majestic death scenes as Lear on stage, the death of Sir is witnessed only by Norman, who bitterly describes it as a failure: "Wasn't much of a death scene. Unremarkable and ever so short. For him" (135). As a spectator, Norman's disappointment comes from an expectation based on spectacular stage deaths, but as a performer in his own private globe, his distress is even more painful. He, who could remember everything about Sir's life and work, does not even get a mention in the single paragraph written from Sir's autobiography, a paragraph of thanks and acknowledgments to everyone but the dresser. And at the end, when Norman has lost the single most important spectator of his own backstage performance, and he is bound to disappear into the darkness of oblivion, he opens his bitter heart to the grief-stricken Madge: "We all have our little sorrows, ducky, you're not the only one. The littler you are, the larger the sorrow. You think *you* loved him? What about me?" (137).

The tragedy of this unremarkable denouement is in turn enhanced by the underlying reality of modern society: that outside the world of the theatre, Norman is a nobody, and precisely because he has spent all his active years in the service of Sir, he has no future anywhere else. "Cultural biases that identify the labor performed by dressers—cleaning and polishing, comforting and coddling—as 'women's work'" performed in "a traditionally feminized domestic space" (Essin 177) are directly responsible for the way their work is undervalued, if not completely ignored. Norman is, like Lear's Fool, left behind without a proper farewell, as if the world has already forgotten about him. But his bitter questions may also recall Edgar's couplet at the end of the *King Lear*, in which the survivors look back on the achievements of the deceased and turn toward their own future with anxiety: "The oldest hath borne most; we that are young / Shall never see so much, nor live so long" (5.3.324-25). As Liebler argues, "Edgar's line is a prediction, of course, and as such has little impact on an unpredictable, as-yet-unknowable future" (120). His anxiety about the expectations he may never be able to fulfil brings us back to the problem of age: "The matter of potency/usefulness and its inevitable link to questions of agency is one of the most compelling—and disturbing—among questions about old age and the reciprocal relations and obligations between one generation and another" (116). Norman is thus the character whose drama is both that of the Fool—lost without his old master—and that of the survivor, who sees no reason to go on living, but he is also an aging character in an environment where age brings vulnerability, rather than wisdom.

Works Cited
Batch, Morgan. *The Loss of Small White Clouds: Dementia in Contemporary Performance*. 2019. Queensland University of Technology, Ph.D. dissertation. Web. 9 Feb. 2022.
Berkowitz, Gerald. "Review: *The Dresser*—Duke of York's Theatre 2005." *Theatre Guide London*, n.d. Web. 9 Feb. 2022.
Chivers, Sally. "The Show Must Go on: Aging, Care, and Musical Performance in *Quartet*." *Modern Drama* 59.2

(2016): 213-30. *Project MUSE*. Web. 9 Feb. 2022.

Essin, Christin. *Working Backstage: A Cultural History and Ethnography of Technical Theater Labor*. Ann Arbor: University of Michigan Press, 2021.

Gendron, Tracey L., E. Ayn Welleford, Jennifer Inker, and John T. White. "The Language of Ageism: Why We Need to Use Words Carefully." *Gerontologist* 56.6 (2016): 997-1006. *Oxford Academic*. Web. 9 Feb. 2022.

Grove, Lloyd. "Olney's *Dresser*: Middle-Drawer." *The Washington Post*, 1 July 1983: 9. Web. 9 Feb. 2022.

Gullette, Margaret Morganroth. "Losing Lear, Finding Ageism." *Journal of Aging, Humanities and the Arts* 1.1-2 (2007): 61-69. *Taylor and Francis Online*. Web. 9 Feb. 2022.

Harwood, Ronald. "The Dresser." *The Collected Plays of Ronald Harwood*. London: Faber and Faber, 1993. 63-137.

Higgins, Jim. "Playing 'Geezers' Easier than Ever for Actor James Pickering." *Milwaukee Journal Sentinel*. *Eu.jsonline. com*. 22 Feb. 2018. Web. 9 Feb. 2022.

Krims, Marvin Bennet. "King Lear's Inability to Grieve Aging." *Journal of Aging, Humanities and the Arts* 1 (2007): 71-83. *Taylor and Francis Online*. Web. 9 Feb. 2022.

Liebler, Naomi Conn. "'The oldest hath borne most': The Burdens of Aging and the Morality of Uselessness in *King Lear*." *Shakespeare and Moral Agency*. Ed. Michael D. Bristol, London and New York: Continuum, 2010. 111-26.

Morley, Sheridan. "Reviving a Dramatic Tradition." *The New York Times* 15 Sep. 1999. Web. 9 Feb. 2022.

Nardo, Anna K. "Dialogue in Shakespearean Offshoots." *Literature/Film Quarterly* 34.2 (2006): 104-12. *Gale Academic Online*. Web. 9 Feb. 2022.

Nora, Pierre. "Between Memory and History: *Les Lieux de Mémoire*." *Representations* 26. Special Issue: Memory and

Counter-Memory (1989): 7-24. *JSTOR.* Web. 9 Feb. 2022.

Norledge, Joanna. "The Various Incarnations of Ronald Harwood's *The Dresser.*" *British Library English and Drama Blog* 12 Nov. 2015. Web. 9 Feb. 2022.

Ottilingam, Somasundaram. "The Psychiatry of King Lear." *Indian Journal of Psychiatry* 49.1 (2007): 52-55. Web. 9 Feb. 2022.

"Quartet." *Variety* 13 Sep. 1999. Web. 9 Feb. 2022.

Rapoport, M. "King Lear and Geriatric Psychiatry: 'Thou Shouldst Not Have Been Old Till Thou Hadst Been Wise.'" *The American Journal of Geriatric Psychiatry* 24.3 (2016): S12. *ScienceDirect.* Web. 9 Feb. 2022.

Reuss, Gabriella. *Shakespeare Londonban és Pest-Budán: Színházi előadások emlékezete.* Budapest: L'Harmattan, 2017.

---. "The Genesis of Macready's Mythical *Lear:* The New Tragic *Lear,* According to His 1834 Promptbook." *Shakespeare en devenir* 9 (2015). Web. 9 Feb. 2022.

Shakespeare, William. *King Lear.* Ed. R. A. Foakes. Walton-on-Thames: Thomas Nelson, 1997. The Arden Shakespeare. Ser. 3.

---. *Othello.* Ed. E. A. J. Honigmann. Walton-on-Thames: Thomas Nelson, 1997. The Arden Shakespeare. Ser. 3.

Truskinovsky, Alexander M. "Literary Psychiatric Observation and Diagnosis through the Ages: *King Lear* Revisited." *Southern Medical Journal* 95.3 (2002): 343-52. *Gale Academic Online.* Web. 9 Feb. 2022.

Zamir, Tzachi, "Watching Actors." *Theatre Journal* 62.2 (2010): 227-43. *JSTOR.* Web. 9 Feb. 2022.

10.2478/9788367405423-006

Part II
Irish Drama

Beckett and the Representation of Age on Stage
Christopher Murray

> *"We too were bonny—once. It's a rare thing not to*
> *have been bonny—once."*
> *Beckett,* Endgame

This essay focuses on Beckett's drama, the form he came to only after he had dedicated some fifteen years to the writing of fiction in the 1930s and 1940s. The respite he intended to find in the writing of drama was to be prolonged to the end of his life after *Waiting for Godot* (written 1947-48) proved an unexpected international success following its premiere in Paris in 1953. Somewhat against his will and strikingly against his temperament—shy, reclusive, and undemonstrative—the theater was to become Beckett's home and the source of his livelihood for the rest of his days, spent in Paris, until his death in December 1989. It is doubtful if the Nobel Prize for Literature, awarded to him in 1969, would have materialized on the basis of his fiction alone; whatever its merits, that work remains firmly in the realms of the avant-garde. Instead, by the 1960s, he had won fame almost exclusively through the extraordinary reception in the Western world (the Eastern bloc remaining hostile or ambivalent into the 1980s, see Kurdi) of his plays to date, particularly those still regarded as his best work, *Godot, Endgame* (1957), *Krapp's Last Tape* (1958), and *Happy Days* (1961). The man who regarded himself primarily as poet and novelist had, like a reluctant celebrity, become a world dramatist *malgré lui*. It was on that basis that he was, in the felicitous title of his biographer James Knowlson, *Damned to Fame.*

To what extent it is necessary in a broad reassessment to explore or even refer in any detail to Beckett's Irish origins is a moot point. After all, as exile, Beckett declared for France and for the French language in the late 1930s. Like the man himself, however, the declaration was misleadingly complex. To use local parlance, he had done with Dublin. The humiliating manner in which he was treated when he returned from Paris to give evidence in a libel case in 1937 gave him no reason to think exile a bad thing. In Knowlson's words, "It was a horrendous episode which he wanted to put far behind him" (281). His work to date was despised in Ireland. *More Pricks Than Kicks* (1934) was dismissed as both Joycean pastiche and obscene, while *Murphy* (1938) did not make it past the newly imposed censorship law. In a piece written in 1934, "Censorship in the Saorstat," Beckett was amused to comment: "France may commit race suicide, Erin will never. And should she be found at any time deficient in Cuchulains, at least it shall never be said that they were contraceived. . . . The pure Gael, drawing his breath from his heels, will never be permitted to defile his mind with even such fairly clean dirt as the *Black Girl in her Search for God* [by G. B. Shaw] so long as he can glorify his body" (*Disjecta* 86-87). Shaw's book was banned in Ireland, reinforcing Beckett's resolve to put the country behind him. And yet, as we shall see below, he was subject to an Irish cultural influence that was inescapable and which permeated much of his work through some form of empathy.

In the 1930s Beckett had grown more comfortable with the literary atmosphere in Paris, in the company of James Joyce himself and of a circle of artists and literary people for whom freedom to experiment was never in question. At the same time, the worsening political situation, especially as it affected Jewish writers and their associates (among whom Beckett counted himself), must have made neutral Ireland seem somewhat less real than France threatened by fascism. As he told his mother during a visit home in 1939, when she tried to dissuade him from returning to Paris, "I've promised so many friends I'd get back" (qtd. in Bair 256). Later, he would comment: "I preferred France in war to Ireland in peace" (qtd. in Brater 42).

In committing himself to France, Beckett also committed himself to the French language. French is more precise, less likely to grant an Anglophone the hiding place that rhetorical skills and stylistic facility in English could afford the aspiring writer. To one like Beckett, well versed in modern languages and with academic experience to boot, the step from writing in English to writing in French was not so great as it might have been for others. Any young man who had written on Marcel Proust for his master's degree (at Trinity College Dublin) was not likely to have had difficulty choosing the French language as his medium. For an Irishman, there was the precedent of Oscar Wilde, another TCD graduate, who had written *Salomé* in French. And there were J. M. Synge and Joyce, adept in French as in other languages. So, in short, it is not too surprising that Beckett's trilogy was written in French and that the early plays, *Eleutheria* (1947), *Godot, Endgame, Krapp*, were all written in French before Beckett translated them into English. Not *too* surprising and yet, surely, surprising. To switch languages was to switch identities. It could be said, then, that from 1939 Beckett preferred not to be regarded as an Irish writer per se.

On the other hand, Beckett retained his Irish friends, drank Irish whiskey, followed Irish rugby and (a quaint oxymoron) Irish cricket, and never turned his back on Irish causes. He accepted an honorary doctorate from his alma mater in 1959. Visitors from Dublin could be sure of a welcome if they formally sought him out in Paris. But as writer he was determined to put a distance between himself and Irish experience. This statement is not to deny the validity of some of the arguments put forward by Beckett's friends Vivian Mercier and Alec Reid, on the one hand, and compilers of essay collections (John Harrington, S. E. Wilmer), on the other, that Beckett's roots were in Dublin, and so his work was accordingly pigmented by his genetic origins. Neither do I underestimate the more precisely documented work (with photographs) of Eoin O'Brien, with its linking up of passages in the plays and prose with specific locations in Dublin city and environs. But it is doubtful if a "pervasive Irishness" suffuses many of Beckett's plays (Junker 28). After all, in the famous interview given to Israel Shenker in 1956, Beckett drew a clear distinction between his own work and that of Joyce, otherwise to be considered his master:

> With Joyce the difference is that Joyce was a superb manipulator of material—perhaps the greatest. He was making words do the absolute maximum of work. There isn't a syllable that's superfluous. The kind of work I do is one in which I'm not master of my material. The more Joyce knew the more he could. He's tending toward omniscience and omnipotence as an artist. I'm working with impotence, ignorance. I don't think impotence has been exploited in the past. (qtd. in Mercier 8)

From this declaration we can say that whereas Joyce expanded, Beckett contracted; where Joyce was inclusive of experience, of the world, Beckett was exclusive. Beckett thus learned to go his own way by developing his style toward attenuation and minimalism, features that are non-Irish. For virtually by definition, Irish rhetoric has traditionally been expansive and cumulative. Tacitus has never been imitated in the pubs; Swift's digressions upon digressions have been more the norm.

Anna McMullan has made the point that "it is in the contradictions and interstices within and between Irish Studies and Postcolonial Studies that a dialogue with Beckett's work can be developed" (90). This approach seems to me a sensible one, and in this article I also wish to situate Beckett between the conflicting aesthetic positions current in his lifetime. Here, for the moment, it may perhaps be sufficient to offer the view that Beckett was not an Irish writer in the same sense that W. B. Yeats, Lady Gregory, and Synge took pains to define themselves as Irish, in the context of cultural nationalism. In the end, Beckett's style, his way of seeing the world in language, was his own. As ever, the style is the man.

The argument I present here is that Beckett's drama is for a "new age" in a double sense: it is a drama that on the one hand defies the conventions of realism as developed by Henrik Ibsen, August Strindberg, Anton Chekhov, and their followers, and on the other, it makes age itself thematic in a new way. The first part of that double claim is obvious and needs little attention. To Beckett himself, who had always wanted to escape his Foxrock origins, "[t]he realisation that art has always been bourgeois, though it may dull our pain before the achievements of the socially progressive, is finally of scant interest" (*Proust* 123-24). What he called "the plane of the feasible" was likewise of no importance to him. Indeed, he turned from it in disgust, "weary of puny exploits, weary of pretending to be able, of being able, of doing a little better the same old thing, of going a little further along a dreary road" (*Proust* 103)—no doubt the road along which Stendhal had in the nineteenth century carried his mirror. Having witnessed a performance of Alfred Jarry's surrealistic comedy *Ubu Roi* in Paris in 1896, Yeats was so appalled that he cried out on behalf of the "tragic generation": "after us, the Savage God" (*Autobiographies* 349). For all that he admired Yeats's work, Beckett was to rededicate modern drama to the very "savage god" Yeats saw as slouching its way to Paris's art theaters. Surrealism and Antonin Artaud's Theatre of Cruelty were far more to Beckett's liking than the tenets of the Irish Dramatic Movement, which Yeats chose for text in accepting his Nobel Prize at Stockholm in 1923.

Despise the form as Beckett might, realism thrived in the twentieth century as "the classic form of modern drama" (Gassner 79). The heights to which Shaw, Eugene O'Neill, Seán O'Casey, Arthur Miller, and later David Mamet, among others, brought the art of realism are now beyond dispute. In turning away from their achievements, Beckett set himself a mammoth task. His own accomplishment in the theater cannot, I think, compare. What counts is the height to which he did manage to bring the unpromising materials of symbolism within the so-called Theatre of the Absurd. In this regard, had Jean-Paul Sartre not existed, it would have been necessary for Beckett to invent him. For existentialism underlies his drama as ideologically as Marxism underlies Bertolt Brecht's. Existentialism was his savage god.

As to the second part of my claim, relating to age itself, it is necessary first to say something of the representation of age on the modern stage. Realism tends to represent age negatively. The roots of this convention run deep in comedy, for example, where the *senex* figure is traditionally a blunderer and a serious blocking agent in the comic plot (Frye 163-86). For the most part, Shakespeare derived this pattern from Roman comedy, old people being funny through their ill-fittedness for the practicalities of life, as witness Leonato in *Much Ado about Nothing* and even Capulet in *Romeo and Juliet*. Of course, Shakespeare, unlike Ben Jonson or any other of his contemporaries, could also highlight the pathos underlying age, as in the portrayal of the old retainer Adam in *As You Like It* (a role he is traditionally thought to have played himself) and above all in King Lear. Prospero is probably a special case and may not be old at all in our sense, and is anything but senile.

In modern realistic drama in general, it may be said, age is either ignored or made an issue of. Shaw's Captain Shotover (in *Heartbreak House* [1919-20]) provides an example of the aged character who, simply because he is over eighty years old, is represented as dangerously senile, although in his inimitable paradoxical style Shaw simultaneously represents Shotover as a sage, indeed, as exceedingly wiser than the younger generation. Shaw is by no means being sentimental. He sees the world in such a parlous state that only the lunatic, the artist, or the saint can put it to rights: Louis Dubedat in *The Doctor's Dilemma* (1906) and the eponymous Saint Joan are the other free spirits capable of signaling the necessary revolution. A believer in the possibility of longevity, as his extraordinary *Back to Methuselah* (1921) clearly demonstrates, Shaw considered that aging could be counter-acted by the exertion of willpower. He himself persuasively exemplified his theory by remaining intellectually active and physically fit until the year of his death in 1950, aged ninety-four.

Let me choose just one more modern playwright before moving to the Irish dramatic scene, which was the point of departure for the young Beckett. In line with the realistic conventions governing the American theater in the first half of the twentieth century, the protagonists of Arthur Miller's plays are often middle-aged, such as the Kellers in *All My Sons*

(1947). But the striking ones are sometimes older. In *The Crucible* (1953), the most powerful man, Governor Danforth, is "a grave man in his sixties" (286). In the early play *A Memory of Two Mondays* (1955), Gus, who has given the best years of his life to an auto-parts warehouse, is aged sixty-eight; his colleague Jim, also still working, is old enough to remember fighting the Indians. In *Death of a Salesman* (1949), Willy Loman is sixty-two, and much emphasis is laid on his exhausted state. His age is significant because it heightens the injustice of his dismissal. As he protests to his boss, "I put thirty-four years into this firm, Howard, and now I can't pay my insurance! You can't eat the orange and throw the peel away—a man is not a piece of fruit!" (181). In *The Price* (1968), the furniture dealer Gregory Solomon is described as "a phenomenon; a man nearly ninety but still straight-backed and the air of massiveness still with him" (312). He is patriarchal in the positive sense, a biblical figure whose age represents wisdom (as the name Solomon immediately conveys). In that regard Miller goes against the realistic convention whereby a man of Solomon's years is inescapably senile. Miller uses age rather like Shaw, but less eccentrically in that he idealizes the elderly. In *Death of a Salesman*, after all, the offstage Dave Singleman, who is Willy's ideal, makes his living at age eighty-four and dies like a king "in his green velvet slippers in the smoker of the New York, New Haven and Hartford [train], going into Boston," the perfect end, as Willy sees it, the seal on a good life, "the death of a salesman" (180). For Miller, child of the Great Depression, work gave a person dignity, and its loss robbed him of the reason to live. He himself maintained the work ethic until his death in his ninetieth year in 2005.

As might be expected, Beckett's characters, though mostly middle-aged and upward, carry with them onstage little of the heroic stature of Miller's characters and none of the mad wisdom of Shaw's. Although he turned his back on the Irish dramatic movement, Beckett inherited the Irish idea of the aged. That notion is "glamorous" in the literal sense, to do with standing outside of the workforce not in idleness but with a kind of magical redundancy. In Yeats's Celtic plays the aged tend to be Druidic, endowed with a wisdom supernaturally empowered. In one of his best plays, *Deirdre* (1906), the aged King Conchubar outwits the young lovers with a guile they fail to counter, and they are consequently destroyed. In *On Baile's Strand* (1904), the same king, while attempting to tame the great hero Cuchulain, argues that he complements Cuchulain's strength:

> You are but half a king and I but half;
> I need your might of hand and burning heart,
> And you my wisdom. (Yeats, *Collected Plays* 170)

In binding Cuchulain to his obedience, Conchubar brings about the hero's exposure to supernatural powers and thence his destruction. The magus is in Yeats's poetics the most powerful figure in society, and the magus is conventionally old. But he is not heroic. The struggle in a Yeats play is thus often between the guile of the magus figure—even a debased form of it, as the Old Man in *Purgatory* (1938)—and the wildness of youth. The best example is supplied by the contest between Cuchulain and the Old Man in the sequel to *On Baile's Strand*, entitled *At the Hawk's Well* (1916), in which the Old Man wins a Pyrrhic victory by literally keeping his head down when danger strikes through supernatural agency and Cuchulain rises fatefully to the occasion.

In Synge's plays the older characters tend to be outsiders. He did not believe, with Yeats, "in the possibility of a 'purely fantastic, unmodern, ideal, breezy, springdayish, Cuchulanoid National Theatre'" (Greene and Stephens 157). Synge was more down-to-earth, closer to naturalism in his dramatic philosophy. His old folk are part of the peasant world he saw as infinitely more attractive than the conventional middle class. Here was real heroism, as old Maurya battles against poverty and the loss at sea of her husband and six sons in *Riders to the Sea* (1904). She ends up "destitute" (the most dreaded state in Synge's lexicon) but stoical, since "[n]o man at all can be living for ever, and we must be satisfied" (12). Yet Synge romanticized the aging process. With all the pathological horror of the neurasthenic, he viewed middle age as encroaching on death. In play after play the plangency of loss of youth is sounded. In *The Shadow of the Glen* (1903), Nora Burke, suddenly released, as she thinks, from a loveless marriage to an old man, and having available a young lover in his place, cannot shake off a mood of morbid awareness of time passing and beauty fading all around her, so she concludes: "Why would I marry you, Mike Dara? You'll be getting old, and I'll be getting old, and in a little while, I'm telling you, you'll be sitting up in your bed— the way himself [her husband] was sitting—with a shake in your face, and your teeth falling, and the white hair sticking round you like an old bush where sheep do be leaping a gap" (23).

Ailing himself in his mid-thirties from Hodgkin's disease, Synge saw death everywhere. In the peasant community and especially among the traveling people, ill-nourished and with a high mortality rate, he saw a reflection of his own condition: the middle-aged sidelined through debility. Every mother in Synge is "old" and close to senility. Every middle-aged man is embittered and afraid of the new generation. Loneliness is the endemic condition, to be allayed only by drink and prayer. Even the Priest in *The Tinker's Wedding* (1909) suffers from this malaise: "It's a hard life, I'm telling you, a hard life, Mary Byrne; and there's the bishop coming in the morning, and he an old man, would have you destroyed if he seen a thing at all. . . . What is it I want with your songs when it'd be better for the like of you, that'll soon die, to be down on your two knees saying prayers to the Almighty God?" (36-37). Then there are Martin and Mary Doul, the two blind people in *The Well of the Saints* (1905), beggars "wrinkled and poor, a thing rich men would hardly look at at all, but would throw a coin to or a crust of bread" (67). Though they lack the *communitas* of the tinkers, Synge tends to identify them with tramps, wandering outcasts.

As he sometimes signed his letters to his fiancée, Molly Allgood, "Your old Tramp," Synge identified with these outsiders, just as he felt himself prematurely old. In his last play, *Deirdre of the Sorrows* (1910), left unfinished through illness, he portrayed his fraught love affair in the jealous relationship between King Conchubor, given an age of "about sixty," and the beautiful Deirdre, aged "a score only" (153), just Molly's age. Synge had written the role of Pegeen Mike in *The Playboy of the Western World* (1907) for Molly, and now he wrote Deirdre for her: she was to play it after his death in 1909 at the age of thirty-eight. The play is suffused with loneliness and despair, offset this time not by drink or prayer but by the richness of a language rising to new plaintive heights. Having run off to Scotland with a young man, Naisi, Deirdre falls into a morbid awareness that she cannot elude the power of time, and she wants to return to Ulster, even if it be to certain death:

> DEIRDRE. (*broken-hearted*). There's no safe place, Naisi, on the ridge of the world. . . . And it's in the quiet woods I've seen them

digging our grave, throwing out the clay on leaves are bright and withered.

NAISI. (*still more eagerly*). Come away, Deirdre, and it's little we'll think of safety or the grave beyond it, and we resting in a little corner between the daytime and the long night.

DEIRDRE. (*clearly and gravely*). It's this hour we're between the daytime and a night where there is sleep forever, and isn't it a better thing to be following on to a near death, than to be bending the head down, and dragging with the feet, and seeing one day, a blight showing upon love where it is sweet and tender? (171-72)

Irish lyricism can rise no higher, and Synge makes clear at last that realism is not what he is concerned with at all. In a draft essay prefaced to this play he wrote: "The real world is mostly unpoetical, . . . [but] there is always the poet's dream which makes itself a sort of world" ("Historical or Peasant Drama" 394). Essentially, this is what Synge did: he created an alternative world in the plays.

Sean O'Casey differed sharply from Synge in temperament, being robust in health and free from Synge's morbidity of outlook. As the inheritor of the Synge tradition at the Abbey Theatre, however, he, too, tended to characterize the middle-aged as on the edge of the grave, largely because he dealt with the urban working class, among whom aging was a brutal factor in the workplace and where the hardship of keeping a family prematurely aged men and women alike. It is striking, however, how easily O'Casey characterizes these figures. Juno Boyle in *Juno and the Paycock* (1924) may stand for many others:

She is forty-five years of age, and twenty years ago she must have been a pretty woman; but her face has now assumed that look which ultimately settles down upon the faces of the women of the working-class; a look of listless monotony and harassed anxiety, blending with an expression of mechanical resistance. Were circumstances favourable, she would probably be a handsome, active and clever woman. (4).

Her husband, "Captain" Boyle, is "about sixty" and a figure akin to one of Synge's tramps in that he is a parasite and outsider, being work-shy to the point of making a career of it.

O'Casey's plays are replete with such men, and the role they are given is that of observer, a kind of chorus to the action from which they are excluded (Sylvester Heegan, aged sixty-five, and his contemporary Simon Norton offer good examples from *The Silver Tassie* [1929]). It is as if Ireland, as Yeats intuited in "Sailing to Byzantium," is no country for old men. Juno puts the case strongly to the Captain in act 3, after their daughter Mary finds herself pregnant out of wedlock, a major problem in the 1920s: "What you an' I'll have to go through'll be nothin' to what poor Mary'll have to go through; for you an' me is middlin' old, an' most of our years is spent; but Mary'll have maybe forty years to face an' handle, an' every wan of them'll be tainted with a bitther memory" (O'Casey 74). In forty years Mary would be sixty-two. In the Irish dramatic tradition life was a vale of tears, a pilgrimage through time to be endured with as much patience as possible. To be middle-aged was literally to be halfway through that journey, longing for release at last. Age was thus nothing but a negative trope.

Beckett, for all his cosmopolitanism, thought of age in the same way as the earlier Irish dramatists. As a young man in Dublin he attended the Abbey Theatre. He knew and liked the plays of Yeats, Synge, and O'Casey. When he came to write plays himself in Paris, even though his bias was against Abbey realism, he tended to favor the mode of characterization he had admired and found amusing in Dublin. But he used it to his own ends, pointedly ironic. In the readings that follow I explore Beckett's representation(s) of age/aging in his plays, using the order of composition offered by *The Complete Dramatic Works*, to which the page numbers refer.

"How old are you? If it's not a rude question," asks Pozzo of Vladimir in *Waiting for Godot.* After Vladimir remains silent, Pozzo resumes. "Sixty? Seventy? [To Estragon.] How old would you say he was?" To which Estragon replies, "Eleven" (27). Internal reference—and it is perhaps surprising to find such in a Beckett play—indicates that Pozzo's estimation is if anything on the conservative side. Vladimir refers to the 1890s, when he and Estragon might have been "among the first" to jump from the top of the Eiffel Tower. "Now it's too late. They wouldn't even let us up" (11). The Eiffel Tower was erected in 1889. If Vladimir and Estragon were to have been among the first to jump from the top, whether hand in hand or not, they should have had to scramble up no later than 1890, one would imagine. That would be some fifty-seven years before the play was written. What age might they have been in 1890 (or thereabouts)? How many children had Lady Macbeth? It is, no doubt, a fatuous line of questioning for a dramatic text.

Leaving it aside, one might transfer one's attention to Pozzo himself. He tells his captive audience that Lucky was once his teacher. "That was nearly sixty years ago. . . . You wouldn't think it to look at me, would you? . . . Compared to him I look like a young man, no?" Here he orders Lucky to remove his hat and reveal his long white hair, which he invites Vladimir and Estragon to compare with his own pate (bald) once he removes his hat: "Did you see?" Whereas Pozzo expected the comparison to redound to his physical credit, his vanity being enormous, it simply enrages the two tramps in bowler hats. Their sympathy is with the "old and faithful servant." "Having sucked all the good out of him you chuck him away like a . . . like a banana skin" (32). Although the response is the righteous indignation toward the neglect of age that Willy Loman implores his boss to exhibit, Beckett is only playing with bourgeois values. In a matter of seconds, during which Pozzo puts on an exhibition of suffering at the hands of Lucky, Vladimir turns on Lucky in fury: "How dare you! It's abominable! Such a good master! Crucify him like that! After so many years! Really!" (32-33). The audience cannot but laugh at the *volte face*. At the same time, Beckett has eluded the iconic, semiotic significance of age-as-sign (inviting pathos) and shown how histrionics can completely reverse not only perception but even action. The result is laughter at the absurdity of human emotion. Beckett exploits the realistic representation of age and uses it to ridicule gullibility.

He goes much further in *Endgame*. There are touches of Synge in the accounts of Mother Pegg, now dead, but "bonny once" (112) and a great one for the men. There is a plangency in Nell's refrain "Ah, yesterday!" in elegiac memory of love and happiness. But the prevailing mood is a long way from Synge's in this play. Here aged parents are ostentatiously imprisoned in trash cans. Even if this is surrealistic imagery, it illustrates Hamm's cruelty. "The old folks at home! No decency left! Guzzle, guzzle, that's all they think of," is his response to his father Nagg's demand for "pap" (96). Nell, his mother, dies in her trash can during the play and is unmourned. Beckett is playing Theatre of Cruelty to the top of his bent.

Hamm, the would-be artist, the failed storyteller, exists to cast in the face of the audience his radical callousness. It is a form of alienation, though not in Brecht's vein. Hamm is crippled and blind, and yet unsympathetic. He is dependent on his servant Clov and yet unloved. After his fashion he "supports" his parents but is palpably indifferent to their welfare and wants his father only as audience to his pointless storytelling. Yet it is Hamm who can address the audience like a satirist of Roman days or a prophet out of the Old Testament: "Get out of here and love one another! Lick your neighbour as yourself" (125). The ambivalence of Hamm's representation is like Pozzo's ability to sway the feelings of Vladimir and Estragon: the pitiably old can also appear as awful nuisances. But now the harshness of the middle-aged protagonist (Hamm is old enough to be Clov's father) is a reflection of the harshness and decline of the universe, where everything is on the way out. "If age but knew" is Clov's comment (97). But Clov, the old retainer in a new guise, is helpless in this universe where the most that can be said is, "What skilled attention they get, all these dying of their wounds" (132).

A quick run through the rest of Beckett's plays would indicate how prevalent age is as a theme, an issue, a factor in the dramatization of the losing game he saw as life. In *Happy Days*, the trapped Winnie is about fifty, and Willie is ten years older. In *All That Fall* (1957), Mrs Rooney is in her seventies, while her husband celebrates, if the word is not too strong, his eightieth birthday. In *Krapp's Last Tape*, Krapp is "a wearish old man" (215), aged sixty-nine. Perhaps the most sardonic contrast to Irish romanticism is to be seen in Krapp's lines: "Fanny came in a couple of times. Bony old ghost of a whore. Couldn't do much but I suppose better than a kick in the crutch.

The last time wasn't so bad. How do you manage it, she said, at your age? I told her I had been saving up for her all my life" (222). In *Rough for Theatre 1* (1976), A, the blind man, calls out "A penny for a poor old man" (227), while his counterpart in this two-hander, B, disabled in a wheelchair, has a son somewhere and seems to be of an age with A. Their violent final encounter is decidedly un-Syngean.

Yet lyricism, however sardonically framed, is not absent. The two officials in *Rough for Radio II* (1976) are middle-aged. The Animator says to the Stenographer at one point, "Oh how bewitching you look when you show your teeth! Ah were I but . . . thirty years younger" (*Complete* 281). In *Words and Music* (1962), one of the themes Words has to elaborate for Croak runs: "Age is . . . age is when . . . old age I mean . . . if that is what my Lord [Croak] means" (291). After some time spent in rehearsal, Words manages a full evocative verse to musical accompaniment:

> Age is when to a man
> Huddled o'er the ingle
> Shivering for the hag
> To put the pan in the bed
> And bring the toddy
> She comes in the ashes
> Who loved could not be won
> Or won not loved
> Or some other trouble
> Comes in the ashes
> Like in that old light
> The face in the ashes
> That old starlight
> On the earth again. (291)

It is a compulsive theme. In another radio play for music and voice, *Cascando* (1963), Opener says: "I have lived on it [composition] . . . till I'm old. / Old enough" (300). The artist figure in Beckett, from Pozzo through Hamm and on to Krapp, is in these radio plays briefly recaptured as obsessional, romantically compelled to attend to his craft into old age. At this point, as with Krapp, memory becomes haunting.

Play (1963) is a more complex case. Within the story, the three characters making up the so-called eternal triangle are youngish, certainly vigorous and sexually active. But what the audience sees are the characters in some afterlife, as they recall each within his or her memory the details of the marriage and adultery that activate the little tragedy. The man, wife, and mistress are encased in large urns with only their heads visible, and *"Faces so lost to age and aspect as to seem almost part of urns"* (Beckett, *Complete* 307). The setting serves to distance the characters, who exist in a Yeats-like otherworld (one might compare Yeats's *The Only Jealousy of Emer*). The characters are under the active, not to say inquisitorial, surveillance of a single spotlight operating, Beckett insisted, within "the ideal space (stage) occupied by its victims" (318). The use of the word *victims* is crucial to the effect of the play. These three figures are victims of middle-class morality, rather like Swift, Stella, and Vanessa in Yeats's *Words Upon the Window-Pane*, which Beckett may have seen at the Abbey in 1930.

In the silent *Film* (1963), the observer E, the camera, is the counterpart of the spotlight in *Play*. The focus is on a single observed figure divided into O (object) and E (eye), "the former in flight, the latter in pursuit" (323). In the street scene that takes place before the protagonist is pursued into his room, Beckett, most unusually for him, includes a great deal of detail: "Period: about 1929. Early summer morning. Small factory district. Moderate animation of workers going unhurriedly to work. All going in same direction and all in couples." O enters and goes against the crowd and "storms along in comic foundered precipitancy" (324), watched by E. In trying to escape E's gaze—for the film is about O's unwillingness to be perceived and hence to exist—O jostles against an elderly couple "of shabby genteel aspect" (325). These being the only street characters singled out, Beckett thereby underlines how he finds older characters intrinsically more interesting. In the script (or "project," as he calls it), Beckett emphasizes how the elderly couple markedly observe the fleeing O: "the woman raising a lorgnon to her eyes, the man taking off his pince-nez fastened to his coat by a ribbon. They then look at each other, she lowering her lorgnon, he resuming his pince-nez. He opens his mouth to vituperate. She checks him with a gesture and soft 'sssh !' " This is the only scripted sound in the whole piece. The elderly couple are given a significant place in the action when they turn to stare at E, and as they do so "the expression gradually comes over their faces which will be that of the flower-woman in the stairs scene and that of O at the end of the film, an expression only to be described as corresponding to an agony of perceivedness" (325).

Film provides a transition to a different use of the "elderly" in Beckett's later work. Apart from *The Old Tune* (1960), where the two old men are O'Casey-like codgers who interminably reminisce and quarrel about the details of the old days, the later plays are all not only straightforwardly sympathetic to the aging characters but also closely involved in what is shown to be their tragic situation. (In any case, *The Old Tune* is not an original piece but Beckett's adaptation of a radio play, *La Manivelle*, by Robert Pinget.) No longer are the aging ridiculous or pathetic; they are the subjects of tragic experience. And all are women, which is significant. The shift in tone from the representation of middle-aged woman like Mrs Rooney (*All That Fall*) to that governing the final plays. This is very striking. Once Winnie begins to see through her own self-deception in act 2 of *Happy Days*, Beckett can no longer find middle-aged women funny. On the contrary, they begin to form in his mind and on the stage images of the deepest, irremediable suffering. They provide metaphors for the tragic condition in the post-*Endgame* world, where the threat of nuclear disaster is no longer the image of catastrophe it once was (and before 9/11 reintroduced terrorism as a comparable image).

Come and Go (1968), with its three older women meeting after some time, is but a "dramaticule," and yet it compresses within its couple of pages the horror of death waiting like an evil presence for us all. There is an echo of *Macbeth* in the opening line, "When did we three last meet?" and the reference serves to highlight a motif in all of Beckett's later plays: not the operation of the supernatural on human affairs but the internalizing within those old enough to have experienced mental pain, the anguish of being itself. Macbeth's line, "O! full of scorpions is my mind, dear wife!" (3.2.40), seems to echo all through these last plays by Beckett.

Joe in the television play *Eh Joe* (1965) is in his late fifties and haunted by a voice tormenting him with memories of a woman he loved and left, who then committed suicide. The voice is suffused in Christian references—"your Lord" and "God," for example—and is at once another woman he jilted and his conscience relentlessly tormenting him. In *Not I* (1972), the protagonist is a woman approaching seventy years of age, whose mouth alone is visible to the audience. Her monologue is one long cry of pain as she tries to piece together her life story, told in the third person. Her sense of guilt is deeply ingrained but without sufficient cause: "first thought was . . . oh long after . . . sudden flash . . . she was being punished . . . for her sins" (Beckett, *Complete* 377). But this explanation is dismissed, and the monologue shows how psychologically she is unable to obtain release from the trap of unearned guilt. She is incapable of saying "I" and thereby claiming her identity as well as taking responsibility for being (always a guilty state in Beckett).

Before he dies in *That Time* (1976), the Listener, the only character onstage, with *"Old white face, long flaring white hair as if seen from above outspread"* (388), lives through episodes of his childhood and youth. Three voices reach him in recollection, blending as he tries, as it were, to untie knots in memories bound in with trauma. If one takes the time to be that of composition (1972), then the Listener's youth belongs well before 1947, according to internal references, roughly corresponding to Beckett's own youth (O'Brien 371). The Listener is thus about sixty-six. The mother (V) in *Footfalls* (1976) is ninety, while May (M) is in her forties and "has not been out since girlhood" (Beckett, *Complete* 401). Both figures may be ghosts (Worth 106), but pain is at the core of the play. In *A Piece of Monologue* (1980), the Speaker, once more theatrically given white hair, refers to his life as amounting to 30,000 nights, which translates into eighty years. For him, as for so many Beckett protagonists, "Birth was the death of him" (Beckett, *Complete* 425).

The protagonist W in *Rockaby* (1981) is "Prematurely old" with "Unkempt grey hair" (433). In *Ohio Impromptu* (1981), both Listener and Reader have—once more—*"Long white hair"* (445) and essentially live mentally in the distant past. In *Nacht und Träume* (1983), the Dreamer (A) has "grey hair" (465), while in *What Where* (1983), all four players, dressed and looking alike, have the "Same long grey hair" (469).The remaining plays in the canon, with the exception of the television play *Quad* (1982), maintain this emphasis on old age. In *Quad*, rapid movement is essential, and, as if writing a job specification, the author says, "Some ballet training desirable. Adolescents a possibility. Sex indifferent" (453). In *Catastrophe* (1982), too, "[a]ge and physique [are] unimportant" for all three characters (457). This is a surprising stage direction. Beckett might have said nothing about age here; the very mention indicates that it was his usual practice to specify. Thus the specification may elsewhere be taken as significant. Stage directions in Beckett, as is widely recognized, carry the status of Holy Writ. Interestingly, in the film version of *Catastrophe* (2000), directed by David Mamet, the role of Protagonist (P) was played by John Gielgud, in his ninetieth year.

In *King Lear* (conflated edition), Shakespeare may have his protagonist declare that "[a]ge is unnecessary" (2036), but in Beckett, age is very necessary indeed. He was no gerontologist, however. Rather, his interest in aging and in age was twofold. It had to do, first, with his Irish puritanical disgust with the body, visible from his earliest publications, the short stories, his first novel, *Murphy*, and even the discarded *From Fair to Middling Women*. Second, the prospect of human decrepitude reinforced Beckett's disdain for the human situation but allowed him a bitterly humorous response not seen since the works of Jonathan Swift.

It is where humor meets, indeed embraces, disgust that Beckett reveals his tragicomic genius. Unlike O'Casey, who made aging merely amusing in its display of crankiness, Beckett made the aged symbols of the rib-tickling absurdity of Will. He is the Jaques of all trades in this respect, that is,

Shakespeare's Jaques, who speaks of the last of the seven ages as "second childishness and mere oblivion / Sans teeth, sans eyes, sans taste, sans everything" (*As You Like It* 2.7.168-69). The sixty-nine-year-old Krapp appears to agree, seeing no more to age than "the sour cud and the iron stool" (222). Although many of Beckett's aging characters are as far from second childishness as they are from their first—or they would cease to be laughable and tug too much at the remnants of our compassion—they serve to represent physical frailty in the tragic satirist's style. They are ostentatious icons, semiotic embodiments of entropy. No modern dramatist, with the possible exception of Edward Albee, can be at once so outrageous and so engaging in representing age in the theater as part of his war against sentimentality.

Works Cited

Bair, Deirdre. *Samuel Beckett: A Biography*. New York: Harcourt, 1978.

Beckett, Samuel. *The Complete Dramatic Works*. 2nd rev. ed. London: Faber, 1990.

---. *Disjecta: Miscellaneous Writings and a Dramatic Fragment*. Ed. Ruby Cohn. London: Calder, 1983.

---. *Proust [and] Three Dialogues: Samuel Beckett and Georges Duthuit*. London: Calder, 1965.

Brater, Enoch. *Why Beckett*. London: Thames and Hudson, 1989.

Frye, Northrop. *Anatomy of Criticism: Four Essays*. New York: Athenaeum, 1966.

Gassner, John. *Form and Idea in Modern Theatre*. New York: Holt, Rinehart and Winston, 1956.

Greene, David H., and Edward M. Stephens. *J. M. Synge*. New York: Macmillan, 1959.

Junker, Mary. *Beckett: The Irish Dimension*. Dublin: Wolfhound, 1995.

Knowlson, James. *Damned to Fame: The Life of Samuel Beckett*. London: Bloomsbury, 1996.

Kurdi, Mária. "Samuel Beckett's Drama in Hungarian Theatre History and Criticism before 1990." *Theatron* 16.4 (2022): 54-69.

McMullan, Anna. "Irish/Postcolonial Beckett." *Palgrave Advances in Samuel Beckett Studies*. Ed. Lois Oppenheim. Basingstoke: Palgrave Macmillan, 2004.89-109.

Mercier, Vivian. *Beckett/Beckett*. New York: Oxford University Press, 1977.

Miller, Arthur. *Collected Plays*. Vol. 1. London: Cresset, 1958.

---. *The Crucible. Collected Plays*. Vol. 1 223-329.

---. *Death of a Salesman. Collected Plays*. Vol. 1 129-222.

---. *The Price. Collected Plays*. Vol. 2. London: Secker and Warburg, 1981. 293-373.

O'Brien, Eoin. *Beckett Country: Samuel Beckett's Ireland*. Dublin: Black Cat; Faber, 1986.

O'Casey, Sean. *Juno and the Paycock. Complete Plays*. Vol. 1. London: Macmillan, 1984. 3-81.

Shakespeare, William. *As You Like It. The RSC Shakespeare/ William Shakespeare/ Complete Works*. Ed. Jonathan Bate and Eric Rasmussen. Basingstoke, UK: Macmillan, 2007. 472-525.

Synge, J. M. *Collected Plays*. Ed. Ann Saddlemyer. Oxford: Oxford University Press, 1995.

---. *Deirdre of the Sorrows. Collected Plays* 165-212.

---. *The Playboy of the Western World. Collected Plays* 101-64.

---. *Riders to the Sea. Collected Plays* 1-14.

---. "Historical or Peasant Drama." *Collected Works*. Vol. 4: *Plays Book 2*. Ed. Ann Saddlemyer. Gerrards Cross, UK: Colin

Smythe, 1982. 393-94.

---. *The Shadow of the Glen. Collected Plays* 15-30.

---. *The Tinker's Wedding. Collected Plays* 31-56.

---. *The Well of the Saints. Collected Plays* 57-100.

Worth, Katharine. *Samuel Beckett's Theatre: Life Journeys.* Oxford: Oxford University Press, 1999.

Yeats, W. B. *Autobiographies.* London: Macmillan, 1961.

---. *Collected Plays.* London: Macmillan, 1953.

10.2478/9788367405423-007

Tom Murphy's *Bailegangaire*: Transcending Despair in Old Age

Csilla Bertha

The Poor Old Woman (the Sean Bhean Bhocht or Shan Van Voght), this long-predominant image personifying the nation in Irish literature and culture, most frequently appears in variants of a seventeenth- and eighteenth-century special Irish genre of poetry, the *Aisling* (dream or vision poem), in which she, after much suffering, will be rejuvenated through the self-sacrifice of men for her sake. The legendary Cathleen ní Houlihan in W. B. Yeats and Augusta Gregory's eponymous play (1902), emblematic of such allegory, inspired and influenced for long the reprsentation of old women in Irish literature, although her figure itself was a portrayal of nation and not of woman, let alone of old woman. Tom Murphy, partly evoking this Mother Ireland figure, partly challenging the iconic image, in *Bailegangaire* (1985) focuses on a poor old woman with a dominating physical presence and a personal story but one who also allows for a reading as an impersonation of the nation.

The play starts out with the stereotypical image of an old woman: Mommo is "senile," querulous, incoherent. The setting itself—the country cottage kitchen—is a revival and, simultaneously, a transformation of the most overused, clichéd, therefore boring setting in Irish drama from the Dramatic Revival on. Murphy and his friend Noel Donoghue famously said before they embarked on writing a play together that one thing was certain: "it's not going to be set in a kitchen" (qtd. in O'Toole, *Politics* 20). And that was true until more than two decades later, when Murphy began to form this play about an old peasant woman in rural Ireland, bedridden, looked after by her granddaughters.

Mommo, declared senile by the stage directions, lives in dire need of generational care in what is often called "deep old age," the "fourth age" (Gilleard and Higgs), or the eighth stage in Erik Erikson's renowned description of the lifecycle in human psychosocial development. Such a person is no longer able to control his/her own attention and bodily functions. Joan Erikson, Erik Erikson's wife and co-researcher, in her extended 1997 edition of his *The Life Cycle* (1982), adds her own chapter on the ninth stage. While acknowledging in it that "the dystonic elements win out as time goes on," she claims that if "elders can come to terms with the dystonic elements in their life experience . . . they may successfully make headway on the path leading to gerotranscendence" (113-14). That is what Mommo reaches at the end, albeit not quite the way gerontologists tend to describe the process.

The term gerotranscendence was introduced in 1989 and later explicated more thoroughly by Lars Tornstam in his eponymous book (2005), greatly building on Erikson's psychosocial approach, and since then it has been deployed by a number of other gerontologists. Tornstam's "gerotrascendence implies a shift in meta-perspective, from a materialistic and rational view of the world to a more cosmic and transcendent one, normally accompanied by an increase in life satisfaction" (Tornstam, "Maturing" 166). This theory, as Tornstam claims, shares with Erikson the view on aging "as a developmental process that, at the very best, ends with a higher state of maturity [which] includes a new form of contentment and a new feeling of affinity with past generations." Yet Erikson's "ego-integrity," in Tornstam's summary, "primarily refers to the integration and possible reconstruction of elements from the life that has passed. The individual reaches a fundamental acceptance of the life lived." Gerotranscendence diverges from that as it implies "a more forward and outwardly directed process, including a redefinition of reality" (144-45).

Despite their differences in direction, both the Eriksons' and Tornstam's theories are basically developmental, suggesting the possibility of gradually maturing into serenity and wisdom, and (as supported by experiments with various groups of aging people) can be helped by caregivers encouraging elderly people and guiding them towards such a positive view on old age. I am taking the liberty of borrowing the term gerotranscendence for marking Mommo's ragged journey of life, not as a gradual developmental process but as it is rendered, in a Murphyan manner, in halts and jolts, through denials, sudden recognitions, courageous leaps over some hindrances, and transcending one's own debilitating faults and sins. The need for that change is certainly made more pressing with aging, hence the special usefulness of the "gero" prefix. Tornstam's theory thus helps to explore how "reminiscence might become part of a much larger reorganization and reconstruction process" (Tornstam, *Gerotranscendence* 145) and how, via reminiscence and with generational encouragement, Mommo arrives at an achieved moral and spiritual liberation from her long-depressing burdens.

Storytelling, remembering
Throughout *Bailegangaire* the audience sees Mommo in bed, struggling to tell her own story, with her granddaughter Mary tending to all her physical needs and the other granddaughter, Dolly—who had looked after her for years earlier—now occasionally visiting. At the opening, Mommo

announces to her imaginary "fondlings" that she will give them a bedtime story and defiantly adds that "no one will stop me! Tellin' my nice story" (Murphy, *Bailegangaire* 92). She shows no concern with her declined bodily state, most of the time oblivious of her immediate environment and position, and denies that she knows Mary. In her ramblings from talking to imaginary hens, then to imaginary small grandchildren, or to herself, some preoccupations shine through in unconnected sentences that will be repeated in the course of the story, such as "but he bet [beat] them" (92), "The cursèd paraffin" (93 and many times again), "Tom is in Galway" (98, 107, and so on). The audience soon begins to feel that something more is going on than dementia or old-age confusion.

Two interrelated themes emerge most forcefully with growing emphasis in both her play-long telling of the story and in the whole play itself: one is home, homecoming, the other is guilt. The image of home is created immediately through the setting of the kitchen with a bed (even if they are somewhat incongruous with each other but the reasonable explanation comes: it is more comfortable and warm than the alternative damp rooms would be). Yet "home" very soon becomes problematized. The homecoming journey of a nameless poor farmer couple from a hugely unlucky fair— where they hoped to sell some of their produce but nothing was sold—provides the structure and forms the spine of Mommo's story that she obsessively starts and restarts telling. As it gradually transpires, her protagonists are actually herself and her late husband, Séamus, and the time is some thirty years earlier. Guilt, on the other hand, concealed behind scattered references, only slowly begins to connect and explain past events and present behavior.

The search for home is a recurring theme with Murphy. He famously said in a 1985 interview with Anthony Roche that he has "a very strong homing instinct" (qtd. in Roche 116), but he qualified it in a later interview where he asserted that home "used to appear in the plays in the literal, geographical way . . . . Now, I see it more as a search for the self, for peace, for harmony" (Kurdi, "Interview" 234). In *Bailegangaire*, that quest constitutes the center of the play in both senses of the word, and the characters take diverging and converging routes for all of them to end up in the family country kitchen. The choices along the physical journey the protagonists face in the story from the past that Mommo is striving to describe in the present, are foreshadowed by the fork in the road where they are forced by the weather to take the longer road because the straight one is too icy for the horse to pull the cart uphill: "One road leading up the incline whence they came, the other to Bochtán. . . . the road to Bochtán, though of circularity, was another means home" (98). Circularity forms the pattern of adventures and sufferings of all the family. The re-routing of the homeward journey gains further emphasis by Mary's and Dolly's contributions with their own life-stories of frustration. Mary emigrated to London and worked there successfully until homesickness drew her back home, which she experiences as a failure because her grandmother refuses to recognize her. Dolly, on the other hand, suffering from her loveless marriage and her emigrant husband's absence during the year and his violence on his home-visits, takes revenge by infidelities and now, wanting to get rid of the child she is pregnant with, tries to persuade her sister to adopt it as her own. The attempts and obstacles of the grandparents' homeward journey in the old story are counterpointed by the grandchildren's waiting for them at home. Due to the delay in the journey, a terrible tragedy happens at home and the two ends of the story meet only in the present of the play when at last the two partial experiences complement each other. Similarly, the two kinds of homecoming trips—the physical and the spiritual-emotional—unite and become a whole. The beauty of the writing is that the geographical and literal voyage in the story retains its physical immediacy throughout while at the same time becomes metaphorical for the emotional, moral, and spiritual homecoming.

Mommo used to be a well-known "professional" storyteller, a *seanchaí* in her community, to whom people came to listen from far and wide. In the present of the play her telling the story, although keeping alive its traditional, ornate, archaic language, interspersed with Gaelic, has become broken, fragmented, unbearably repetitive, referred to by the granddaughters as "video" or "gramophone" (Murphy, *Bailegangaire* 143). Her obsessive storytelling seems to have no connection whatsoever with the present and with those present. Yet, as it becomes apparent, her starting and restarting, her difficulties in proceeding originate not so much in her old-age loss or confusion of memory, as in her manifold trauma and guilt. The continual storytelling proves an excellent dramatic means of revealing her oscillation between wanting to confess something and trying to conceal it. The distancing technique is obvious, for instance, in her talking about herself and her husband in the third person as a "decent man and his decent wife the same," or "strangers." When Mary from time to time tries to switch to the first person, Mommo does not respond. Yet now and then she drops some hints of her eagerness to face her guilty conscience. Of the many "misfortunes" that surface in the course of the story, several were caused by herself, for instance, about her children she almost casually says early on that those that "weren't drowned or died they said she drove away" (98). And again: "An' *did* she drive them all away? Never ever to be heard of, ever again" (164, emphasis in the original).

The storytelling tradition and her own long practicing of it makes keeping memories alive easier for Mommo. But although her embellished, sophisticated, complex language comes as a routine from her past, she still needs to remember the right words and the innumerable details in their order— and there seems to be no problem with that part of her consciousness. Her story, even in its fragmentariness and brokenness, is nothing like confused blathering but a structured, many times repeated narration—yet only as far as it is comfortable for her. Omitting certain details appears to have become also part of her routine, and when challenged by Mary's persistent questions, all her alertness is needed to evade what might become traps to force her to face the truth. She even cunningly uses her fragility as a disguise (for instance, pretending she is sleepy). It is hard to see how much of her hide-and-seek game is deliberate, yet her efforts to escape are noticeable.

"Repetition . . . is an obstacle to remembering," in Paul Ricoeur's statement ("Memory" 6), using "remembering" in its meaning of recollection, deliberate action (the Greek *anamnēsis*)—as differentiated from "simple" memory or evocation (Aristotle's *mnēmē*). Recollection, because it "is a way of doing things, not only with words, but with our minds" (Ricoeur, "Memory" 5), "an active search" (*Memory, History* 17), has its ethical dimension. Mommo's endless storytelling seems to be mostly such recollection and her repetitions arise from her need yet reluctance to name her trauma. Although Ricoeur talks about the "duty to remember" primarily in a historical context ("Memory" 9), the moral imperative can also apply to the individual. It is necessary to remember truly and not sufficient to simply retell selected parts of memories if liberation from the psychological weight is to be achieved. Ricoeur also calls attention to the "duty to forget," not in the sense of general amnesia and forgetting the past, but as "a duty to go beyond anger and hatred" and "be reconciled with the past" ("Memory" 11), to move towards forgiveness. Perhaps the most difficult is to be reconciled with oneself, but the miracle in Murphy's play is that Mommo will arrive at that point by its end.

Storytelling itself has been a dominant Irish genre of communication and self-expression, long before postmodern drama discovered it as a way of revealing psychological states without the openly theatrical monologue. But, as Roche maintains, in *Bailegangaire*, the relationship between story and play is complicated, and the audience becomes aware of the "discrepancy between the rambling Christmas story of Mommo . . . and the present-tense conditions of the play itself." This "gap" is, Roche suggests, what "has to be filled in and made meaningful by a sustaining process of dramatic interaction" (120). The stumbling block in the narration remains invisible for long even to the best-intentioned Mary, and only Mommo herself can bring to light certain components. One so-far hidden part of the truth is revealed in the crucial confession uttered in a simple sentence, in the midst of relating a host of other happenings: that Mommo and her husband "could have got home" (140) before the tragic turn. This fact is entirely new to the granddaughters, who know the rest of the story by heart now. From Mommo's narrative we learn that while waiting for the thaw, the couple stopped at a pub in the remote village of Bochtán—the Irish name denoting the "village of poor people"—where the husband got involved in a laughing contest with Costello, the local "giant" laughter-champion. And, as in folktales, the hero "must slay [the giant] in order to reach home" (O'Toole, *Politics* 189). The story recounts, as Mommo announces at the beginning, "how the place called Bochtán . . . came by its new appellation, Bailegangaire, the place without laughter" (92), similarly to an origin-myth or a folktale. More exactly, fitting in the specifically Irish genre of *dinnsenachas* (or *Dindsenchas*): the lore of the place that recites or sings out the formation of the placenames, their deriving from local figures, events, stories, legends. Tradition within tradition—dinnseanachas within storytelling. But the storytelling actually is a circuitous road to confession.

Although Mommo's frustration primarily derives from trauma and guilt, and not really from incapabilities caused by old age, the moral-psychological dilemma of how to face and name the truth is obviously aggravated by the considerable urgency that aging brings to look back and get ready to give an account of life. Guilt renders it near-impossible to evoke and tell—basically to herself and whoever is there to listen—what happened in the past. What she goes through is similar to what the renowned gerontologist who coined the term "ageism" in 1969 and revolutionized gerontology, Robert N. Butler, names the "life review." He protested as early as in the 1960s against the general "tendency to identify reminiscence in the aged as psychological dysfunction," dementia or escapism, "aimless wandering of the mind," "unselective and unbidden," "of dubious reliability," and beyond the control of the person. In contrast, he conceives of it as a "naturally occurring, universal mental process, characterized by the progressive return to consciousness of past experiences, and, particularly the resurgence of unresolved conflicts" (65, 66). With the exception that Mommo's guilty memories do not "progressively" return but have been torturing her for long as her continual storytelling bears witness, she follows the trajectory Butler describes: "As we grow older and approach death, it becomes enormously important to strengthen our intimate relationships, . . . to come to grips with guilt and shame, experience remorse and . . . effect reconciliations" ("Prologue" qtd. in Bengtson). Mommo, at one point soberly, skeptically meditates about how strange life is: "'Tis. An' if we could live it again? Would we? . . . In harmony? Aah, I don't know" (119).

The laughing competition that the narration circles around, itself compresses a long "life review" into the events of an evening. The laughter is rooted in defiance—an ancient, oximoronic, grotesque response to the blows of fate; the ability to laugh at one's tragedies, to laugh death in the face. Murphy said about his characters in an interview that in their search for home they "seem to fly but then come back to fight," since reality, "as it is, unbearable because it's inadequate to deal with whatever the spirit of man is looking for" (Billington 111). Laughter is a mode of that fight; a confrontation with the "unbearable" reality. The more tragic the events are, the more laughter. And it is chiefly Mommo, who supplied the two champions with the "topic" of the continual laughter: euphemistically called "misfortunes" (163-64). Those range from the miserable potato crop through fights within the family, babies, "unbaptized an' stillborn in shoe boxes planted at the dead hour of night" in the fields (a well-known scandalous phenomenon in the reality of the 1980s in the West of Ireland), to the many deaths including all her children—an unending litany of horrible tragedies. She recalls that she herself "made great contributions, rollcalling the dead," cataloguing "their nearest an' dearest. Her Pat was her eldest, died of consumption . . . . Soft Willie inside, quiet by the hearth . . . An' for the sake of an old ewe was stuck in the flood was how she lost two of the others . . . . An' the nice wife . . . one of them left behind him? . . . Died tryin' to give birth to the fourth was to be in it. An' she herself left with the care of three small childre waitin'" (163-64). One of the two sons that drowned and his "nice wife" are, Mary recognizes, their parents—the missing generation. The list goes on in the tale and so does the mad laughter, joined by all present, the "wretched and neglected, . . . ragged an' dirty, impoverished, hungry, . . . ridiculin' an' defying of their lot on earth below—glinting their defiance—their defiance an' rejection, inviting of what else might come or *care* to come!" (164, emphasis in the original). That is what Vivian Mercier calls the "noisy desperation" of Murphy's characters when he talks about Mommo as a "female Job who longs to unburden herself of all her grievances before she dies" (18-19).

Recurring images of circularity abound in the story and reinforce the closed circle of despair: the circuitous route home, the husband drawing curlicues with his glass on the pub counter while forming his decision to challenge the local laughing champion (127), then Costello "began to walk circles screechin'" (138), and the "two gladiators, circling the floor, eyes riveted together . . . " (154). The circular movement is repeated by the young generation: as Mary says to Dolly, "you're running round in circles," to which Dolly retorts: "*I'm* running round in circles? Suitcase packed—How many times?" (151, emphasis in the original)—referring to Mary's hesitant intention to go away again. The circle may well become a trap of repetition.

It is contemplating the nature of freedom that leads Mary
to the decision that she would help Mommo to break out of the
repetitions and finish her story. Asking Mommo, "Give me my
freedom" (120)—that she did not have when far away, in
England—she answers herself with "What freedom? . . . No
freedom without structure" (120, ellipsis in the original).
Freedom does not exist without defining what from.
Significantly, her meditation on freedom and home is inspired
by Thomas Hardy's poem "Silences." The lines she reads out
aloud reflect Hardy's pessimist determinism in emphasizing
that what happened in the past cannot ever be changed or
remedied in the present:

> But the silence of an empty house
> Where oneself was born,
> Dwelt, held carouse. . .
> . . .
> Is of all the silence most forlorn.
> It seems no power can waken it—
> . . .
> Or the past permit
> The present to stir a torpor like a tomb's. (122)

To which she responds with a definite "[i]s that so? Well, I
don't agree with you" and wakes up Mommo with her offer to
cooperate with her in finishing the story and then to achieve
some relief. She not only faithfully repeats Mommo's words,
turns of speech, but also imitates her accent, and enters into
the story and storytelling, creating almost a dialogue with
Mommo. Moreover, from this moment on the audience
witnesses "an increasingly theatrical collaboration between
Mary and Mommo in the generation of the narrative, with

Mary performing more of a directorial function than just urging the action forward" (Roche 124).

Fintan O'Toole, talking about the "double narrative," the "double time frame" of many a Murphy play, with "things happening simultaneously but in different time frames" ("Preface" xii, xiii), asserts that Murphy constantly destabilizes the notion of time's linearity in favor of its circularity and threatens that the past may return as the future (xiv). Yet *Bailegangaire* (along with *The Gigli Concert*, written around the same time, in the early '80s) differs from most Murphy plays in its more optimistic resolution. The doubleness of the time frame is obvious here, too: the pastness of the story told in the present, the sin committed thirty years prior to the confessing of it now, and the granddaughters' contemporary lives, conflicts, problems unfolding parallel with Mommo's reviving the past. In Peter Crawley's words, Murphy's "plays are poised exquisitely between despair and hope" ("Tom Murphy"). That is true of his plays with characters of any age, and particularly so of the old Mommo, although for long despair seems to prevail. That duality constructs Erik Erikson's definition of the fundamental antithesis of "integrity vs. despair" (61), typical of the psychosocial development in the last (eighth) stage of life. Integrity consists in peace, "a sense of *coherence* and *wholeness*" (albeit at constant danger of breaking down due to the somatic processes), and, above all, wisdom: an "informed and detached concern with life itself even in the face of death itself" (61), whereas its antithetical counterpart is disappointment, disgust, disdain, bitterness, ruminating over mistakes. He suggests that these "syntonic" and "dystonic" elements should be in balance in order to successfully resolve crises (8). With Mommo that balance is sorely missing for most of the play as the palpable despair and bitterness seem to be the only "integrating" force of her being.

One direction in which the play's dynamics work is a jolt out of the circles returning exactly to themselves and being entirely determined by the past. That takes huge effort from the family members, who must accept and absorb the changes, the losses, the passing of time with all its debris. There is no return to the past but the past values and feelings are necessary to sustain the present. Mommo's senile-appearing repetitive circularity, her return to the same moments of the past sounds futile until it proves more than a self-serving "gramophone." She needs and receives Mary's help to break out of the enclosed story at Bochtán to arrive back home and acknowledge how greatly it has changed due to the grandparents' delay. The earlier repeated phrases now gain their tragic context: Tom, the little grandson, having suffered a mortal accident (caused by "[t]he cursed paraffin"), died in the hospital in Galway ("Tom is in Galway"), and the grandfather died within two days from the wounds given by the Bailegangaires infuriated by his victory over their hero, Costello ("but he bet them"). Costello's death ended the laughing contest, and changed the name of their village to one without laughter. Again, as in folktales: a threefold death comes as punishment for evil intentions. The punishment is certainly out of proportion with Mommo's evil, which only consisted in impulsively urging the continuation of the laughing contest in her desire to revenge the many years of silence and coldness in her marriage and all the fatal losses in their lives. That competition, indeed, lasted to the end of life (three lives). But the burden cannot be lifted until she acknowledges her part in causing all that.

The moment of Mommo's stepping out of the gramophone groove on Mary's prompting, encouraging, insisting, happens when she, after admitting that "they could have got home" because the thaw was settling in (140), adds that she herself demanded that the contest continue although both her husband and Costello would have given it up. And reluctantly, she discloses her motivation:

> But what about the things had been vexin' *her* for years? No, a woman isn't stick or stone. The forty years an' more in the one bed together an' he to rise in the mornin' (and) not to give her a glance. An' so long it had been he had called her by first name, she's near forgot it herself . . . Brigit . . . Hah? . . . An' so she thought he hated her [. . .] but she'd renege matters no longer [. . .]—she hated him too. (140, ellipses in square brackets added)

As the competition goes on and the local people's mistrust of the strangers turns into welcoming and cheering them on, she rejoices: "'Twas the best night ever!" (131), "'Twas the nicest night ever" (156, 159, 164, repeated many times).

In his interview with Mike Murphy, Tom Murphy talks about how he did *not* do research into the traditional Irish storyteller's ornate, elaborate language interspersed with Gaelic-Irish words and phrases and Elisabethan turns of speech, but rather he absorbed it from his mother's extraordinary vocabulary. He describes with admiration her ability to compress into one sentence an amazing range of emotions, "hateful, vindictive, loving, tender, elated, depressed." All that "would be regurgitated and come out later in a play," as he tried to "achieve in writing" that kind of "emotion and the sudden changes that can happen in the space of a sentence" (Mike Murphy 176). The evocation of the grotesque, tale-like laughing contest amply shows that kind of complexity which creates the frame for the coexistence of the "syntonic" and "dystonic" elements in the psyche, of despair and mirth, defiance and affection, and facilitates the compression of excesses of feelings in a short space. Thus soon after Mommo's expression of resentment, anger, frustration, being hurt, desire for revenge, and hatred of her husband, she suddenly arrives at a moment of great tenderness and the unexpected re-emerging of love between them:

> An' didn't he ferret out her eyes to see how she was fairin', an' wasn't she titherin' with the best of them an' weltin' her thighs. No heed on her now to be gettin' on home. No. But offerin' to herself her own congratulations at hearin' herself laughin'. An' then, like a girl, smiled at her husband, an' his smile back so shy, like a boy he was in youth. An' the moment was for them alone. Unawares of all cares, unawares of all the others. An' how long before since their eyes have met, mar gheal dhá gréine, glistenin' for each other. Not since long and long ago. (161-62)

Her urging him on with the contest gave rare joy and triumph to both of them. It provided him with the opportunity to win a fairy-tale-like heroic victory against the giant Costello backed by his own community. Proud of his clever riposte to Costello's words that even the community admired and changed their first hostile attitude to warm welcome, she became enabled to laugh with such abandon as never for a long time. Indeed, "twas the nicest night ever." This "nicest night" though, caused the triple death of Costello, the Bochtán laughing champion, that of Tom the grandson at home, and that of Mommo's husband.

Guilt and its expiation

Although it all sounds like Erikson's "retrospective mythologizing that can amount to a pseudo integration as a defence against lurking despair" (65), Mommo's deliberate distancing of her oft-repeated story would contradict a self-mythologizing intent. In an intertextual form Murphy even validates the "truth" of what Mommo is saying in his companion play, *A Thief of a Christmas* (1985), which focuses on the laughing contest itself. Set some thirty years earlier than *Bailegangaire*, when Mommo was obviously not senile, it dramatizes the same characters and displays many similar details of behavior, relationship, circumstance that will return in Mommo's memory-story. Not that Murphy would write *A Thief* to justify Mommo's memories (and the resolution is radically different in the two plays), yet it also indicates that the problem is not with her forgetfulness and dementia. To a great extent, her dementia itself appears to be related to, and originating from, her sense of guilt. Her ongoing recounting of her story with her distanced self in the centre, carefully omitting moments that prompted the events towards the tragedies, evidently derives from a compulsion to dig deep in the consciousness and conscience to reveal the truth below the surface under her decades-old repression.

The haunting presence of Mommo's guilt and devastating trauma could be explained by Freudian repression, yet a more subtle view is offered for her trauma treatment by the psychiatrist whom Murphy worked with for long, Ivor W. Browne. Browne confesses:

Having been led astray for a long time by Freud's notion of "repression" I have finally come to realise that when a person . . . is faced with an experience which is so painful, so threatens to engulf him or her, rather than go through the pain and the suffering, which would be too much at that time, the person brings into play a capacity . . . to deny, to quite simply put the experience on ice so that it remains unlived, . . . waiting to be experienced with all its pain and immediacy at some later time . . . [when they] work them through . . . with all the immediacy, detail, pain and suffering . . . . And in this way they manage to become more at ease within themselves. (133)

In most of the play Mommo is still trying to keep her painful "experience on ice" by distancing the story while from time to time the truth forcefully surfaces. This struggle makes the relief and liberation from her secret sin at the conclusion almost miraculous: she recognizes Mary, giving the feeling of homecoming to her granddaughter, who in turn agrees to accept her sister's plan, and all three can unite in the warmth of a re-found home and love. A rebirth becomes possible, the new baby will replace Tom; as forecast by Dolly's earlier persuading remark that if Mary accepts it, "if it's a boy you can call it Tom, and if it's a girl you can call it Tom" (147).

Mommo tells all her story with amazing consistency in the details, including moments of immense turbulence of contradictory emotions: anger, frustration, revenge, defiance, a will to burst out of (mostly self-generated) silence—the kind that Murphy describes as his mother's unique capability. Mary's relentless efforts to get Mommo through her tale, empowers the old woman to tell it all and revive the shameful and hurtful moments as well as the deeply emotional ones with the same clarity as the neutral, descriptive details. Except for the final blows of Tom's and her husband's death, which must be spelled out by Mary, but with Mommo's consent. The confession by way of storytelling becomes a therapy, a kind of psychotherapy. The awareness of unacknowledged guilt and unresolved sin is as great an emotional obstacle in the telling as the physical obstacle of the icy road was in the journey towards home. As in the story she transcends her estrangement from her husband in moments of high tension, so now she transcends her repression. She reaches gerotranscendence after long and arduous efforts, suffering, fighting, if not a gradual development. The battle is with herself, the others move in and out of her horizon, and she will be able to re-establish real contact with them, but only after she faces and names her guilt and integrates the past into the present. This is indeed close to Erik Erikson's "ego-integrity": "wisdom," "a sense of coherence and wholeness," possible to achieve in the last phase of life.

Gerotranscendence, in addition, opens up a broader view of life that Tornstam calls the "cosmic" dimension, feeling as part of, and in contact with the universe. That includes becoming "less self-occupied," "transcending borders and barriers that had circumscribed [such people] earlier in life" ("Maturing" 168). Indeed, Mommo, locked into herself for long, now places herself in "the flow of generations" (169); contemplates and quotes her father's pieces of wisdom, renews her relationship with her granddaughters, transcends her estrangement from her immediate environment, recognizes Dolly and then, more miraculously, Mary. She also finds her place in the universe (reminded by her father's philosophizing of how humans should find their place on earth, like the snail knows its own) and becomes able to pray. Out of uniting the personal and the metaphysical arises love. Which constitutes a real, manifold homecoming. Similarly to the resolution of crises in several (not all) Murphy plays, his characters may experience sudden moments of enlightenment and recognition, miraculous strokes of light, unexpected grace that change their behavior. Mommo's tansformation after a long time of torturing herself and her granddaughters is such a miracle. As she sheds her dementia in recognizing the surrounding reality, and surprisingly assesses her present condition addressing Mary (now by her name): "haven't we everything we need here, the two of us" (169), she eventually transcends the despair about the human condition being "unbearable." As her writer-creator confirms in an interview, she finds peace through "accepting that it is a valley of tears, and as is said in *Bailegangaire*, 'And sure a tear isn't such a bad thing?'" (Billington 112).

"The story of Bailegangaire began with a laughing contest and ended in tragedy. The story of *Bailegangaire* begins in the fruitless grief of mutual isolation and achieves its healing atonement through moments of shared laughter" (Roche 127). Holding laughter and tears, laughter and tragedy together— here mirthless laughter as desperate defiance, tears of bitterness and tears of gratitude—is a feature of the most characteristic Irish dramatic genre, tragicomedy. The sisters' first moment of reconciliation in laughter "brings Mommo back to life, enabling her to resume and . . . [finally] bring the family narrative to a conclusion" (Roche 127). Both acts end in tears, but with a great difference: at the closing of act 1 Mary and Dolly are crying over their seemingly unsolvable troubles with the only relief that they can share their suffering and console each other while Mommo still continues, irritatingly, telling her story. In the concluding scene of act 2 the tears are those of Mary: "tears of gratitude" that "brim to her eyes, fervently" but "her crying is infused with a sound like the laughter of relief" (Murphy, *Bailegangaire* 170) while Mommo is assuring her that "a tear isn't such a bad thing" (169). To the miraculous transformations that bring some kind of resolution to all the three women's problems, the only response can be gratefulness and prayer. Mommo's prayer—"To thee do we cry. Yes? Poor banished daughters of Eve" (169)—is the prayer of the "painfully orphaned" people (Murray, "Rough" 14) in their metaphysical homelessness after the expulsion from Paradise. The beautiful closing stage image, however, shows the threesome in a union of love and peace with the old woman in the middle of the bed and the two granddaughters going to sleep on her two sides. An unholy trinity, having found home in the old place but with the future beckoning with the possibility of renewal, in sharp contrast with the opening image in which the lonely Mommo was imperiously sitting up in the middle of the kitchen, in bed, like on a throne, ordering real and imaginary people around her. The final words are given by Mary in her relief and joy—an unsentimental, hard-earned conclusion: "To conclude. It's a strange old place, alright, in whatever wisdom He has to have made it this way. But in whatever wisdom there is, in the year 1984, it was decided to give that—fambly . . . of strangers another chance, and a brand new baby to gladden their home" (Murphy, *Bailegangaire* 170).

Murphy's creating their home in the cottage kitchen is a *tour de force*. This setting, on the one hand, makes tangible Mommo's multiple (in time, space, and spirit) isolation from the contemporary world; on the other, is both a desirable fixed point in the lives of the lonely and frustrated granddaughters, who bring in the shifting outside reality, and an ironic revival of the nostalgic image of Western Ireland. This richly associative site works as a *lieu de mémoire* both in the sense of an all-too-familiar iconic place in rural Ireland and as its long-lived traditional representation on the stage. Sites of memory are created and revered when memory itself is fading, precisely "because there are no longer *milieux de mémoire*, real environments of memory" (Nora 7). Still, what is questioned more than the existence of the country cottage in reality is, as Christopher Morash and Shaun Richards remind us, the Irish sense of place itself, long considered a strong component of Irish identity. In the process of disappearing in the 1980s, it no longer supplies playwrights with "stage spaces that are already invested with meaning" (116). Murphy, however, while destabilizing this ready-made sense of place, also fills the setting with meanings, old and new; he turns this most commonplace space into a womb-tomb-like ritualized area where existential transformation, even transubstantiation can happen.

A great truth-seeker, Murphy, as often in other plays, brings his characters to the point of crying out, shouting out, naming the evils that bother them, to expose the truths that have been carefully concealed, confront their own selves and, consequently, find relief from the burden of their sins. "No other Irish playwright grapples as intensely as he with matters of guilt, sin and redemption" (Murray, "Reading" 7). Guilt, sin, repentance, forgiveness, rebirth—central to Murphy's work— are also at the core of Christianity. Elsewhere, I explore how several Murphy plays, in his unconventional, undogmatic, faithless faith, dramatize such a trajectory of the soul from the darkness in sin, void, desperation, to a sudden transformation through arriving at some light of hope. It could be identified as magic or alchemy, where matter must be dissolved into its parts in order to be reshaped into precious gold or, as the pagan, shamanic notion of (the artist's) having to go down to the darkness of the underworld and be ripped apart in order to be reborn. It is also consistent with the idea of St. John of the Cross's "Dark night of the soul" and, of course, with Jesus

Christ's passion, death, and resurrection. I argue that "Murphy's discourse leaves his plays open to readings of his human miracles as manifestations of the divine presence within the human, especially in interpersonal relationships" (Bertha 288). Murphy allows some of his characters, often full of anger, defiance, revolting, doubting, questioning, talking back, to also come to moments of sublime beauty when suddenly they will show empathy and love transcending their sinfulness. The human goodness and forgiveness that surface from some unlikely sources, radiate glimpses of divine grace—the peace which passeth all understanding. Or, as Richard Cave maintains: "what is often profoundly moving in Murphy's plays is his conviction that even in a godless world humanity retains some religious instinct which compels them for good or ill to shape their own strange rituals of belief behind which one can still sense as it were a palimpsest of Western traditions of faith and practice" (qtd. in Bertha 276).

Transcendence and relief, however, does not follow the defiant laughing at disasters in the community of Bailegangaire, "the place without laughter." The host of the "wretched and neglected, dilapidated an' forlorn, the forgotten an' tormented, the lonely an' despairing, . . . impoverished, hungry, emaciated and unhealthy" (164) people at the laughing contest broadens to encompass the whole nation. Shaun Richards, reading together Murphy's trilogy, *The Mommo Plays: Brigit, Bailegangaire, A Thief of a Christmas* (published together in this volume as late as 2014) along with earlier drafts and notes, traces Mommo's individual drama back to the national trauma of the mid-nineteenth-century Great Famine. His comparative study of the three plays that focus on different moments in the life of the same family, brings plenty of evidence that "it is against [the] backdrop of physical deprivation and the concomitant emotional consequences, that the story of Mommo and Séamus can be fully comprehended" (Richards 326) and that Mommo "is always seen as a link to an earlier generation of suffering and loss" (331). Thus she gives voice to her fellow sufferers—in Murphy's words—the "silent," "hungry and demoralised" people ("Introduction" xi). One psychological distortion the Famine is responsible for is what Kevin Whelan describes as "a certain amount of iron [that] entered the Irish soul in the Famine holocaust" (qtd. in Richards 332), which shows up in Séamus's "famine-hardened fatalism" (Richards 333) and in Mommo's toughness that sometimes looks like cruelty. Murphy himself remarks that "[w]omanhood becomes harsh. Love, tenderness, loyalty, generosity go out the door in the struggle for survival" as a long-lasting effect ("Introduction" xi). Quite a few signs indicate that once those affirmative values were there, such as Mommo's sudden switching from her story to singing the song "Once I loved with fond affection" (134).

Like his heroine, Murphy himself answers the call for the "duty to remember" in "keep[ing] alive the memory of suffering over against the general tendency of history to celebrate the victors" (Ricoeur, "Memory" 10). His *Bailegangaire* itself preceded by ten years the first publication of a selection and edition of oral testimonies of the last generation who still heard famine-surviving relatives' personal experiences, and his Mommo, due to her age, could have been one of those giving testimony from her own family's history. Indeed, she begins her list of "misfortunes" with the "potatoes, the damnedable crop was in that year" (163)—an unquestionable immediate reminder of the Famine. In this way she connects not only the past and the present but also personal, communicative memory (which lasts only through three or four generations) with cultural memory (in Jan Assmann's differentiation, 56) and the individual with the community—with disaster lurking always behind, even, or especially, in the mirth of the laughing contest. As Nicholas Grene sums it up, "by recuperating the history of that family in all its psychic deformation, in forcing through the mythic story of the laughing-contest to its end, the play enacts a sort of family therapy that expresses the trauma of a nation for all of us who share in it" ("Talking It" 81). Growing to represent the nation, she assumes the role of Mother Ireland, without losing or diminishing her subjectivity. This must have been apparent to theatre-goers as, for example, Fintan O'Toole praises Siobhán McKenna's brilliant performance of Mommo in his review of the premiere of *Bailegangaire*, for "[t]he scale of her style, the fact that Mother Ireland hovers in the background of her stage persona, is exactly right here, precisely because she *is*, in one dimension of Mommo, Mother Ireland. But it is not the Mother Ireland of long and noble suffering, weeping and wailing. It is a Mother Ireland who spits and urinates" (qtd. in Grene, *Theatre* 14, emphasis in the original).

Thus, through this miserable yet still dominating Mother Ireland figure encapsulating the nation's suffering and defiance, *Bailegangaire* brought into public debate the vastness of the national trauma and its legacy. The play suggests that a belated coming of age is necessary however much courage it takes from the older generation. Generational help is mutually needed by the old and the young—for the latter to avoid depthlessness and spiritual homelessness in the hugely changing world of modernizing Ireland. Mary's yearning for the recognition of her belonging to the family, for an "anchor" to confirm her identity is only answered when Mommo, herself liberated from dementia, at last calls her by her name. By the end the three women will succeed in bridging the vast gaps and making room for continuity, for the future metaphorized by Dolly's to-be-born child.

Conclusion

Evoking the traditional Mother Ireland figure in Mommo, Murphy shapes her to be radically different from Yeats and Gregory's Cathleen, who steps into the cottage from outside, carrying the air of another dimension of existence. Mommo, by contrast, is as deeply rooted in the place and in her physical being as anyone possibly could be. Although she does, similarly to Cathleen, demand heroism and causes deaths but being an earthly woman, badly suffers from the consequences, and her final renewal will not turn her into a "girl with the walk of a queen," but into a loving grandmother. This ailing, bedridden old woman, wracked by historical and personal disasters, long nurturing very earthly anger and hatred—partly through the sacrificial help of the young, partly due to her courage to face her past—while remaining literally a poor old woman with all her frailty and arrogance, transcends all that and metamorphoses into an indomitable yet far-from-idealized Poor Old Woman.

The *seanchaí*, being an old—in everyday behavior mostly—senile woman, whose listeners first pay no attention to her, and then later nudge her into finishing her tale only to "have done with it," despite all, carries vivid energies from the past. *Bailegangaire* is not a memory-play in the sense that, for instance, Brian Friel's world-famous *Dancing at Lughnasa* (1995) is, where the narrator, Michael's childhood memories of his parents, aunts, and uncle will be projected onto the stage. The people, places, and events in Mommo's tale come to life merely by way of her words and through their power in the "eye of the mind" of the audience. Whilst the narrating creates images of the past, the audience all along sees the storyteller staying in the same spot, sitting up or lying down in bed, time travelling in her mind, and experiences not only the double timeframe but also the double space-place dynamics. Mommo's storytelling may be broken, repetitive, incomprehensible, but it connects generations of the Irish and centuries of Irish history. The play suggests that "the national tradition of storytelling may gain a new function: acknowledging the past, which is a key issue both in finding Irish identity and feeling at home in the world" (Kurdi, *Nemzeti* 204, my translation from the Hungarian).

The hope in "the transmissibility of culture" through art (including the art of storytelling) may sound "romantic" and "utopian," but I do not think Murphy in *Bailegangaire* wants it to look also "just not possible" as Declan Kiberd's reading suggests (87). It is true that Mommo's healing into gerotranscendence takes a miracle such as Murphy often works in his plays: "The ending of a Murphy play . . . involves transformation. The lights do not go down on stasis but on a new dynamic. Liberation is usually incorporated, if not always hope or transcendence (though these are certainly emphasized more in the later work" (Murray, "Reading" 8). Tom Murphy— with great courage in the modernizing Ireland and Irish theatre—powerfully shaped the figure of a tradition-bound old woman in her traditional environment, engrossed in her own storytelling, battered by memories of past blows of fate and endangered by the (then) present tendency of the Irish to forget them, who will reach psychologically viable equilibrium in gerotranscendence and dramatically earned transformation that is the essence of theatre.

Works Cited

Assmann, Jan. *A kulturális emlékezet* [Cultural Memory]. Budapest: Atlantisz, 1999.

Bengtson, Vern L., and Frank J. Whittington. "From Ageism to the Longevity Revolution: Robert Butler, Pioneer." *The Gerontologist* 54.6 (Dec. 2014): 1064-69. Web. 25 Oct. 2021.

Bertha, Csilla. "'Rituals of a Lost Faith'?: Murphy's Theatre of the Possible." *Alive in Time: The Enduring Drama of Tom Murphy.* Ed. Christopher Murray. Dublin: Carysfort, 2010. 273-90.

Billington, Michael. "Tom Murphy in Conversation with Michael Billington." Grene, *Talking About Tom Murphy* 91-112.

Browne, Ivor W. "Thomas Murphy: The Madness of Genius." *Irish University Review* 17.1 (1987): 129-36.

Butler, Robert N. "The Life Review: An Interpretation of Reminiscence in the Aged." *Psychiatry* 26: 65-76. Web. 21 Oct. 2021.

Crawley, Peter. "Tom Murphy: 'How do you write a play? I don't Know'" *The Irish Times.* Web. 23 Aug. 2021.

Erikson, Erik H. *The Life Cycle Completed: Extended Version with New Chapters on the Ninth Stage of Development by Joan M. Erikson.* Ed. Joan M. Erikson. New York, London: W.W. Norton, 1997.

Grene, Nicholas. *The Theatre of Tom Murphy.* London and New York: Bloomsbury Methuen Drama, 2017.

---. "Talking It Through: *The Gigli Concert* and *Bailegangaire*." Grene, *Talking About Tom Murphy* 67-81.

---, ed. *Talking About Tom Murphy.* Dublin: Carysfort, 2002.

Higgs, Paul, and Chris Gilleard. *Rethinking Old Age: Theorising the Fourth Age.* New York: Palgrave Macmillan, 2015.

Kiberd, Declan. "Response." Grene, *Talking About Tom Murphy* 83-87.

Kurdi, Mária. *Nemzeti önszemlélet a mai ír drámában (1960-1990)*. [National Self-Perception in Contemporary Irish Drama]. Budapest: Akadémiai, 1999.

---. "An Interview with Tom Murphy." *Irish Studies Review* 12. 2 (2004): 233-40.

Mercier, Vivian. "Noisy Desperation: Murphy and the Book of Job." *Irish University Review* 17.1 (1987): 18-23.

Morash, Christopher, and Shaun Richards. *Mapping Irish Theatre: Theories of Space and Place*. Cambridge: Cambridge University Press, 2013.

Murphy, Mike. "Tom Murphy." *Reading the Future: Irish Writers in Conversation with Mike Murphy*. Ed. Cliodhna Ní Anluain. Dublin: Lilliput Press, 2000. 163-87.

Murphy, Tom. "Introduction." *Plays: One*. London: Methuen, 1992. ix-xxi.

---. *Bailegangaire*. *Plays: Two*. London: Methuen, 1993. 89-170.

Murray, Christopher. "The Rough and Holy Theatre of Thomas Murphy: Introduction." *Irish University Review* 17.1 (1987): 9-17.

---. "Reading Murphy Reading Ireland: Introduction." Murray, ed. *Alive in Time* 1-13.

---, ed. *Alive in Time: The Enduring Drama of Tom Murphy*. Dublin: Carysfort, 2010.

Nora, Pierre. "Between Memory and History: Les Lieux de Mémoire." *Representations* 26 (Spring 1989).

O'Toole, Fintan. *The Politics of Magic*. Dublin: Raven Arts, 1987.

---. "Preface: Tom Murphy's Times." Murray, ed. *Alive in Time* xi-xvii.

Richards, Shaun. "From *Brigit* to *Bailegangaire*: The Development of Tom Murphy's Mommo Trilogy." *Irish University Review* 46.2 (2016): 324-39.

Ricoeur, Paul. "Memory and Forgetting." *Questioning Ethics.* Ed. Richard Kearney and Mark Dooley. London: Routledge, 1999. 5-11.

---. *Memory, History, Forgetting.* Trans. Kathleen Blamey and David Pellauer. Chicago and London: University of Chicago, 2004.

Roche, Anthony. *"Bailegangaire:* Storytelling into Drama." *Irish University Review* 17.1 (1987): 114-28.

Tornstam, Lars. *Gerotranscendence: A Developmental Theory of Positive Aging.* New York: Springer, 2005. Web. 25 Sept. 2021.

---. "Maturing into Gerotranscendence." *The Journal of Transpersonal Psychology* 43.2. (2011): 166-80. Web. 25 Sept. 2021.

10.2478/9788367405423-008

Old Age and Aging: Presence and Absence in the Plays of Brian Friel

Giovanna Tallone

The process of aging and the condition of old age may not seem to be an immediate priority in Brian Friel's dramatic work. Critical attention has been paid to aspects such as national identity, community, and gender, along with deranged and disabled characters that have been highlighted in his plays, whether "at the centre of the action or, more frequently, in peripheral roles" (Niel 143). Yet, the companion categories of old age and aging remain relatively unexplored in his *oeuvre* as they are quite a new area in literary studies at large, too, a "missing category in current literary theory" (Ingman 8). The growing attention to studies on aging features in a variety of fairly recent publications, such as Heather Ingman's study on fiction, *Ageing in Irish Writing: Strangers to Themselves* (2018) and the special issue of *Nordic Irish Studies* devoted to women and aging, where Margaret O'Neill and Michaela Schrage-Früh point out in their "Introduction" how aging "has, until recently, been curiously overlooked in Irish literary and cultural criticism" (1). Female aging is at the center of both Jeanette King's *Discourses of Ageing in Fiction and Feminism: The Invisible Woman* (2013) and *Ageing Women in Literature and Visual Culture* edited by Cathy McGlynn, Margaret O'Neill, and Michaela Schrage-Früh (2017). Groundbreaking studies on aging in literature and drama are represented by the pioneering work of Valerie Barnes Lipscomb, both in the volume published jointly with Leni Marshall in 2010, entitled *Staging Age: The Performance of Age in Theatre, Dance, and Film*, and in her own more recent book, *Performing Age in Modern Drama* (2016). Lipscomb highlights the special role of aging in drama, pointing out that "issues of age and aging arise in all aspects of a play, from the script to casting and staging choices" ("Performing the Aging Self" 285). Furthermore, she underlines that if "age is performative in nature," "drama most specifically highlights age as performative" (*Performing Age* 1). The concept of performativity, first described by John L. Austin, refers to the overlapping of utterance and action: "the issuing of an utterance is the performing of an action" (6). The closeness of the adjective "performative" and the noun "performance" is embedded in Lipscomb's quotation from Aagje Swinnen and Cynthia Port's work: "Performativity defines age not only as a state of being but through acts of doing . . . [as a] repetition of behavioral *scripts*" (qtd. in Marshall, *Performing Age* 4, emphasis added). Lipscomb's significant use of the word "script" sheds light on the expectations of behavioral social prescription(s) in old age and in any age, implying that age is also socially and culturally constructed (Lipscomb and Marshall, "Introduction" 5).

Relying on Marvin Carlson's work *Performance: A Critical Introduction* (2004), Adele Anderson and Sofia Pantouvaki remind us that "performance can be recognized in the physical presence of one or more agents demonstrating some skills before and to an audience" (vii). Thus physical presence and acts of doing which are distinctive features of performance seem to be at odds with aging and aged characters, often invisible on stage, virtually absent. Likewise, the "growing cultural visibility of older people" (Ingman 1) contrasts with their invisibility as useless members of society: they are physically present, yet invisible. In a similar way, Safi Mahmoud Mahfouz points out the importance of "offstage characters" as "driving forces of the dramatic onstage action," and if they are "denied a stage presence" (392), absence as a theatrical device marks offstage characters as potential catalysts for action. In the case of aged and aging characters, however, the theatrical choice of absence might highlight the elderly being on the periphery of the society. Those who are unseen may often be marginalized, rendered nearly non-existing.

These assumptions can be stimulating when approaching Brian Friel's plays through a "gerontological lens" (Ingman 1) and provide new ground in the study of his dramatic production. This paper takes into account some of Brian Friel's plays with no strict chronological order and considers the variety of ways in which the playwright introduces or openly deals with the issues of aging and of old age through stagecraft and varied dramatic choices, in particular the manipulation of mimetic and diegetic space in terms of presence and absence. Especially an elderly character's presence on stage is generally revealed through his/her absence, which arouses reflection on the role of old age. Friel's elderly or aging characters range from dominant figures like Columba in *The Enemy Within* (1962), to even tyrannical ones such as Manus in *The Gentle Island* (1971) and Father in *Aristocrats* (1979), to social outcasts including the Mundy sisters and Father Jack in *Dancing at Lughnasa* (1990). Clear distinctions may be blurred; for example, Cass in *The Loves of Cass McGuire* (1967) tries to impose herself as dominant to counteract the actual abandonment and neglect she faces in the family home.

Brian Friel investigates the issue of old age and aging in a variety of ways and in a variety of plays; memorable characters of old, elderly, aging, or declining people feature throughout his career in primary or secondary roles, representing the fragility and decline of aging, the mental disorder that often accompanies old age, the contradiction between an aging body and a still fresh mind. Examples range from the elderly monks in Iona in *The Enemy Within* to Screwballs, Madge, Aunt Lizzie, Canon O'Byrne, and Master Boyle in *Philadelphia, Here I Come!* (1966), Cass, Gran McGuire, and the guests at Eden House in *The Loves of Cass McGuire*, District Judge O'Donnell in *Aristocrats*, the middle-aged Mundy sisters and the demented Uncle Jack in *Dancing at Lughnasa*, the middle-aged couples stranded on Ballybeg pier in *Wonderful Tennessee* (1993), Tom Connolly's expectations of assessment as an elderly writer in *Give Me Your Answer, Do!* (1999), to landowner Christopher Gore in *The Home Place* (2005). Occasionally, elderly characters are powerful patriarchs, such as Manus in *The Gentle Island*, while the fragility and bitterness of old age appear in the debilitating illness and deranged mind of Judge O'Donnell in *Aristocrats*, or in Maggie's degenerative arthritis in *Give Me Your Answer, Do!*

Two of Friel's early plays, *Crystal and Fox* (1968) and *The Enemy Within* (1962), deal with the process of aging in different ways. In the former, Friel sheds light on the bitterness of aging by juxtaposing it to performance. The play features a fit-up or traveling show of no particular distinction belonging to the eponymous and dominating Fox Malarkey, whose awareness of aging makes him cynical and emotionally empty. The company includes Fox's wife, Crystal's elderly and ailing father, Papa, who occasionally takes part in performances. Speaking of Papa in act 1, episode 2, Fox reflects on aging and acting, thus providing insight into the issue of performance and performers underlying Friel's later plays: "Your father's a real sage, my sweet . . . . All clowns become sages when they grow old, and when young sages grow old they turn into clowns" (23). The stylistic chiasmus underlying Fox's words combines the self-consciousness of acting and the process of aging, thus anticipating the performative nature of aging embedded in a number of Friel's plays. Relying on Judith Butler's formulation of performativity, Anna McMullan terms it "a regulatory force" (142), a "reiteration of norms, which precede, constrain and exceed the performer" (Butler 234 qtd. in McMullan 142). Therefore, it works as a sort of behavioral script, so that considering aging characters as performers is likely to have a particular relevance for drama in terms of characterization, dramatic construction, and metadramatic reflection.

In *The Enemy Within*, Friel deploys different shades of old age and aging as *leitmotifs*, taking into account both the strong and outstanding figure of the protagonist and his impending senility. Columba dominates the scene, both offstage in the diegetic space while he is being spoken about and onstage in the mimetic space. Iona is a stage where Columba is to perform a double role, as a warrior faithful to his family and as a man of God. He is in turn "a priest or a politician" (34), "Columba of Iona," and "Columba of Kilmacrenan" (62). His two identities are embedded in the double performativity expected of him, interlacing with the performativity of his body, from which he feels alienated as his health does not match with his age. When he first appears on stage, the stage directions highlight this kind of contrast and duplicity: "Columba is sixty-six but looks a man sixteen years younger. There is vitality, verve, almost youthfulness in every gesture" (15). Columba himself reiterates the contradiction between age and body: "I cannot *feel* my 66 years . . . . I am burdened with this strong, active body that responds to the whistle of the fight of the sail, the swing of the axe, the warm breadth of a horse beneath it, the challenge of a new territory" (48). The stylistic choice of the passive form "I am burdened" is magnified by the accumulation of physical activities in the form of a list, all of them belonging to the behavioral script of Columba the warrior. The "complexity of aging identities" (Ingman 2) and the "sense of alienation from their aged bodies" are often reported by elderly people to the point of "misrecognition of their mirror image" (Lipscomb, "Performing the Aging Self" 286). In this respect Columba's standpoint reflects Kathleen Woodward's theory of "this reaction as the mirror stage of old age" as "an inversion of Jacques Lacan's mirror stage of infancy" (67). In the play this kind of alienation from the body is highlighted also when Columba is absent from the stage; at the beginning of act 1, Dochonna remarks: "he thinks he's young enough at sixty-six to be out at the corn" (12), with the implication that Columba does not conform to the script of his age and is not behaving his age. If "each of us performs the actions associated with a chronological age" (Lipscomb and Marshall, "Introduction" 2), Columba eludes this behavioral script, yet gradually becomes aware of himself as an older man—a process which intensifies in the development of the play. As he gains ground in the mimetic space, Columba views himself as unworthy of God for yielding to the "enemy within," leading him to the world of tribal war he is expected to take part in. The stage directions highlight a growing consciousness of unavoidable realities: *"For the first time he looks his years. Tired, weary, apathetic. His face is drawn and worried"* (*The Enemy Within* 58). *"At last he is old"* (59).

Old age and aging represent a structuring principle in *The Enemy Within*. Not by chance is the play set in autumn (8, 11): it is a late phase of the year and a late phase of human life, the beginning of decline, the beginning of the end. This acts as a catalyst and anticipates the recurring insistence on the aging community in dialogue and stage directions. The age of the various monks is pointed out, the scribe Caornan, who opens the play, is "*a frail old man of seventy-one years*," whose "*eyesight is weak*"; Dochonna, the "*domestic manager*," is sixty-six and "*he is deaf*" (11). Their physical ailments, typical of old age, are counterpointed by Grillaan the Prior, who is "*in his sixties but straight and well preserved*" (13), and in a conversation between Columba, Grillaan, and Dochonna, the monk Fintan from Cork is mentioned as being "ninety-six" but strong "like a boy" (41).

The community itself is referred to as "a number of senile crones" (35), and when he first arrives, the novice Oswald asks: "Are all the monks old men?" (14). Similar references recur increasingly in the play, the monks in the community are "old doters" (17), and the same expression is used by Dochonna speaking of the scribe Caornan in reiterated clichés: "the old doter was five years older than me" (46). The word "doter" is a cognate with the verb "to dote," implying a decline of mental faculties, especially associated with old age, with "wet chins and shapeless feet" (48). The intensity and frequency of such patterns of references throughout the play contribute to casting attention on a reading of the play that links the protagonist's progressive inner debate, the tension between his double roles and his growing consciousness of aging. The play is thus an early, contextualized study of aging in Friel's dramatic work, which will be further developed throughout his career.

Another play dominated by the pervasiveness of aging is *Losers* (1967), in which Friel exploits metadramatic conventions, at the same time having an absent character interact with the characters onstage. The play is the second part of the diptych *Lovers*, whose first part, *Winners*, features the young love of a couple of teenagers. The contrast in age between the youth of Mag and Joe and the process of aging in

Andy and Hanna, the middle-aged lovers, interlaces with the condition of old age and ailing in Mrs. Wilson, Hanna's invalid mother. *Losers* makes use of distinctive elements of farce (Higgins 21) to present "a kind of cartoon of Irish sex life before the country was transformed" (Kilroy 15) and to approach the issue of aging in the double perspective of middle-aged and elderly characters. Here Friel experiments with metadramatic devices: fifty-year-old Andy addresses the audience recounting his courting Hanna *"in her late forties"* (53) and the intrusion on the part of her bedridden mother. This will be enacted on stage with Andy as both external and internal narrator (Higgins 20) as he turns to the audience to introduce his story at the beginning of the play and comment upon it as the play develops, also providing a conclusion.

When the play begins, Andy is *"staring fixedly through a pair of binoculars at the grey stone wall," "watching nothing"* until *"he becomes aware of the audience"* (51). A "symbol of escape and isolation" (Dantanus 113), the binoculars are a dramatic choice creating a distance between the present of Andy's condition and the story he is going to tell, a sort of "confidential monologue" (Higgins 20). They also represent a sort of commentary on the observation and control enacted by Hanna's mother, Mrs Wilson, and Cissy, her next-door neighbor, who together watch the relationship and the lovers constantly. They find the middle-aged romance socially unacceptable, thus confirming that aging is socially and culturally constructed. In fact, Andy and Hanna are expected to act or perform their age, while Andy both gives voice to and subverts the unwritten but generally accepted normative script, which prescribes the couple should follow certain standards of behavior: "people think that when you're . . . well, when you're over the forty mark, that you're passified. But aul' Hanna, by

God, I'll say that for her, she was keen as a terrier in those days" (53). Hanna's old mother, Mrs Wilson, acts as a controlling agent in the two lovers' courting, obsessively ringing her handbell to summon her daughter in moments of intimacy, as she does not think it is appropriate for Hanna and Andy's relationship to continue. The old woman remains invisible in the first part of the play, absent from the mimetic space and relegated to the diegetic space offstage. Her temporary lack of visibility turns into a sort of performing omnipotence as Friel manipulates space boundaries, and the absentee, alive in the diegetic space, invades the mimetic space through the reiterated and obsessive sound of her bell. Mrs Wilson is thus present and absent at the same time before actually appearing on stage—she is audible before being visually perceived. The interaction between presence and absence increases the comic stance of the play in a sort of play-within-a-play as Andy's performance of Thomas Gray's "Elegy Written in a Country Churchyard" is the only way to pretend that innocent conversation is going on in the living room, alongside the recitation of "bloody shopping lists" and "multiplication tables" (64), and thus prevent the offstage intrusion of Hanna's mother. The stage directions highlight the forced game pointing out that "[h]*is recitation is strained and too high and too loud—like a child in school memorizing meaningless facts. Throughout his recital, they court feverishly*" (57).

If the lovers try to elude the script ostensibly imposed on them as a middle-aged couple, old Mrs Wilson performs her age and acts her role as an invalid, looking "*angelic*" (65) when her unseen presence is first visually revealed to the audience. The stage directions emphasize her conscious performance as she is "*propped against the pillows*," she is "*a tiny woman, with a sweet, patient, invalid's smile*," and yet "*her voice is soft and commanding"* (65), which identifies the old lady as the propelling force in Hanna and Andy's life in the dominant role she has chosen for herself. She is emblematic of the general moral picture, albeit her role is not so much chosen as a result of social construction. Even her bigotry manifest in her obsessive devotion to Saint Philomena is a form of control expressed by the cliché that "the family that prays together stays together" (66); therefore, Andy's dethroning of the saint when fully drunk is an overt act of rebellion against the *status quo*. His momentary reaction, however, does not dispel the subtext of sadness and pessimism underlying the play, as he and Hanna are stuck in an unhappy marriage, too old to free themselves from Mrs Wilson's bondage, and will probably spend their own old age in bitterness, which makes them the losers of the play. *Losers* has a circular pattern, as it closes in the same way as it begins, with Andy staring at the wall through his binoculars. His closing words highlight the selfishly subtle but overpowering authority of Hanna's mother: "By God, you've got to admire the aul' bitch. She could handle a regiment" (77), which emphasizes the power of the elderly absentee, representative of the moral rigidity of the society, as a force preventing the couple's attempt to reach a fragment of happiness.

In *Aristocrats* (1979), Friel reworks and enlarges his experiment with the presence and absence of the elderly character as it appears in *Losers*. In this case, District Judge O'Donnell's authority as a patriarch intertwines with the decline of old age, and in a dramaturgically similar yet more complex way, the occasionally farcical stance of *Losers* is replaced by the sad reality of a disintegrating house and a disintegrating dynasty. The protagonists, all members of the O'Donnell family, come back to their father's decaying house,

Ballybeg Hall, epitome of the Catholic Big House, to celebrate the wedding of their young sister, Claire. This planned event is, however, strategically and ironically replaced by the funeral of the father, whose death marks the "collapse of Ireland's patriarchy" (Boltwood 127). A parallelism is evident in the double decline of the old house and the old man, which frustrates and nullifies the work of the American historian Tom Hoffnung, engaged in research on the Hall. The only male son, Casimir, is a "pivotal character" (O'Brien 93), a master of fiction and words, who invents an impossible past in which people like Gerard Manley Hopkins, Daniel O'Connell, George Moore, Sean O'Casey, and W. B. Yeats allegedly visited the house. By doing so, he is keeping alive the spirit of the house, in an attempt to preserve its "aristocratic ethos" (Corbett 76-78).

The absent ghosts of the past in Casimir's "phoney fiction" (Friel, *Selected Plays* 278) have a counterpart in Father, relegated upstairs by an invaliding stroke. He never appears on stage, save very briefly at the end of act 2, when a second stroke causes his death. In his physical fragility, Father is not only a symbol of past authority, but also a catalyst for aging off and on stage. All his physical needs are attended to by the eldest daughter Judith, an "automaton of duty" (Higgins 49), and his privacy and intimacy are violated, as "the most intimate exchanges in which his soiled body is cleaned" are publicly exposed, "broadcast" by the baby-alarm, a counterpart of Mrs Wilson's handbell, acting as a loudspeaker (Roche 44) that Willie Diver, the factotum, sets up in the first scene in act 1. Such a mechanical trick is the vehicle to convey on stage the voice of the invisible Judge in his incontinent and dependent senility, making him present in his physical absence. "He is the voice of past authority, a voice without a body" (Corbett 75):

amplified by the baby alarm the absent Father relegated offstage to the diegetic space takes possession of the mimetic space, invading it aurally in spite of no visible actions. In Friel's experimentation with absence, the baby-alarm connects offstage to onstage, and the first sound coming from it is "the sound of static from the speaker," followed by "Father's laboured breathing," expanded into "incoherent mumbling" (Friel, *Selected Plays* 256). The absent character has agency in both the diegetic and mimetic space as Friel manipulates spatial boundaries, thus Father's performing self makes him both present and absent at the same time, real and unreal—not unlike Mrs. Wilson—and his second childhood in the fragility of old age does not dispel his patriarchal control. In fact, Casimir "jumps to attention" when he hears his father's "clear and commanding voice" (282) through the baby alarm, regressing to childhood powerlessness and a state of terror before patriarchal authority. On hearing his name called by the voice of his absent father, Casimir's verbal reaction is a triple repetition: "God, it's eerie—that's what it is—eerie—eerie" (263). This touches the semantic areas of the no man's land of the living dead, and from this limbo Judge O'Donnell returns time and again to interact and interfere with the action onstage imposing his oppressive authority *in absentia*.

The absent aged man performs the role he used to have, in his disorientation in time and space he addresses present people as if they were absent and behaves as if he were at court when his "very loud and very authoritative voice" (258) breaks into the stage space through the baby alarm:

> Are you proposing that my time and the time of this court be squandered while the accused goes home and searches for this title which he claims he has in a tin-box somewhere? . . .

Because I can tell you I won't have it—I will not have it! . . .
And I will not endure it a second longer. Case dismissed.
Court adjourned. (258)

When he finally appears on stage only for a few seconds leaving
the diegetic space to enter the mimetic space, he is a terrifying
presence: the stage directions define him as "*a grotesque and
frightening figure,*" who has nothing human left in him in his
"*almost animal roar*" (304), announcing the end of an era. The
damaging effects of patriarchal dominance, however, still
remain with the family, for instance, in the immaturity of the
"pivotal" character, Casimir.

In *The Loves of Cass McGuire* (1966), Friel deals with old
age openly and directly, as the protagonist is the elderly
returned emigrant Cass McGuire, and part of the play takes
place in the setting of an old people's home sarcastically called
Eden House. The play's stage directions are obsessively
dominated by references to aging, prominence given to the
characters' age and the assumed correspondence of their looks
to their age, which each of them is expected to perform
according to the socially constructed rules of behavior. Friel's
second greatest success after *Philadelphia, Here I Come!*, the play
is concerned with emigration, home, and love, but its formal
and experimental complexity highlights the play as a
sociological, behavioral, and psychological study of old age and
aging. In fact, it opens with an impressive image of old age,
eighty-nine-year-old Gran McGuire, a matriarchal figure
"*almost totally deaf,*" sitting in a wheelchair (11). Though
appearing only at the beginning, Gran McGuire establishes the
mood of the play and its concern with aging. Her senile
dementia causes her to be present and absent on stage at the
same time. Her presence is pervasive in act 1, yet everybody

ignores her, she is virtually invisible and inaudible, by being old and useless, which anticipates her daughter Cass's position in the family. She is isolated by her deafness and senility, and her present immobility anticipates the disappointment and lack of perspectives the elderly returned emigrant Cass will experience after returning home. Rather than receiving the warm welcome Cass has been looking forward to for over fifty years, she becomes displaced in her own home (Corbett 2).

Cass worked in a depressed area of New York for fifty-two years (Friel, *Selected Plays* 19), annihilating herself to earn the money she thought the family would need. However, the money Cass sent over the years in a tangible act of love and care had never been used and upon her return was a "nest-egg" waiting for her (41). "Nest-egg" is ironically ambiguous, as the nest of home refuses her any gesture of love. In this respect, Cass followed a certain kind of prescribed script all her life; she behaved as a decent Irish emigrant used to be expected to. The years of hardship in New York made her an old woman at seventy, a disagreeable character, vulgar, embittered, and aggressive. Her grotesque physicality marks the rupture with family and community, she now resists the "forces of normalizing performativity" (McMullan 142), and her unruly presence shatters the respectability of the family home: Cass does not act her age, rather her "performance falls outside behavioral norms" (Lipscomb, *Performing Age* 2) and is therefore socially unacceptable.

Invisible in the first part of act 1, Cass shouts, swears, smokes, and drinks offstage and when first entering the mimetic space she "charges" on the stage (14), which underlines her resistance and disruptive energy. Her banishment to Eden House is a form of imprisonment for Cass, where she identifies the place as the old workhouse it used to be in the past. The play's strategic Pirandellian metatextual organization highlights Cass's struggles with Harry over the power on her life and on her story (Coult 36): "The story begins where I say it begins, and I say it begins with me stuck in the gawddam workhouse! . . . What's this goddam play called? *The Loves of Cass McGuire*. Who's Cass McGuire? Me! Me! And they'll see what happens in the order I want them to see it" (Friel, *Selected Plays* 15-16). If Cass tries to make herself heard as an elderly woman, she also dominates the mimetic space, as the stage space is fluid and transforms from Harry's respectable middle-class house to Eden House "at Cass's command" (Cave 134). In a similar way, Cass "refuses to be contained" in others' story and by social norms, which involves her enhanced presence and her role at large, as she embodies a form of "resistant performativity" (McMullan 142) in relation to the text she is part of. Her escape from the script of the play overlaps with escaping from the behavioral script that prescribes her role as an elderly woman expected to behave her age. She shouts "in her Irish-American voice" (Friel, *Selected Plays* 14), she can be heard "singing at the top of her voice half the night" (12), and her verbal outburst when coming onstage is an attack to the "polite speech" (Kilroy 13) of Harry's household. Likewise, when at Eden House, Cass eludes the rules of the place by asking to have drink brought to her, yet her resistance to prescribed norms gradually deteriorates when she loses contact with the audience: at first they are *"her friends, her intimates,"* while the other people on stage are *"interlopers"* (Friel, *Selected Plays* 15). By the end of the play, seduced by the verbal fantasies of Trilbe and Ingram, two residents of Eden House, Cass loses contact with the world and the audience disappears: "And I could ov swore there were folks out there"

NEGOTIATING AGE

(59). Presence and absence overlap as her contact with reality slowly disintegrates.

With *Dancing at Lughnasa*, Friel integrates age and aging into the dramaturgy of presence and absence, creating a connection between themes and staging techniques. Michael, the narrator, opens the play introducing a *"motionless . . . formal tableau"* (1) featuring all the characters involved in the play. According to the staging technique, Michael changes ages very rapidly by being himself in middle age recalling scenes of his childhood and his younger self, bodily absent on stage. The stage directions underline the relationship between adult Michael and Boy Michael in terms of presence and absence: *"The convention must now be established that the (imaginary) BOY MICHAEL is working at the kite materials lying on the ground. No dialogue with the BOY MICHAEL must ever be addressed directly to adult MICHAEL, the narrator"* (7). The "incorporeality of the child" (173), to use Prapassaree Kramer's words, and his "physical elision" from the stage implicitly shed light on the aging body on stage (Lipscomb, "Performing the Aging Self" 302), since Michael, introduced as "a young man" in the list of characters, is perceived by the audience as someone either in middle age or older. "The adult's aging body displays the passage of time," while the adult's presence and the child's absence "prevent the audience from slipping fully into the present action" (302). Aging as a process and as a condition pervades the whole play, and the stage directions accurately underline the age of each character. Father Jack, the elder brother recently returned from his missionary work in Africa, is fifty-three; the Mundy sisters' ages range between twenty-six and forty. None of them is thus actually old, yet health issues and economic difficulties have a significant impact on their aging. "Shrunken and jaundiced with malaria" (Friel,

138

Dancing 2), Jack is immediately perceived as old and the stage directions point out the contrast between his actual age and his appearance, while having forgotten his mother tongue adds to the confusion of senile dementia: "*He looks frail and older than his fifty-three years. . . . He walks—shuffles quickly—with his hands behind his back. He seems uneasy, confused*" (17). The verb "to shuffle" is repeatedly used in the stage directions to describe Jack's movements; it is the walk of an old man, and the subtext of confusion embedded in the verb anticipates the mental confusion of his senility. The twenty-five years spent in a leper colony in Uganda absorbed Jack and transformed him, a respected member of society into an "outcast" in disgrace gone "native" (39), who has abandoned his faith for African religion and rituals. His return to Ireland for unspecified reasons accelerates his decline, deriving from the clash between his imposed original culture and the behavioral freedom he experienced in Uganda.

Jack's confusion is reiterated, the expression "his mind is confused" (11, 12) is repeated in slightly different forms within a few lines and emphasized in his actions on stage, as he "doesn't know the difference" between the sisters (12). Moreover, he has difficulty remembering words and speaks in fragmented sentences verbally reproducing his fragmented mind: "I expected to enter my bedroom through that . . . what I am missing—what I require . . . I had a handkerchief in my pocket and I think perhaps I—" (17).

Jack's aging and physical ailing have a counterpart in the sisters' awareness that the broken mirror in the house shows only "more and more wrinkles" (3). A sense of impending old age, of life having been wasted, obsesses the Mundy household as the sisters gradually become aware "that they are no longer considered marriageable because of their age" (Boltwood 170).

The topography of the house, "two miles outside the village of Ballybeg" (Friel, *Dancing* n. pag.), neither inside nor outside the village community, marks the sisters as outcasts or outsiders, and being unmarried they do not conform to the status required of women in 1936 Ireland. This makes them socially invisible, and so does the fact that Chris, the youngest sister, has mothered an illegitimate child, Michael, whose adult self as the narrator displays awareness of having had a role in the family's becoming "ostracized for its transgression" (Boltwood 170). Because of Chris's having broken the rules, the unconventional family of the Mundy sisters raising a child without a father does not conform to the prescribed and accepted behavioral norms rooted in the postcolonial social milieu of control and repression.

Kate, the eldest of the sisters, acts as the authority in the family, and as a school teacher she reproduces at home the regulatory and normative social and cultural control characterizing her job, reminding her sisters of the behavior expected of them at their age and in their position, of the social script they are expected to follow. Her reaction to Agnes's suggestion to go to the harvest dance of the festival of Lughnasa is haunted by a rigid insistence on respectability: "We're going nowhere! . . . Just look at yourselves! Dancing at our time of day? . . . Do you want the whole countryside to be laughing at us?—women of our years?—mature women, dancing?" (Friel, *Dancing* 13).

However, the sisters, even Kate, manage to momentarily elude the social script while making their wild dance in act 1, which is not only a powerful element of dramaturgy but also an unspoken act of subversion. Their dance is a wordless response to impending aging and social invisibility, a form of resistance and liberation from "confining gender roles" and from the "normalising performativity" of village life in Ireland in the 1930s (McMullan 142), a form of escape by means of the unruly body, a statement of youth and survival, a challenge to ideological and social discursive constructions. From this point of view, considering age as socially and culturally constructed (Lipscomb and Marshall, "Introduction" 5), the unruly dance is a denial of the imposed sense of impending aging. The lack of control embedded in the dance is highlighted in the stage directions: Maggie has "*a look of defiance, of aggression,*" her face is a "*crude mask of happiness,*" she metamorphoses into "*a white-faced, frantic dervish*" (Friel, *Dancing* 21). In spite of this brief interlude, the subtext of aging haunts the play and overlaps with the perception of "things changing too quickly" in the Mundy house and in the social context of Ballybeg (2), but certainly not for the better with regard to the sisters.

In the same way as in society the elderly become invisible, Friel plays with the explicit and implicit absence of aging and aged characters onstage caught up in different phases of physical and mental decline and the consciousness of aging. Old age and aging are still fairly new approaches in literary and drama studies, but "[t]heatre can show us different perspectives on age" (Lipscomb, *Performing Age* 154), being a catalyst that certainly has value in Friel's plays. The plays taken into account point out age and aging as a *fil rouge* throughout his dramatic work, underlying the subtext of several of his plays as pivotal features since the early stages through further developments in his career, thus displaying a recurrent interest in the topic. Friel exploits the interaction of presence and absence off and on stage as an aspect of his stagecraft, responding to the various conditions of old age. If in some plays elderly characters remain in the background, in others issues of age and aging gain ground and become pivotal to dramatic construction, and what Heather Ingman calls "gerontological lens" (1) can provide new insights in the study of Friel's dramatic production. His exploration of age, aging, and the elderly either as dominating characters or on the periphery of the social context shows his treatment of this *leitmotif* as a recurring tendency to shed light on the culturally and discursively inflected complexity of aging identities throughout his career.

Works Cited

Anderson, Adele, and Sofia Pantouvaki. *Presence and Absence: The Performing Body.* Oxford: Inter-Disciplinary Press, 2014.

Austin, John L. *How to Do Things with Words.* Cambridge: Harvard University Press, 1962.

Boltwood, Scott. *Brian Friel, Ireland, and the North.* Cambridge: Cambridge University Press, 2007.

Butler, Judith. *Bodies that Matter: On the Discursive Limits of "Sex."* London: Routledge, 1993.

Cave, Richard Allen. "Friel's Dramaturgy: The Visual Dimension." Roche, ed. *Cambridge Companion* 129-41.

Corbett, Tony. *Brian Friel: Decoding the Language of the Tribe.* Dublin: Liffey, 2002.

Coult, Tony. *About Friel: The Playwright and the Work.* London: Faber, 2003.

Dantanus, Ulf. *Brian Friel: A Study.* London: Faber, 1988.

Friel, Brian. *Crystal and Fox.* London: Faber, 1970. Loughcrew: The Gallery, 1984.

---. *Dancing at Lughnasa.* London: Faber, 1990.

---. *The Enemy Within.* 1975. Loughcrew: The Gallery, 1979.

---. *Lovers: Winners and Losers.* 1968. Loughcrew: The Gallery, 1984.

---. *The Loves of Cass McGuire.* 1967. Loughcrew: The Gallery, 1984.

---. *Selected Plays of Brian Friel: Philadelphia, Here I Come!; The Freedom of the City; Living Quarters; Aristocrats; Faith Healer; Translations.* Intro. Seamus Deane. London: Faber, 1984.

Higgins, Geraldine. *Brian Friel.* Tavistock: Northcote, 2010.

Ingman, Heather. *Ageing in Irish Writing: Stranger to Themselves.* London: Palgrave, 2018.

Kilroy, Thomas. "The Early Plays." Roche, ed. *Cambridge Companion* 6-17.

Kramer, Prapassaree. *"Dancing at Lughnasa*: Unexcused Absence." *Modern Drama* 43.2 (2000): 171-81.

Lipscomb, Valerie Barnes. *Performing Age in Modern Drama.* New York: Palgrave Macmillan, 2016.

---. "Performing the Aging Self in Hugh Leonard's *Da* and Brian Friel's *Dancing at Lughnasa*." *Comparative Drama* 47.3 (Fall 2013): 285-308.

---, and Leni Marshall. "Introduction." Lipscomb and Marshall, eds., *Staging Age* 1-7.

---, and Leni Marshall, eds. *Staging Age: The Performance of Age in Theatre, Dance, and Film.* New York: Palgrave Macmillan, 2010.

Mahfouz, Safi Mahmoud. "The Presence of Absence: Catalytic and Omnipresent Offstage Characters in Modern American Drama." *The Midwest Quarterly* 53.4 (2012): 392-409.

McMullan, Anna. "Performativity, Unruly Bodies and Gender in Brian Friel's Drama." Roche, ed. *Cambridge Companion* 142-53.

Niel, Ruth. "Disability as Motif and Meaning in Friel's Drama." *Hungarian Journal of English and American*

Studies 5.1 (1999): 143-59.

O'Brien, George. *Brian Friel.* Dublin: Gill and Macmillan, 1989.

O'Neill, Margaret, and Michaela Schrage-Früh. "Introduction: Women and Ageing in Irish Literature and Film." *Nordic Irish Studies* 17.1 (2018): 1-13.

Roche, Anthony. "Family Affairs: Friel's Plays of the Late 1970s." Roche, ed. *Cambridge Companion* 41-52.

---, ed. *The Cambridge Companion to Brian Friel.* Cambridge: Cambridge University Press, 2006.

Swinnen, Aagje, and Cynthia Port. "Aging, Narrative, and Performance: Essays from the Humanities." *International Journal of Ageing and Later Life* 7.2 (2012): 9-15.

Woodward, Kathleen. *Aging and its Discontents: Freud and Other Fictions.* Bloomington: Indiana University Press, 1991.

10.2478/9788367405423-009

The Tyranny of the Old: Destructive Generational Relations in Brian Friel's *Lovers* and Martin McDonagh's *The Beauty Queen of Leenane*

David Clare and Mária Kurdi

A great number of critics have already traced influences on Martin McDonagh's dramatic world, highlighting, for instance, the mark that J. M. Synge and Samuel Beckett as well as British avant-garde theatre and gothic horror cinema have left on his work. With regards to the first piece in the Leenane trilogy, *The Beauty Queen of Leenane* (1996), Fintan O'Toole claims that "[i]n it, Harold Pinter and Joe Orton blend seamlessly with Tom Murphy and John B. Keane to create a vibrantly original mixture of absurd comedy and cruel melodrama" (379). José Lanters similarly sees a blending of Synge and Murphy, suggesting that what ties their work to McDonagh's is the use of storytelling as a characteristically "Western" device, "but through that device, each dramatist reflects the concerns and anxieties of his age" (221). Werner Huber notes the script's debts not only to Synge's West of Ireland plays but also to Beckett's *Rockaby* and *Footfalls* (20, 25) and Laura Eldred demonstrates the influence of Alfred Hitchcock's 1960 film *Psycho* on the play (111-14). *The Beauty Queen* stands apart from the author's other works set in Ireland as it mixes several modes including one which is unusual within the canon of Irish drama: a thorough embracing of the tragic. [1]

---

1 Modern and contemporary Irish playwrights have had a tendency to "soften" fully tragic endings by adding vague hope or a touch of dark humor to works that are otherwise tragedies. Consider the extra leaves on the tree in act 2 of Samuel Beckett's *Waiting for Godot* (1953), the sons' mutual recognition of the role that their father has played in their flawed reliance on toxic masculinity in the final moments of Tom Murphy's *A Whistle in the Dark* (1960), the bittersweet romance (overshadowed by the specter of death) in Martin

This mixture of modes may explain why critics have been tempted to enlist very disparate playwrights and filmmakers as important for the genesis of this McDonagh play. However, in their attempts to identify the DNA of the postmodern "mash-up" that is *The Beauty Queen*, these critics have failed to note the important parallels between this play and the work of an Irish playwright that is not often mentioned in connection with McDonagh: Brian Friel.

This essay suggests that McDonagh's *The Beauty Queen* echoes Friel's pre-1990s work in taking on and twisting a key trope found in much postcolonial writing: strong parental dominance and young people's futile, even self-destructive rebellion against it. The topos of generational conflicts dates back to the Revival period in Ireland when playwrights' creation of old, vicious patriarch characters reflected what Ania Loomba and other theorists have noted is a particularly damaging aspect of colonialism: specifically, that foreign rule "intensified patriarchal relations in colonized lands, often because native men, increasingly disenfranchised and excluded from the public sphere, became more tyrannical at home" (Loomba 16). For men, especially older men, the sole compensatory way to acquire and demonstrate some power in the home was to dominate the "weaker" bodies in their households, that is, the young and/or female. Synge's *The*

McDonagh's *The Cripple of Inishmaan* (1996), and the sense of catharsis experienced by the main characters (as opposed to merely the audience, as would be the case in traditional Greek tragedy) in Brian Friel's *Faith Healer* (1979) and Christina Reid's *My Name, Shall I Tell You My Name?* (1989). Marina Carr—in classic plays such as *By the Bog of Cats...* (1998) and *Woman and Scarecrow* (2006)—arguably embraces the tragic mode in a thoroughgoing way; however, both of those plays also prominently feature (brilliant) dark humor. For a further discussion of this, see Dan McGovern's "Eugene O'Neill's Place in Irish Theater Today: Interviews with Irish Theater Scholars." *Eugene O'Neill Review* 39.1 (2018): 140-62 (146-48).

IRISH DRAMA

Shadow of the Glen (1903) and *The Playboy of the Western World* (1907) are set in contemporary colonized Ireland and stage domineering old husband and father figures respectively, both wielding harsh patriarchal rule. Seamus Deane claims that in these plays social victory is given to age, but "the existential victory to youth. Society is not redeemed, and the traditional function of comedy remains incomplete" (53). Older male bullies are also a feature of other Revival-era classics: prominent examples include King Finn from Lady Gregory's *Grania* (1912) and the Old Man (who literally *kills* his son) in W. B. Yeats's *Purgatory* (1938).

Some postcolonial plays from Ireland have demonstrated that patriarchy and its oppressive ideologies are able to work even without men. Cormac O'Brien has described this phenomenon by pointing to the tendency that "subtextual patriarchy is ubiquitous in Irish theatrical history and performances, even when there are no men present on stage" (202). Having internalized the constricting expectations and double standards of the patriarchal system, the female characters police each other. In some plays, internalized misogyny leads a relatively young woman to encourage a female peer to accept the gender status quo, even as both women acknowledge the injustices endemic in a patriarchal society. Consider Mrs Nolan and Mrs Feeney commiserating about the fact that they have to have sex with their husbands whenever asked—and to bear children even when it's dangerous—in Maura Laverty's *Tolka Row* (1951). But much more often, it is an older woman who willfully curtails the dreams of greater personal freedom cherished by young women. A famous and important example of this is Mrs Marks in Teresa Deevy's *The King of Spain's Daughter* (1935). Whenever she comes on stage, Mrs Marks preaches to the young protagonist Annie about her duty, strongly encouraging her to stifle her imagination, to follow the prescribed ways of "good" (that is, narrowly Catholic) morals, and to accept the unalterably subordinate position of women to male dominance—even when they are, like Annie, being physically abused by a dominant male in their lives.

To add a new perspective to the critical investigation of McDonagh's links with his prominent Irish predecessors, in the present essay we are going to explore affinities between characterization strategies and their social and cultural embedding in the part entitled *Losers* from Friel's diptych play *Lovers: Winners and Losers* (1967) and McDonagh's *The Beauty Queen of Leenane*. In both works, the elderly parent who is sticking to the inculcated ideals and norms of patriarchy as well as exercising power over a middle-aged daughter is the mother and not the (apparently long-dead) father.

Parallels between the two plays

Losers adapts one of Friel's own short stories, "The Highwayman and the Saint" (1966), for the stage with only a few alterations. In the drama, the first-person narration of the short story is replaced by the monologue and dominant viewpoint of Andy, first lover and later husband of Hanna, the fortyish daughter of the invalid Mrs Wilson. Time and again, the forward progress of the drama is interrupted by scenes recollected and acted out from the past. Andy's retrospective narration is not a chronological one, mentioning later outcomes early in the monologue, which creates suspense as in traditional storytelling. Concurrently, his monologue offers a both external and internal view of the mother-daughter dyad since he is part of the action he conjures up and comments on—similar to Tom in Tennessee Williams's *The Glass*

Menagerie (1944), which also includes a dominant mother eager to plan arrangements for her daughter's future life. In *Losers*, Mrs Wilson is elderly and bedridden, although able to walk if she feels like it—as one of the evoked scenes shows. As a household rule, she rings a bell whenever she wants the services of her daughter. Mrs Wilson—with her worshipping of Saint Philomena (for whom she has created a mini-altar surrounded by candles in her bedroom), her insistence on the nightly recitation of the rosary, and her repetition of the mantra she learned from an American celebrity priest ("The family that prays together stays together" [Friel 303])—is the very embodiment of Catholic piety almost ubiquitous in Ireland well into the mid-to-late-1960s, when the play was conceived. She is also keen on policing the morals of the younger generation, as prescribed and expected by the Catholic Church in conjunction with the rigid patriarchal system of the post-independence period. [2] Mrs Wilson disturbs the courting of Hanna and Andy by ringing her brass bell when she hears no noise from downstairs, since, to her mind, silence is a sign that the lovers must be up to something morally wrong. Andy comments: "That's the way with a lot of pious aul' women—they have wild dirty imaginations" (299).

Regarding form, *The Beauty Queen* features what is effectively a reverse of the narrative structure of Friel's play.

---

2 It should be noted that we are not told in the script if *Losers* takes place in the Republic of Ireland or in the six counties still under British rule, Northern Ireland. (The syntax and colloquialisms suggest Ulster, but that could include the three counties in that province that are part of the Republic: Cavan, Monaghan, and—the county where Friel lived for most of his adult life and where he set most of his plays—Donegal). Regardless, during the decades after independence, patriarchal values were strongly dominant on both sides of the Irish border. It should be noted that the *Winners* portion of *Lovers* takes place in Northern Ireland: specifically, in a fictional town in Co. Tyrone called Ballymore—a counterpart to Ballybeg, the fictional town in Co. Donegal, where many of Friel's plays are set.

Almost the entire plot is acted out for the audience through dialogue. The only interruptions are two, brief, narrated sections that employ direct address: the reading out of a letter and an account of an imaginary farewell scene at a railway station. In McDonagh's drama, the mother, Mag, is not an invalid but she keeps on complaining about her age and various bodily pains to stress that she is entitled to expect her daughter, Maureen, to take care of her. For example, Maureen is expected to serve Mag a daily portion of Complan (a nutritional supplement in the form of a mix-at-home powder), and she insists that it must have no lumps in it. Maureen is a forty-year-old, embittered woman, who used to work as a cleaner in England; towards the end of her time there, she was treated for mental health difficulties brought on by loneliness and anti-Irish bullying. (The English cleaners she worked with made her feel awful, which led her to feel like an inferior being in the other country— formerly, for colonized Irish people, the *mother* country). The English mental health facility released Maureen into her mother's "care," even though the reality is that it is Maureen who slaves for Mag.

In Eamonn Jordan's wording, mother and daughter have a parasitic relationship, in which both use "manipulative methodologies." As Jordan further notes, when Mag refers to her damaged hand (on which, we later learn, Maureen poured heated oil as punishment),"Mag seems initially dominant, in part because of her seniority," but "the status shifts quickly when Maureen opts to confront her about the smell of urine coming from the kitchen sink. Indeed, Maureen raises the stakes higher by responding to Mag's story of a woman strangled by a stranger in Dublin. This is the type of man Maureen suggests she would like to meet and to bring home with her" (77). Obviously, she would love for Mag to die—or even be murdered—so that she does not have to be her mother's slave anymore.

While Mrs Wilson from *Losers* is characterized by ostentatious and very vocal Catholic piety, Mag's relationship to her religion in more subtle—and a reflection of a change in Irish society between the 1960s and the 1990s. The outward manifestations of Mag's Catholic faith are limited to two objects hanging on the wall of the living room/kitchen in which all the visible action of the drama takes place: the (inevitable) crucifix and a Stage Irish, *"touristy-looking embroidered tea towel . . . bearing the inscription 'May you be half an hour in Heaven afore the Devil knows you're dead'"* (McDonagh 1)—demonstrating a less sincere and perhaps wryly self-aware Catholicism. However, the deeper imprint of Mag's Catholic upbringing is very clear from her prudery around sex and her prizing of virginity (she even claims to be able to recognize "the look of a virgin" [47]). The prudish Mag regards Maureen as a "whore" for having merely kissed (and not slept with) two men in her life, adding "two men is two men too much!" (15); she detests the "skimpy dress" (25) that Maureen wears to a party and thinks it is disgraceful to go around the house "half-naked" in front of "stray men" (by which she means Pato, someone Maureen has known for many years who is back in Leenane on a visit from London; 29); she gets *"disgust[ed]"* as she watches Maureen kiss Pato (27) and whenever her daughter discusses sex in a frank way (43-47). In other words, in deference to changing social mores and less genuine belief in Catholic "mysteries" and doctrines, older Catholic people in Ireland in the 1990s like Mag may no longer signal their piety in flashy ways like Mrs Wilson. However, much of what they were taught about religion and morals during their Catholic upbringing remains strong. As Tom Inglis claims, there was an effective and long-lasting "inculcation of Victorian prudery" in Ireland and what "made Ireland unique was how deeply Victorian attitudes and practices penetrated into the Irish body and soul" (21); it was the Catholic Church, with its extensive influence over Irish society both before but especially in the decades just after independence, that is credited with successfully inculcating these sexual values into a large majority of Irish people. As McDonagh's play suggests, this prudery outlasted genuine Catholic faith in Ireland.

The most obvious link between *Losers* and *The Beauty Queen* is the depictions of the two mothers, with their hyper-Catholic prudery and their sexual infantilizing of a middle-aged daughter (out of fear that they will lose the daughter as a carer and get sent to a home for senior citizens). However, there are several other, subtler parallels between the two scripts. These commonalities, as outlined below, suggest that *Losers* may have been used by McDonagh as an intertext when composing *The Beauty Queen*; at the very least, they demonstrate interesting similarities in how Friel and McDonagh depict twentieth-century Irish matriarchs who have internalized patriarchal values.

One important and easily overlooked parallel between the plays is that the narcissistic natures of the two mothers (with their obviousness regarding the happiness of their daughters) often manifests itself in their voracious desire for food. When Mrs Wilson rings the bell for her daughter, she is not only breaking up Hanna's courting sessions with Andy: she is also looking to satiate her colossal appetite. At one point, Hanna returns from upstairs with *"her mother's soiled tray"* and says to Andy: "Look at—the invalid tray! Not a crumb on it! Six rounds of sliced pan and a boiled egg! Thank God she gets no fresh air or she'd eat up the town!" (Friel 304). Similarly, in *The Beauty*

Queen, Maureen is constantly having to provide her mother with porridge, the aforementioned Complan, biscuits, and her beloved cod in butter sauce. Rebecca Wilson notes that "[l]ike all intensely narcissistic creatures, Mag is oblivious to anyone else." "Mag's world revolves around food. Typical of the infant personality craving constant feeding, Mag is obsessed with being fed," Wilson adds (31), while Mag reminds Martin Middeke of "Nagg's wish for 'Me pap!' in Samuel Beckett's *Endgame*" (215). It is very reasonable to conclude that Mag's real need for her unmarried daughter has nothing emotional about it; she wants Maureen to serve her food and drink whenever she orders her to do so.

The two put-upon daughters are linked by their rebellion against the sexual repression represented by their prudish mothers, and there are similarities in how the plays depict the strong sexual appetites of these younger women. Both daughters seem to be hungry for sex with a partner that they feel very lucky to have at their age. In the first recollected courting scene in *Losers,* the stage directions tell us, *"Very suddenly, almost violently,* HANNA *flings herself on him* [Andy] *so that he falls back, and she buries her face in his neck and kisses and caresses him with astonishing passion"* (Friel 301). In *The Beauty Queen,* Maureen's sexual keenness is not only obvious from, as previously discussed, her frank discussions about sex after her night with Pato (which we later learn was unconsummated) and by her parading in front of him and her mother "half-naked." It can also be seen *before* the party where she picks him up, when she responds to her mother's taunt that she is a "whore" for having kissed two men by saying: "'Whore'? (*Pause.*) Do I not *wish,* now? Do I not wish? (*Pause.*) Sometimes I *dream...*" (McDonagh 16). This, of course, greatly disturbs Mag.

In Friel's play, Hanna and Andy want to prevent Mrs Wilson's frequent calls for her daughter in the midst of their courting sessions, and they hit on a unique solution: they decide that, in order to avoid the silence that will result in the bell being sounded, Andy should recite the only poem he knows by heart—Thomas Gray's "Elegy Written in a Country Churchyard" (1751)—in the midst of their lovemaking. This creates a situation both humorous and sinister at the same time, with the atmosphere of death that pervades the poem foretelling the death of their relationship. (In the original short story, the poem was "The Highwayman" by Alfred Noyes, a less well-known text than Gray's, hence its replacement for the stage by Friel). In *The Beauty Queen*, songs are playing on the radio at various points throughout the script. One which plays during the first kissing and fondling session between Maureen and Pato (and which is commented upon by them) is "The Spinning Wheel" by Delia Murphy, which was recorded in 1939 but which remained quite popular in Ireland up through the 1960s. The sentimentality of the song fails to impress Pato: "She does have a creepy oul voice. Always scared me this song did when I was a lad. She's like a ghoul singing. (*Pause*) Does the grandmother die at the end, now, or is she just sleeping? . . . They don't write songs like that any more. Thank Christ" (McDonagh 23). The song has a similar function to Gray's poem in *Losers* in that it evokes the mood of death, which is reinforced by its repeated playing on the radio at the end of McDonagh's drama as a belated greeting from Mag's other daughters after the old woman had already been struck dead by Maureen. Similarly to *Losers*, here the laughable combines with the macabre, although more disturbingly than in Friel's play.

There is another parallel between the plays which involves song. In both works, the male lover enters an important scene intoxicated and singing. In *Losers*, it is when Andy comes home late one night, having gotten drunk to celebrate the Pope's decree that there is no saint called Philomena, which means that the old lady's worshipping of her image on the bedroom altar must cease. Andy, in a reckless and humorous mood, is ironically singing "God Save Ireland." In *The Beauty Queen*, Pato enters the house that Maureen shares with Mag after they connected at a party to celebrate "Yank" relations who have been in Leenane and who are now heading back to Boston. Pato is singing "The Body of an American" by the London-Irish trad-punk group The Pogues. This is part of McDonagh's focus and reflections on the Irish Diaspora throughout the play and is of a piece with the numerous other "Diasporic" references. That includes Mag's suggestion that the Irish language wouldn't be "any good to you" (McDonagh 5) when looking for work in England or America (and Maureen's anger over those remarks), as well as the allusions to the Kennedys, Spike Milligan, *The Sullivans* (an Australian soap opera), the Birmingham Six, and—arguably—Paul Brady's song about anti-Irish racism in England, "Nothing But the Same Old Story" (1981). [3] While the songs are used for different purposes in the two plays, it is noteworthy that McDonagh decided to follow Friel in having a scene that begins the downward slide towards calamity involving the lead male drunkenly singing.

The tragic denouement to *The Beauty Queen* includes, of course, Maureen's slaying of her mother with a poker between scenes 7 and 8; this murderous assault comes after the many verbal and non-verbal threats made by Maureen towards her

---

3 In Brady's song, an Irish immigrant who has been working on building sites in England has been offered a job in Boston by his brother. In *The Beauty Queen*, Pato—who similarly works on building sites in England—has been offered a job by an *uncle* in Boston.

mother earlier in the play. One of the most notable ones is already discussed above: that is, when Maureen tells her mother in scene 1 that she would like to bring home a man like the Dublin strangler. Maureen's darkly comic elaboration on this reveals the frustration she feels regarding her life and foreshadows the hatred for Mag that eventually leads Maureen to torture and kill her mother for sabotaging her relationship with Pato:

> MAG.   (*pause*) Sure why would he [the murderer] be coming all this way out from Dublin? He'd just be going out of his way.
>
> MAUREEN. For the pleasure of me company he'd come. Killing you, it'd just be a bonus for him.
>
> MAG.   Killing you I bet he first would be.
>
> MAUREEN. I could live with that so long as I was sure he'd be clobbering you soon after. If he clobbered you with a big axe or something and took your oul head off and spat in your neck, I wouldn't mind at all, going first. Oh no, I'd enjoy it, I would. (6)

In *Losers*, Hanna does not physically assault or kill her mother. However, there is a parallel with McDonagh's play in that she repeatedly threatens violence against her mother in her pre-marriage conversations with Andy. For example, her anger over her mother's constant ringing of the bell on inane pretenses leads her to exclaim with menace: "One of these days I'll do something desperate" (300). Later, she gets more explicit about what she plans to do to the woman she calls "that 'aul bitch" (306), proclaiming: "One of these days I'm going to strangle that woman . . . with her rosary beads" (308).

In the end, whether such threats are carried out (as in Maureen's case) or not (as in Hanna's), the result is the same. In *The Importance of Being Earnest* (1895), Oscar Wilde uses the witty Algernon as a mouthpiece when he has him say: "All women become like their mothers. That is their tragedy" (362). And that is effectively what happens decades later in both *Losers* and *The Beauty Queen*. Hanna's threats of violence against her mother, as voiced to Andy before their marriage, are contrasted by her tears, her rebellion seeming to be only the helpless outburst of a desperate child who cannot find the solution to a puzzle. Once they are married, things change and the old lady rings her bell to call Hanna when she hears the couple talking, presumably because she is afraid that they might discuss a plan for abandoning her. As they postpone moving out to Andy's newly refurbished house at Riverview, Mrs Wilson's influence over her daughter gradually increases, and it gets even stronger after Andy comes home drunk celebrating the deposing of Saint Philomena. For this one transgression, Hanna turns away from Andy and starts sleeping in her mother's bedroom. Hanna's visibly increased piety at this point in the play (she is more interested in "the [nightly] prayers" than talking with her husband over the state of their relationship [Friel 321]) is an indication that she is becoming quite like Mrs Wilson. As Andy remarks: "[T]o see a woman that had plenty of spark in her at one time and then to see her turn before your very eyes into a younger image of her mother, by God, it's strange, I tell you, very peculiar . . ." (303).

Similarly, in *The Beauty Queen*, we see Maureen go from fighting her mother to becoming her. Maureen's pouring heated oil on Mag's hand in punishment for the old woman's emptying of her potty into the sink causes terrible pain for Mag, which she returns by secretly reading then burning the letter Pato has written to Maureen in which he asks her to join him in emigrating to America. This ruins Maureen's chances to have a lover, and perhaps husband, in Pato, who actually liked her and showed friendly understanding for her even when her mental health issues were disclosed to him by an interfering Mag. Maureen's loss of a grip on reality due to the shattering of her hopes is notable first in her self-deceptive monologue about following Pato to America soon, at the man's bidding. Her striking Mag dead with the heavy poker does not happen on stage (and it is uncertain when and how it was carried out), suggesting that Maureen may have acted when not in full control of her mental faculties. In the final scene, after the funeral, Pato's younger brother, Ray, communicates Pato's condolences to her, as well as the news that he is engaged to another woman. This adds to Maureen's psychological crisis, and Ray rudely remarks, in response to Maureen's deepening confusion and her unconscious repetition of her mother's verbal ticks, "*You're* a fecking loon! . . . The exact fecking image of your mother, you are, sitting there pegging orders and forgetting me name!" (58, 60). She has become a murderer like her "slyly oppressive" mother (Billington 390), who killed her daughter's dreams out of selfishness. As a sure sign of continuity, Maureen takes her mother's usual place in the rocking chair. With the mother and then the daughter idly rocking in the rocking-chair on stage, *The Beauty Queen* conspicuously nods to Beckett's *Rockaby* (1981).

That is not the only Beckettian element in *The Beauty Queen*—and, perhaps more surprisingly, *Losers* has important Beckettian aspects, as well. Both plays explore the potential destructiveness of the strictly defined familial roles and religious dogmas that the respective mother figures have internalized through education and social experience and now incarnate by sticking to conventional ideals and routines. Their behavior toward the young people reveals their self-centered dispositions, including enduring behavioral patterns which, according to Geraldine Moane, can be attributed to the alienating effects of colonialism on the Irish psyche and people's interpersonal relations, manifest in, for example, internal tensions between generations and gendered individuals (36-37). These two dramatizations of rigid, unequal familial relationships have a close kinship with Beckett's *Footfalls* (1975), a play in which a forty-something-year-old daughter is haunted by the voice of her dying (or possibly dead) mother—something which ties her like an umbilical cord to the restricted, routine-based world they inhabited together. As in *Footfalls*—and *Rockaby*—the plays by Friel and McDonagh problematize the lack of energy in the younger generation to stop fate from repeating itself. Andy the storyteller's perspective is dominant in *Losers,* and the play primarily represents his tragedy: from the unfriendly and unloving indifference of his wife, he escapes to the backyard. As Thomas Kilroy claims (16), [4] Friel's description of the initial scene of *Losers* is very Beckettian: "ANDY TRACEY *is sitting upright and motionless on a kitchen chair in the backyard. He is staring fixedly through a pair of binoculars at a grey stone wall which is only a few yards from where he is sitting. It becomes obvious that he is watching nothing"* (294). While the image of Melville's Bartleby the scrivener staring at a wall aimlessly might come to mind, this

---

4 Thomas Kilroy's view of the Beckettian in Andy's silent behavior at the beginning and the closure of the drama is quoted by Stephen Watt in *Beckett and Contemporary Irish Writing* (Cambridge: Cambridge University Press, 2009): 87.

eerie situation in *Losers* may also remind the reader/spectator of Clov's activities in *Endgame*—for example, his staring at the wall of their offstage kitchen, his climbing up to two small windows to look out, and his claim that through his telescope he can see a joyful multitude, i.e., the audience in the often metatheatrical Beckettian universe. The fact that Andy from *Losers* engages in the same meaningless routine on a regular basis in the backyard is yet another Beckettian touch.

Conclusion

Endgame, of course, pre-dates Friel's *Losers*, and *Footfalls* and *Rockaby* post-date it— whereas all of Beckett's dramatic oeuvre pre-dates (and has clearly had a profound influence on) McDonagh's work. But the specific Beckettian elements in *Losers* and *The Beauty Queen* reinforce the notion that Irish postcolonial anxieties are a key feature of these two works and in modern and contemporary Irish drama more generally.

In the Ireland where Beckett and Friel were born (and where McDonagh, the London-born son of Irish parents, spent his childhood summers), the idealization of family life and the emphasis on the sanctity of motherhood have been long-standing and important aspects of both normative discourses and individual mentalities, thus affecting the ethos and practices of the society. Indeed, the Irish Constitution *still* conflates "womanhood" and "motherhood" in Article 41. It states:

> In particular, the State recognises that by her life within the home, woman gives to the State a support without which the common good cannot be achieved. . . . mothers shall not be

obliged by economic necessity to engage in labour to the neglect of their duties in the home. [5]

A prominent factor in creating this strong emphasis on family and motherhood was the Roman Catholic Church's deep and long-standing moral influence over a large majority of Irish citizens. While this influence was partially related to the Church's crucial role in helping to keep the Irish Catholic community together during the harsh colonial era (especially under the cruel Penal Laws), it arguably deepened after independence. In the twenty-six counties, the Church effectively replaced the British in ruling over Irish education and health and even in playing the role of "big Daddy" in the not-yet-decolonized Irish psyche. (The weak but conservative new state allowed the Church to possess this overweening power for decades). In the six counties of Northern Ireland, the Church continued to provide succor to Catholic Nationalists who were suffering from the curtailing of their civil rights—but, at the same time, it kept enforcing patriarchal values that were also prized by the new statelet's ruling, Protestant, conservative, "Ulster-British" authorities. Much of twentieth- and twenty-first-century Irish literature and theatre has problematized the destructive fixities of family life and the rigidly defined roles within it.

Both *Losers* and *The Beauty Queen* represent elderly mothers not as self-sacrificing and long-suffering Irish "mammies" who may even represent "Mother Ireland" itself (as famously featured in works such as Patrick H. Pearse's "The Mother" [1916] and Seán O'Casey's *Juno and the Paycock* [1924]), but in a subversive way: as domestic tyrants

---

5 *Bunreacht na hÉireann / Constitution of Ireland (Dublin: Oifig an tSoláthair).* Article 41.2.1-2.

confirming what Nancy Chodorow describes as a "narcissistic" attitude of mothers to their daughters in patriarchy, considering them "as one with themselves" (195) without being entitled to a life of their own. Mrs Wilson acknowledges her daughter's services by thanking God and Saint Philomena for them, yet is suspicious of anything Hanna might be doing to satisfy her own emotional needs. Thus, it is the old lady who is most responsible for the actual undermining of the endlessly repeated pious slogan that "[t]he family that prays together stays together," since the family's togetherness is only a surface phenomenon. Moreover, Mrs Wilson's piety and orthodox moral convictions are doubled and strengthened by her neighbor, Cissy Cassidy, who visits her every evening to take part in her devotion to Saint Philomena and pray the Rosary with the family—and who calls all men "brute animals" (Friel 319). Under the surface, as Andy's narration suggests, both Mrs Wilson and the courting couple were trying to outwit each other: the latter by reciting the poem during their lovemaking sessions, and the old woman by using strategically timed bell ringing and guilt-inducing religious rituals and dogmas. This power struggle is a sign that the younger generation knows it must fight back against the rule of conservative elders (though, of course, Hanna—and then Andy—eventually give up the fight).

In *The Beauty Queen*, even the thin veneer of a tolerably good relationship between mother and daughter is shown to have worn away, and they fight battles in which both are viciously picking at each other's most sensitive points like birds of prey. But, again, Maureen's willingness to do battle with an oppressive mother shows a desire to push back against the sexual repression and narrow gender roles associated with patriarchy, even if the rebellion of the child—like that of matricidal "the Kid" in McDonagh's Oscar-winning short film, *Six Shooter* (2004)—turns murderous.

About *Lovers* as a whole, comprising the parts *Winners* and *Losers*, Ulf Dantanus says that it "presents a rather depressing view of life. In spite of the energy and the will to live and love that these characters so obviously possess, circumstances combine to frustrate them. These circumstances are all expressions of various kinds of societal pressures, and, as always in Friel, the individual suffers" (114). [6] Elmer Andrews goes further than Dantanus, stating (and echoing Yeats) that "in *Losers* Friel concentrates on the lack of courage equal to desire," and thereby "touches on a distinctively Irish theme: the willingness to acquiesce fatalistically in one's own enslavement" (115, 118). Critics, thus, anchor the play written in 1967 among literary and cultural representations of the long-lasting and paralyzing psychological effects of Irish colonialism on the individual. The backyard where Andy retreats is a refuge from the house, but its stone walls and small size mirror the fact that in *Lovers*, as F. C. McGrath has noted, Friel is depicting Ireland "at the end of the age of DeValera as claustrophobic and suffocating" (72). A more recent monograph about Friel by Scott Boltwood looks at the two parts of *Lovers* as texts which portray characters lingering in social death (69), as if in purgatory. In *Losers* the individual and social levels combine: the binoculars Andy has with him used to belong to the late Mr Wilson, which suggests continuity

---

6 In *Winners*, teenage lovers die, and they can therefore be called winners because they will not have to face the more destructive effects of the hostile circumstances in which they find themselves. This idea has its grotesque resonance in McDonagh's *The Pillowman* (2000), in which the kind and helpful pillowman shows comforting love when he strangles children, thereby preventing them from the vicissitudes and tragedies life would bring for them later.

without change, Andy's fate repeating that of another probably unhappy and certainly quiet man suffering from his wife's, the mother of Hanna's, religious mania.

Losers may be a work of social realism, but *The Beauty Queen*, set in the early 1990s, shortly before the Celtic Tiger boom, does not aspire to give a realistic picture of life in Connemara at that time. As Patrick Lonergan writes, the place in the play "does not correspond to geographical, political, or social realities" (115). However, in addition to the parallels outlined above, the two plays do share the creation of a general feeling, an affect of an all-encompassing human failure, which confirms their hauntedness by Beckett again. The style of *Losers*, as Dantanus describes it, is a "bold farce with tragic undercurrents" (109), the polarization of which anticipates the oscillation of the comic and the cruel in *The Beauty Queen*. In McDonagh's play, the continuity between Mag's tyrannical selfishness and Maureen's equally insensitive reactions to it provide an even more profound sense of failure than in *Losers*: the two women do not recognize the other as a human being with distinct needs and problems and thus make no attempt at achieving mutual understanding. This leads to the tragic outcome of death for Mag and death-in-life for Maureen. Does this deserve the label of failing better or failing worse in the Beckettian sense? What emerges as certain is that, by representing the tyranny of selfish old women and its impact on younger family members, *Losers* and *The Beauty Queen* thoroughly dismantle idealizing views about Catholic piety, Irish motherhood, and the peace of the rural Irish home.

Works Cited

Andrews, Elmer. *The Art of Brian Friel: Neither Reality Nor Dreams*. London: Macmillan, 1995.

Boltwood, Scott. *Brian Friel, Ireland and the North.* Cambridge: Cambridge University Press, 2007.

Chambers, Lilian, and Eamonn Jordan, eds. *The Theatre of Martin McDonagh: A World of Savage Stories.* Dublin: Carysfort, 2006.

Chodorow, Nancy J. *The Reproduction of Mothering: Psychoanalysis and the Sociology of Gender.* Berkeley, Los Angeles, London: University of California Press, 1978.

Dantanus, Ulf. *Brian Friel: A Study.* London: Faber, 1988.

Deane, Seamus. *Celtic Revivals.* London: Faber, 1985.

Eldred, Laura. "Martin McDonagh and the Contemporary Gothic." *Martin McDonagh: A Casebook.* Ed. Richard Rankin Russell. New York: Routledge, 2007. 111-30.

Friel, Brian. *Losers. Brian Friel: Collected Plays.* Vol. 1. London: Faber, 2016. 294-321.

Huber, Werner. "The Early Plays: Shooting Star and Hard Man from South London." Chambers and Jordan 13-26.

Inglis, Tom. "Origins and Legacies of Irish Prudery: Sexuality and Social Control in Modern Ireland." *Éire-Ireland* 40.3-4 (Fall/Winter 2005): 9-37.

Jordan, Eamonn. *From Leenane to L. A.: The Theatre and Cinema of Martin McDonagh.* Sallins Co. Kildare, Ireland: Irish Academic, 2014.

Kilroy, Thomas. "The Early Plays." *The Cambridge Companion to Brian Friel.* Ed. Anthony Roche. Cambridge: Cambridge University Press, 2006. 6-17.

Lanters, José. "Playwrights of the Western World: Synge, Murphy, McDonagh." *A Century of Irish Drama: Widening the Stage.* Ed. Stephen Watt, Eileen Morgan, and Shakir Mustafa. Bloomington and Indianapolis: Indiana University Press, 2000. 204-22.

Loomba, Ania. *Colonialism/Postcolonialism.* London and New

York: Routledge, 1998.

McDonagh, Martin. *The Beauty Queen of Leenane*. London: Methuen, 1996.

McGovern, Dan. "Eugene O'Neill's Place in Irish Theater Today: Interviews with Irish Theater Scholars." *Eugene O'Neill Review* 39. 1 (2018): 140-62.

McGrath, F. C. *Brian Friel's (Post)Colonial Drama: Language, Illusion and Politics*. Syracuse, NY: Syracuse University Press, 1999.

Middeke, Martin. "Martin McDonagh." *The Methuen Guide to Contemporary Irish Playwrights*. Ed. Martin Middeke and Peter Paul Schnierer. London: Methuen, 2010. 213-33.

Moane, Geraldine. *Gender and Colonialism: A Psychological Analysis of Oppression and Liberation*. London: Macmillan, 1999.

O'Brien, Cormac. "Unblessed amongst Women: Performing Patriarchy without Men in Contemporary Irish Theatre." *Ireland, Memory and Performing the Historical Imagination*. Ed. Christopher Collins, Mary P. Caulfield. London: Palgrave Macmillan, 2014. 190-206.

O'Toole, Fintan. "*The Beauty Queen of Leenane*." Chambers and Jordan 379-81.

Watt, Stephen. *Beckett and Contemporary Irish Writing*. Cambridge: Cambridge University Press, 2009.

Wilde, Oscar. *The Importance of Being Earnest. Oscar Wilde's Plays, Prose Writings, and Poems*. Intro. Hesketh Person. London: J. M. Dent and Sons, 1955. 345-402.

Wilson, Rebecca. "Macabre Merriment in McDonagh's Melodrama in *The Beauty Queen of Leenane*." Chambers and Jordan 27-41.

10.2478/9788367405423-010

Perspectives on Lifespan and Regeneration in the Plays of Conor McPherson

Maha Alatawi, Eamonn Jordan

Introduction

During the early part of his career Conor McPherson (1971) had mainly written monologues featuring predominantly young adult male narrators: in *Rum and Vodka* (1992), *The Good Thief* (1994), and *This Lime Tree Bower* (1995). The landmark turning point in McPherson's career happened in 1997; firstly, with *St Nicholas*, which features a suburban, middle-aged, self-indulgent, and paunchy theatre critic and his encounters with vampires that are regenerative, and, secondly, with *The Weir*, a play which uniquely featured rurally based characters who neither shared his own age profile nor wider social/cultural, urban experience. While it can be argued that the Irish playwriting tradition to which McPherson belongs is heavily if not predominantly past leaning, this essay maintains that McPherson's dramaturgy re-imagines that orientation more towards the present, but also the future by means of a focus on the notion of aging.

Simone de Beauvoir has stated, "Nothing should be more expected than old age: nothing is more unforeseen" (10), yet in McPherson's work, aging, we will argue, is brilliantly anticipated and foreseen. If as Mária Kurdi has claimed, "Characteristically, a significant portion of the critical literature on aging focuses on women's aging" ("Introduction" 81), accordingly, McPherson's work allows us to focus our analysis not just on women's aging, but on male aging as well, as there are no deficits on male aging in his work. With one exception, we focus on characters that are over fifty, some central to the dramas but others less so. In the first part of the essay, we deal with Jack in *The Weir*, John in *Dublin Carol* (2000), Joe in *Port Authority* (2001), John in *Shining City* (2004), Tommy and his uncle Maurice in *The Night Alive* (2013), Mr Perry in *Girl from the North Country* (2017), and, in the second, we discuss Valerie in *The Weir*, Margaret in *Come on Over* (2001), Grandie in *The Veil* (2011), and Elizabeth in *Girl from the North Country*. While these characters are singled out, we emphasize their connections and interdependencies on others, and by so doing we establish that the mix-gendered life-narratives that shape McPherson's characters are critically determined and informed by their specific experiences of and attitudes and responses towards the aging process. While optimism does not displace death-phobic narratives, McPherson's writing moves against a notion of aging as is scripted culturally and socially as a process of decline and diminution, degeneration or abjection, towards something more positive, optimistic, recuperative, even ageless. Category-wise, for example, across the plays, narrative elements vary from intradiegetic narration in *The Weir* to extradiegetic in *The Seafarer*, to the combination of both in *The Veil*; *Girl from the North Country* includes Bob Dylan songs and homodiegetic narration (see Alatawi 177-86).

Age-aware male articulations and mutualities

Research in cultural gerontology emphasizes, as noted by Julia Twigg and Wendy Martin, among other things, the individuality and agency of older people and the importance of their voices through narrative (*3*). Cultural gerontology aims not to focus on the problematic social, personal, or mental consequences of old age, but to maintain the subjectivity and depths of older people's lives. The construction of this subjectivity and the wide and deep experiences of old age, we argue, are prompted by the power of narration and recollections of memory in McPherson's work. His male characters' experiences of aging are informed by social notions regarding masculinity, marriage, and relationships and the associated consequences of success or failure. Increased risk of loneliness and vulnerability is linked to aging, or so it appears.

In *The Weir*, Finbar, as the successful businessman and the only married male character, describes his lonely drinking companions as desperate, old, single, and dreadful "fellas" who change the bedsheets every Christmas (48). While elderly relatives are mentioned in the play, Jack, the oldest of the four male characters, relates a story about the impact of loss and absence in his life, prompted by Valerie's question as to whether he has children. Jack, now an elderly bachelor and childless, tells the story of his girlfriend, who left the countryside for Dublin. Jack, at that time, rejected the idea of moving away and stopped responding to his girlfriend's letters. He reminisces about attending the wedding of his beloved as just another guest, how drunk he became the night before the wedding, and how he left the wedding to visit a bar where a barman and stranger offered him a sandwich as a kind gesture which was overly appreciated by Jack. The girl he loved is now with another man and "there's not one morning I don't wake up with her name in the room" (69). Younger characters such as Brendan can learn from the experiences of their older counterparts, for example, when Jack advises Brendan not to end up a "cantankerous old fucker" like himself (66). Jack tries to compensate for loss by making the best of the changes in his life.

As they undergo continual change, notions that communities have altered historically is a fact that Jack rejects at first. Yet the play's ending demonstrates initial acceptance of such change. Towards the end, Jack, whose reluctance to even venture to Dublin costs him a life partner, has shown unexpected enthusiasm to engage with tourists: "If Valerie is willing to come in and brave the Germans then I'm sure me and Jim'll come in and keep yous company, how is that now? . . . I think that is the right attitude. You should stay with the company and the bright lights" (73). That trajectory towards renewal is evident in the play's optimistic ending, in which there is a sense of communal solace offered, significantly prompted by Jack's age-informed initiative, awareness and acceptance.

Like Jack, Joe in *Port Authority* (2001) is the oldest of the three narrators in this play, but unlike Jack, he is married and has two children. The other characters are Kevin, in his twenties, and Dermot, in his thirties. The three men represent three different stages in the life cycle and in performance witness each other's stories unresponsively. Joe is a pensioner who lives in a home for the elderly, and no longer seems to have a substantial purpose in life. The stories told by the three characters embody the physical and emotional transformation and accompanying anxieties related to aging, through the recurrent presence of the three characters on the stage. Joe's nostalgic narration reflects a succession of losses: loss of health, past life relationships, opportunity, and prior purpose. His narration draws attention to the physical changes that come with age and management of daily lives.

Abandonment and desertion in the life of elderly people who relocate to a nursing home also occur as an issue in the play as families fail to provide the necessary care. Joe describes the residents in the home, including himself, some of whom are agile while others rely on sticks and wheelchairs. The residents spend their time in a variety of pursuits such as chatting about the weather, discussing the racing results, family gossip, and the recounting of memories: Joe says, "me and Jackie'd wander around to the bookies and get a bottle of stout in Tighe's" (140), but for Joe not all matters can be shared, "when you live in close proximity to people in a home like me, and you're fairly private, you don't let on if you've got news, especially if it is of a highly personal nature" (183). Joe has not received a birthday present for years, asking "who would be sending an old curmudgeon birthday presents?" (139). He also has a son but not once is there mention of a visit in his narrated story.

Joe's experience reflects the uncertainty of beliefs and commitments through his narrative about the unexpected twists and turns of his life. His narration treasures the simplicity of a past life and his naiver self, in relation to identity, gender roles, and domestic life. In Ireland at that time, "you didn't have a lot of the issues that you do now" and "you didn't need to be asking all the questions you do now" (150-51). All the simplicity of his past life and significant hope for the future are now suspended, and he is left with an unexplainable affection for his married neighbor, Marion, which forms the majority of his narrative. The conflict between loyalty to his wife and his affection for Marion causes him to question whether it is God's plan to take his wife away because Joe is supposed to be with someone else or whether his unrequited love for Marion is an illusion. His indecisiveness is starkly illustrated as he lies down holding Marion's picture and his wife's rosary beads. Joe lived long enough to reflect on his life with neither regret nor worry because "when you get to my age, you give up on them because they don't help anything" (186).

Dublin Carol presents John's checkered past through his reminiscences of alcohol addiction. Now in his late fifties, he recalls how he would drink at all hours of the day, and the associated sights and smells, such as "the stink of all those dirty bastards leaning into you" (90) and "filthy dirty places" where the barman sleeps on a mattress behind the bar (91). As an alcoholic estranged from his family, John, in his conversation with his daughter Mary, says, "I was in a very bad state . . . I was in hell. I was in agony" (105). In a similar situation, John in *Shining City*, who is also in his fifties, is a widower who regrets his emotional unavailability and detachment from his wife, Mari, before her death in a car accident. As he still grieves over her death, John tells Ian, his therapist, about Mari's ghost, haunting the house. Both Johns have desperate longing for communication and intimacy; John in *Dublin Carol* through an affair with Carol, although he admits he was a liability to her, while John in *Shining City* first with a woman named Vivien and then later during another scenario in a brothel that does not work out, says "I just needed to connect with something, or someone, you know?" (McPherson, *Shining City* 35). In this respect, together these two plays can be interpreted as a meditation on loss and duties and obligations towards others and how to cope with changes in relationships through time. The moments at which they feel listened to by someone else represent, for both Johns, brief moments of clarity in an otherwise lonely elderly existence. *Shining City*'s John has a sense of his own exoneration as he can see "a new chapter is opening up" (51), while evidence of hope transpires in *Dublin Carol*'s John's life as he returns the Christmas decorations from storage while thinking of visiting the dying wife he has abandoned.

In 2013's *The Night Alive*, Uncle Maurice takes in his middle-aged, fifty-year-old nephew, Tommy, after his marriage ends, giving him a home within his own home. Tommy does not show gratitude towards his uncle, and instead keeps the place untidy, jimmies the electrical supply, gripes about hot water and allows his friend and colleague, Doc, to stay over. Although Maurice, an elderly man with a walking stick, is curmudgeonly, suspicious, depressed, alcohol dependent, and hostile towards Tommy, Maurice wonders, as a father substitute of sorts, why Tommy has gone from being someone who was full of life and exuberance to someone who is sneaky, unmotivated, and dishonest.

Drunk and depressed, Maurice fills the narrator's role as he speaks to Tommy, blaming him for forgetting to be a part of Maura's memorial, Maura being Maurice's late wife who helped Maurice to raise Tommy. His monologic expression of disconnection, loss, grief, and death also reflects on how age influences perceptions about life passing: "Death is real, Tommy! Yeah! You're just knocking the days off the calendar . . . just another invisible man, knowing that the end is sneaking in on you and knowing it is gonna be the worst part of your life" (79). Three concerns about ageing can be discerned within Maurice's quote. Firstly, death and dying are critical factors in late life. Maurice's opening up to Tommy perpetuates the emotional toll of decline and physical illness. Secondly, guilt and regret are also fundamental to Maurice's feelings about his dead wife. Maurice was not talking to his wife the night she slipped on ice and died. His final concern is the length of time and the number of people who will remember you after death. Maurice is enraged about the fact that only eight people managed to attend Maura's memorial service.

During this same moment of honesty and revelation between Maurice and Tommy, Maurice judges Tommy's irresponsibility and carelessness, advising that "the country is a shambles and we're crying out for people like you. That can lead us into the light" (80) and that people "don't get endless goes. Two, three goes maybe" (83). Guilt is an uneasy burden for Maurice; his affliction is connected to his perception of chaos and limited opportunity. When Maurice offers to sign over his house to Tommy, his gesture is one signal of the play's shifting of consciousness, as it coincides with Doc's reflections on the Magi that were present during the birth of Jesus Christ, but also those who gave him a gift, an insight into black holes, life after death, and infinity. Maurice's aging features initially as disappointment in life, rage against chaos, and disgust at the disregard that Tommy affords him. However, these are not constants, and in the age of toxic masculinity, both Doc's fortitude and resilience, despite an intellectual disability in the face of multiple life challenges, and Maurice's generosity serve as substantial supports to Tommy's life. Maurice's gift is to transform Tommy's economic reality and safeguard his future. In *The Night Alive*, stereotypes of aging are defied, and instead aging is almost regenerative, offering opportunities en route to hope, change, or new realizations.

Set during America's Great Depression and prompted by the songs of Bob Dylan, *Girl from the North Country* (2017) has considerable things to say about aging. Loneliness in this play is synonymous with aging and has a causal link to psychological and mental distress. Mr Perry in *Girl from the North Country* represents the correlation between losing a partner and experiencing loneliness, leading to his pursuance of a young woman despite her rejection of him. A shoe mender in his sixties, Mr Perry offers nineteen-year-old Marianne a win-win deal—Marianne is Nick and Elizabeth's adopted African American daughter, who is pregnant. Mr Perry lives alone and needs someone to ease his loneliness, so he offers himself to Marianne in return for the house after his death.

Mr Perry envisions an inferior life for Marianne if she is not married to him and tells her that his dead wife comes to him in a dream prompting him to get married. In a hot-tempered monologue, he confronts Marianne with her situation as an African American young woman living in Duluth, Minnesota; her father is losing the family home to the bank and Mr Perry envisages her ending up working as a maid. His fear of aging and loneliness renders Mr Perry desperate for someone to share his home, as he explains: "Nobody chooses to get old. Everybody fights it . . . You move slower and slower ' cause you can't go fast! It hurts! Pain got ya surrounded. Your back and your legs and your hands in here in your got?! You wake in the night, there's no one there. Only the cold" (74). Loss of close relationships can lead to feelings of emptiness and depression. Mr Perry clearly misses the warmth of family, closeness and intimacy. In the eyes of Marianne, however, Mr Perry is simply a predator who takes advantage of her foster father's need for money. Mr Perry uses Nick's need for money and Marianne's potential downfall as motivating factors to find a warm human presence in his house to help him get through physical pain, haunting past memories, and, what scares him the most, the feeling of being alone, as it distorts notions of choice and consent.

Dublin Carol's John's words—"Boredom. Loneliness. A feeling of basically being out of step with everybody else. Fear. Anxiety. Tension" (111)—define many of the reminiscences of McPherson's negative-leaning male characters. Kevin Wallace maintains that the telling of stories gives McPherson's male characters "a sense of control, a power over their place in the world, their history and their identity" (95). According to Patrick Maley, McPherson's characters are presented to the audience through the global context of revelation related to a requirement for sociality and a limit on their ability to self-determine that is made distinct (208). These views stand in contradiction to Brian Singleton's argument that McPherson's male narrators are frozen and submissive, focused, as it is, on passive masculinity. McPherson's males, he argues, are only aware of their failures. Even if this is observed as a process of self-awareness, this argument is still not sufficient as it does not prompt progress or change (272-73). However, in McPherson's work, such feelings are always accompanied by the possibility of subversion and change. McPherson debunks long-standing stereotypes and fears of aging through such possibilities with a sense that there would be more to life if only his characters could work out how to access it. This sense is usually realized through their storied experiences.

Age-aligned female visibility, defiance, and consent
On aging and femininity, Margaret O'Neill and Michaela Schrage-Früh write that "the gendered dimensions of ageing are particularly trenchant in Irish literature and culture, where images of a beautiful young girl or poor old woman have often been conflated with that of the nation" (1). They explain how passive constructions of such images contribute also to the cultural invisibility of women, thus reinforcing the traditional gender roles of women and men. However, complex constructions and empowered representations of women in older age exist in all genres of Irish writing and dominant images of aging can be countered and revised. McPherson's work is more in line with this second view of aging.

If Marianne, in *Girl from the North Country*, as a nineteen-year-old captures the energy of youth, and risks a great deal by running away with Joe Scott, aging also finds perspective in the experiences of many of McPherson's female characters in midlife or old age. Although Valerie in *The Weir* is only in her thirties, grief has prematurely aged her. If it seems that Valerie has little in common with the male characters in the plays, by the play's end that viewpoint is shattered. She narrates the story of how she had to encounter the ghostly visits of Niamh, her dead daughter, leaving Dublin, her husband and her job, and taking a house in the countryside to cope with the traumatic loss of her little girl. Loneliness after loss has haunted Valerie's present life at a younger age than other characters, yet the shared telling of stories helps her to overcome. She now takes comfort in company and the knowledge that she is not alone: "Something happened to me. That just hearing you talk about it tonight. It's important to me. That I'm not . . . bananas" (57). Clearly, loss prompts her to re-evaluate her life, question her sanity, and the experience of death triggers her to deal with things she might not have expected to do at her relatively young age. Valerie, then, exemplifies McPherson's female characters with her strong presence, value, and influence over male characters, but also someone who responds to a recognition of co-dependencies and the responsibility to transact unselfishly.

An aging Margaret in *Come on Over* (2001) delivers a passionate and nostalgic monologue which merges remote and recent past incidents. Margaret's monologue centers around her loss of love and her relationship with Matthew, a Jesuit, who left her many years before, and now is investigating miracles for the Catholic Church. Her monologic account reflects her memories, thoughts, regrets and female instincts. Matthew provides his own monologue first, which considers the events of the past from his—very different—perspective. Margaret's monologue, on the other hand, is more concerned with her feelings for Matthew, as she recollects an encounter, some thirty years prior, when the pair were walking in a rose garden. Margaret's remembrance of sensual details such as her clothing and her desire for Matthew's touch are clearly strong memories for her and have remained a conscious part of her life over the intervening three decades. Aging has not diminished the intensity of her feelings, memory is activated and animated in the now, on his return. Going on to recount more recent experiences, such as her husband's death from leukemia, her daughter's graduation and subsequent travels, and caring for her husband's father, Margaret's narrative is more passionate and nostalgic than Matthew's, relating to the experience of life's passing and remembrance of details of the past, and how heartbreak affected Margaret's later life after Matthew left. In the here and now, his face is scarred, wounded by a young African woman, Patience, whom he had sexually assaulted when she was eleven, for which he tries to disown moral and criminal accountability.

At various moments during their narrations, Matthew and Margaret interject and interrupt each other, for example, when Margaret removes a straw hood that both wear in performance during a moment of intensity and Matthew repeatedly asks her to replace it. Or Margaret's emotional and somewhat confused interjections during some of Matthew's most open and honest moments:

> MATTHEW   (to MARGARET). I was lost.
> MARGARET   (to MATTHEW). Stop.
>   Keep going, I'm sorry. (198)

At the same time, the transition from monologue into interrupted dialogue implies a closeness between the characters and a shared desire to cover up the story from the past, which nevertheless continues to affect the lives of the characters in their older age. The background to this detail is only implied within the narration, but the implication becomes clear as the monologues end with Matthew's reflections on his experience and Margaret's interjections.

The Veil includes characters with a range of ages, some of them elderly, including Reverend Berkeley and Mrs Goulding. While *The Veil* is ostensibly about economics, material decline, asset transfer, conflicts between the indigenous Irish and the Ascendency landlord class, complex and materially led inter- and intra-class relationships and arranged marriages, as every character knows that it is not Hannah's fiancée but his father who is especially attracted to her. *The Veil* is also a play about the past, the future, hauntings, guilt, ghosts, and death. End of life intrudes across all stages of life. Hannah had found her father, Edward, dead, hanging over the mantelpiece; Audelle had lost a wife and child; Berkeley's wife is dead and local children are dying from scarlet fever and hunger, while others die due to the collapse of accommodation belonging to the Lambroke estate. Berkeley is particularly manipulative and self-indulgent in how he uses collective prayer and a séance to invoke the dead. Madeline suggests that his vocation as a priest was vanity-led and that he has not sufficiently grown up: "I'm not your child, Berkeley. You *are* old, I don't deny it. Age has racked your body, but it is your brain that has suffered most! I hear you speak and I believe you are like a man with an infant's toy box in his head," to which Grandie responds with a reinforcing, mocking "Woah!" (93).

Superstitions, trauma, alcohol, and the laudanum that Audelle inappropriately provides Hannah with to alter her psyche also adjust the play's register or genre signature, moving it away from something grounded in naturalism towards the supernatural. Its equivalence, character-wise, is found in Grandie's almost constant, otherworldly presence on stage, which counters any sense of age invisibility. Although Grandie interacts minimally, "while she makes eye contact and smiles from time to time, she rarely speaks," displaying an awareness and articulating insights that the others cannot access (23).

Throughout *The Veil*, Grandie is variously steered, guided, shushed, shunted, monitored, indulged, and absorbed within the play's character collective, which is Chekhov-like in many respects. A stage direction curiously indicates: "The lights change as everyone but Grandie drifts out to the hallway. An afternoon materializes around Grandie as she sits there" (115), and in that unusual conception of focus, in the materialization of the afternoon around her, there is a distinctive indicator of her centrality to the play's consciousness. If Berkeley wants to claim authority and dominance within the family's tradition of gender and aging norms, Grandie disrupts Berkeley's séance, having connected with Hannah's gaze, and seen the need to protect her. Grandie's first verbal intervention is to signal the presence of a ghostly dog at the door (50), indicating her multi-focality, absorbed simultaneously in the here and now and in another dimension of knowing or being. Just prior to Audelle's suicide, Grandie again feels the presence of a barking blind old dog that long ago lived with them, suggesting levels of awareness that her illness does not discommode, rather perhaps accentuates. Later, when distressed, Grandie screams at Audelle, then laughs at, mocking, striking him with a stick, and eventually terrifies him in the process, because she knows that he has seen a ghost (79-80). If a young Hannah is the play's protagonist through her challenging of gender norms, duties, obligations, and her willingness to embrace the visions that come to her, the aging Grandie is also central to the forging of the play's gender-norm instabilities, and she serves as an additional force of power, energizing and monitoring the matrilineal line.

If Audelle and Berkeley, respectively, provide plagiarized philosophy and religious belief as patriarchal master narratives of sorts, united in their faith in the otherworldly, Grandie's storytelling is far more embedded and embodied as a rival gendered belief system, based around communal values, duty, integrity, manipulation, displacement, and injustices. Times and spaces amalgamate in Grandie's comments that echo with Hannah's reality: "A boy once proposed to me who was from Northampton, but Daddy wouldn't brook it. He had a kind face. He wasn't good-looking but he was kind. It will be nice to be near him. Won't it?" (118).

Grandie has one vitally significant narrative moment. She is fixated on a story told to her by the king with mirrors instead of eyes, who stated that St Patrick was a gold prospector, who preached about Jesus Christ and Christianity to the indigenous population, while intent on stealing their gold (63). Likewise, the Lambroke's Ascendancy-class took ownership of indigenous Irish lands, and now they are to be displaced to Northampton and replaced by Colonel Bennett, the new owner of the estate. Because of maturity and expanded consciousness, Grandie's age-related awareness is to resist greed and dispossession. Berkeley also reflects and expands on the notions of God, mirrors and infinity, expressing ideas on consciousness and self-aware subjectivity, which link back to Grandie's concepts, but Grandie's is the more substantial philosophical claim. Grandie serves as a peculiar witness and observer, contributing a degree of dispassion, indifference, and confusion, while responding to situations ranging from aggressive behavior and "the slightest of smiles" (90) to applause (100) or by being supportive and affectionate towards Hannah, kissing her. She also "sings with confidence" on two occasions (101).

Grandie benefits from emotionally protective gestures, evident in the willingness of Mrs Goulding to offer to keep her in Ireland, so that she would not have to relocate to Northampton. Equally, Grandie acknowledges Madeleine as a good mother. Moreover, the conditions and circumstances of Grandie's Alzheimer's disease and the license it affords, facilitates a fraught and complex understanding of character interactions and co-dependencies, delivering a perspective that is simultaneously multiple, discrete, forgiving, forbidding, and enabling, far from being mere issues of visibility and invisibility, agency or restraint. If illness seems to be the source of Grandie's random thoughts, and her confusion as to whether it is night or day, yet her observations bring past, present, future, and the eternal into play. Grandie's presence is one that engages with, comments, reflects, and substantiates viewpoints. She is simultaneously excessively present and vaguely absent, someone who might be indulged, shushed and dismissed, but is never silenced or marginalized. Even in illness, Grandie's instinct is to protect the matrilineal line, supporting Hannah by exposing Berkeley and Audelle's fraudulent beliefs. If an Irish tradition of writing unduly connects the matrilineal to the past by way of madness or senility, or wayward performativity (see Tom Murphy's *Bailegangaire* [1985]), McPherson uses Grandie's Alzheimer's not to orientate the play towards a recurring and inescapable past, but to suggest something more freeing and focused about his understanding of existences inside and outside of time, a viewpoint which chimes with the sensibility of the eternal in *The Night Alive*.

Grandie is not the only female character with a mental condition in McPherson's work. Elizabeth in *Girl from the North Country* is a woman in her early fifties with dementia. McPherson presents Elizabeth as an aged, demented woman with a degrading cognitive capacity but, at the same time, with a consciousness that can still be valued and appreciated: "People with dementia continue to be participants in and co-creators of the lived lives of others, whether those others are paid carers, relatives, or friends. In short, just like people who do not have dementia, they continue to be active subjects who create meaning for themselves as they encounter the external world" (Millet 9). Cognitive impairment does not always entail losing oneself and personal worth to mental decline in old age. Demented elderly people can still maintain their importance and appreciation in their changed status in the life of their families even if on a different scale. Elizabeth's awareness of the hazards around her are witnessed at various times in the play, in the same way as her judgments of the other characters' personalities and behaviors can also be perceived.

Elizabeth's expressions and reactions throughout the play suggest both "her absence, [and] her presence" (McPherson, *Girl* 12). As the play opens, the fact of Elizabeth's dementia is revealed by Dr Walker, Elizabeth's doctor and the play's narrator. The situation is hard on her husband Nick, who is Elizabeth's primary family carer, with help from their daughter Marianne. Elizabeth's clumsy behavior at times irritates Nick and leads to his frustration and harsh words and actions, creating a new lifestyle for Nick, Marianne, and Gene, her other child—one in which Nick, Marianne and Gene perform primarily as carers rather than husband and children. However, there are also moments in the play when it is clear that Elizabeth has a good understanding of the actions of those around her, as well as the ability to argue her opinion and discuss the lives of their dependents, thus continuing to contribute to the life of the family, albeit in a less predictable and less routine fashion. For example, Elizabeth is clearly aware of the advances of Mrs Nielson towards Nick, and their assumed relationship, which presumably fulfils the function of a release or respite for Nick from his new life as a caregiver. She also conveys clarity in her conversation with Marlowe the preacher about the various destinies of her family members and the box of money she is keeping hidden as a safeguard under her chair. That is the only thing left with her at this stage of life.

Despite her frequent relapses, Elizabeth is also coherent in her disapproval of the suggestion of marrying Marianne off to Mr Perry for money, continuing to contribute her voice to the decision-making processes of her family. Elizabeth's moments of lucidity stand in sharp contrast to her moments of dementia, Nick's somewhat harsh reactions to his frustrations and his statement that in not taking Elizabeth to "some old lady's home," she should be grateful (66). Then there are the moments when Elizabeth sings so passionately and coherently Dylan's *Like a Rolling Stone* towards the end of act 1 and *Forever Young* towards the end of the play. The singing of such classic sounds, the positioning of them dramatically, and how the mood of the songs counters the circumstances of their lives is hugely significant to McPherson's use of lucidity and musical numbers to hint at alternative realities, even as characters continue to age.

The play also reflects on non-functional marital relationships and the loss of family connections as a result of losing material security during the Great Depression. The threat of losing their home complicates the relationship between Elizabeth and her husband, with the result being Nick's plan to end both of their lives. Elizabeth, despite her weak position and her illness, manages to change his mind by narrating what seems to be the story of how they first met. Dr Walker's last act of narration shows that Nick does not proceed with his plans and that Nick "took care of her best he could" (101) before taking her to a home for women on the banks of the Missouri and remaining in a hostel nearby so as to be with her every day until the morning she died. Lisa Fitzpatrick views McPherson's female characters as elements of disruption of the male world whose presence can be harmful and deadly ("Conor McPherson's Haunted Women" 170-74). She argues that "The evocation . . . of the male characters' darkest regrets and most painful, buried memories suggests that female characters function in McPherson's work as a recurring trope for the exploitation of grief and regret" (177). For us, McPherson uses narrative in a wide variety of forms, with very different intentions, particularly in relation to aging.

In recognition of the fact that Elizabeth and Grandie have dementia or Alzheimer's, one is cautioned by the idea that there may be a type of gendered inclination to associate women characters with illness or dysfunctional consciousness, but our discussions on both characters and on Marianne and Valerie decline that connotation. Furthermore, in *The Birds* (2009), a production inspired by Daphne Du Maurier's novella *The Birds* (1952), the relationship between Nat and Diane is threatened and complicated by the arrival of the younger Julia. Even as predatorial birds signal destructive attacks and possibly human extinction, Diane's ruthless actions are more to do with the play's chaotic dystopian worldview, and less due to aging or jealousy surrounding Julia's possible pregnancy.

In particular, characters, especially women, do not stand for anything else, do not exclusively carry the burden of meaning that the males cannot access. As Anne Fogarty notes of Anne Enright's *The Green Road* (2015), "Recalcitrance, waywardness and discomfiting reminders of the incomplete are fundamental characteristics of the aging maternal Others that populate Enright's work. Old age is circumscribed by her [Enright] not through images of wholeness or debility but through tropes of the gapped and the unfinished" (133). For McPherson more generally, however, there is less debility and less of the unfinished, and more completeness for aging maternal and paternal figures. Where there is stubbornness, it is rewarding, and there is less obstinate waywardness, even if there is cussedness, but a degree of flexibility and mobility, prompted by openness and a partiality towards acceptance, the new and the novel.

Conclusion

In response to concerns like those of Fitzpatrick, what we have identified in this article is a range of actions and narratives of different aging female and male characters in McPherson's work. For us, McPherson's various aging characters' stories, both male and female, give pain and trauma, pleasure and success a degree of meaning denied under postmodern thinking, as they render from the life narratives details and connections that affirm purpose. The McPherson characters we have isolated may be aging and less mobile but are nevertheless energetic. In theatre, low energy characters ruin performance intensity. Buoyancy, flamboyancy, and vibrancy, especially for an elderly character appearing even for short spans of time, must be the order of the day. McPherson's elderly characters may show signs of confusion, but never dissociate too easily from the past—there is no fugue state, no living without accountability. The McPherson plays evaluated here problematize the notion of agency, belonging and community, querying how characters have contributed to, shaped, or responded to their own story. Across the works we have discussed, characters attest to various ideological viewpoints, gender norms, expectations, and contraventions, and these are particularly acute when viewed from the perspective of elderly characters whose significance is not necessarily aligned with their prominence or dramatic centrality.

McPherson's aging characters are less intent on unnerving other characters, delivering life lessons or standing in their way, and more about displaying a degree of tolerance, indeed generous gifting and protectiveness towards younger characters. Accordingly, their narratives are not so much therapeutic, confessional, or burdening, but more a confident sharing of deliberations or viewpoints, prompted by inquisitiveness, uncertainty, and enthusiasm. With plays such as *Port Authority*, the young/old binary is tampered with, McPherson's three seemingly different characters capturing and breaching the notion of there being either three distinct stages of life or of them representing three versions of the same character in alternative dimensions of time. Acts of subjective remembrance in old age help to interpret and situate aspects of life and in so doing can illuminate both the past and the present. McPherson presents through character narration, actions, and interactions how the personal past is always latent within the present, enhancing the experience of aging and different life stages with changing personalities, ways of thinking and growing maturity.

As McCormick notes, "Humans know how to live longer; it is the ability to live better that remains a challenge" (20), and for characters it is likewise. Accordingly, the age-related stories referred to in this essay are less about frail bodies and more about their vigorous embodiment, less about stereotypes of aging and decline, and more about a kind of maturation informed by life lessons, less about ageism, acting one's age, or the performance of aging and more about centering on a sense of self that is formidable, self-aware, self-depreciatory, but absolutely aware of its interconnectedness.

McPherson's characters revisit the past, reclaim the narratives of their youth, emphasize the costs and consequences of loves won and lost, limited agency, poor and good choices, illustrate how they deal with those close to them passing away, even as they express what might seemingly amount to life lessons of sorts, delivered raucously, crudely, defiantly, and despairingly. Few of these aging characters tend to be self-serving, self-deceiving, or bent on self-justification. These characters find purpose and presence in age-inappropriate behavior and thinking, in a jouissance associated with growing old. As argued here, differences between characters, between spaces and times do not always hold. By tinkering with time in particular the past is accommodated, the present is abundant, and the future serves as a form of an eternal performative. Time passes non-linearly, and as characters age, there are declines but also recuperations, there are losses but also regenerations, thereby ensuring that the plays are neither age-denying nor age-defying feats.

Works Cited

Alatawi, Maha. "Narrativity and the Narrator Figure in Conor McPherson's *Port Authority*, *The Veil* and *Girl from the*

North Country." Eamonn Jordan. *The Theatre and Films of Conor McPherson: Conspicuous Communities.* London: Methuen, 2019. 177-86.

De Beauvoir, Simone. *Old Age.* Middlesex: Penguin. 1970.

Fitzpatrick, Lisa. "Conor McPherson's Haunted Women: *The Weir, The Veil,* and *Paula.*" Jordan, 165-77.

Fogarty, Anne. "'Someone whose kindness did not matter': Femininity and Ageing in Anne Enright's *The Green Road.*" *Nordic Irish Studies* 17.1 (2018): 131-44.

Kurdi, Mária. "Introduction." Special Section: Negotiating Ageing and Ageism in English-Speaking Fiction and Theatre." *Hungarian Journal of English and American Studies* 26.1 (2020): 81-84.

Maley, Patrick. "'The play is set in the theatre': Conor McPherson and the Late-Modern Humanism of the Theatrical Event." *Irish Studies Review* 22.2 (2014): 207-23.

McCormick, Sheila. *Applied Theatre: Creative Ageing.* London: Methuen, 2017.

McPherson, Conor. *The Birds.* McPherson, *Plays: Three* 153-210.

---. *Come On Over.* McPherson, *Plays: Two* 187-206.

---. *The Dance of Death* (an adaptation of August Strindberg's play). McPherson, *Plays: Three* 310-71.

---. *Dublin Carol.* McPherson, *Plays: Two* 75-128.

---. *Girl from the North Country.* London: Nick Hern, 2017.

---. *The Good Thief.* McPherson, *Plays: One* 75-128.

---. *The Night Alive.* London: Nick Hern, 2013.

---. *Plays: One.* London: Nick Hern, 2011.

---. *Plays: Three.* London: Nick Hern, 2013.

---. *Plays: Two.* London: Nick Hern, 2004.

---. *Port Authority.* McPherson, *Plays: Two* 129-86.

---. *Rum and Vodka*. McPherson, *Plays: One* 7-48.

---. *The Seafarer*. McPherson, *Plays: Three* 57-152

---. *Shining City*. McPherson, *Plays: Three* 1-56.

---. *St Nicholas*. McPherson, *Plays: One* 135-78.

---. *This Lime Tree Bower*. McPherson, *Plays: One* 85-132.

---. *The Veil*. McPherson, *Plays: Two* 211-306.

---. *The Weir*. McPherson, *Plays: Two* 9-74.

Millett, Stephan. "Self and Embodiment: A Bio-Phenomenological Approach to Dementia." *Dementia* 10.4 (2011): 509-22.

O'Neill, Margaret, and Michaela Schrage-Früh. "Introduction: Women and Ageing in Irish Literature and Film." *Nordic Irish Studies* 17.1 (2018): 1-13.

Twigg, Julia, and Wendy Martin. "The Challenge of Cultural Gerontology." *The Gerontologist* 55.3 (2015): 353-59. Web. 19 July 2021.

Singleton, Brian. *Masculinities and the Contemporary Irish Theatre*. Basingstoke: Palgrave, 2011.

Strehler, Bernard L. *Time, Cells and Ageing*. New York and London: Academic, 1962.

Wallace, Kevin. "'Shame shame shame': Masculinity, Intimacy and Narrative in Conor McPherson's *Shining City*." *The Theatre of Conor McPherson*. Ed. Lilian Chambers and Eamonn Jordan. Dublin: Carysfort, 2012. 89-102.

10.2478/9788367405423-011

Part III
American Drama

Aging and Death in Edward Albee's *The Sandbox* and Tennessee Williams's *The Milktrain Doesn't Stop Here Anymore*
Réka M. Cristian

Tropes of aging and death abound in two American dramas, Edward Albee's chamber piece, *The Sandbox* (1960), and Tennessee Williams's *The Milktrain Doesn't Stop Here Anymore* (1963), yielding a negotiation of the protagonists' identities through specters of age and the means of encountering death. Both plays were written in the early sixties by playwrights who excelled in the depiction of controversial themes, including the representation of age. It was the time when the last tide of the Baby Boom generation—the generation between 1946 and 1964, which shaped most of twentieth-century US society —was born. The representation of senior citizens in these dramatic plots, ranging from Albee's Mommy, Daddy, and especially Grandma to Williams's Mrs. Flora Goforth, challenges mainstream cultural constructions of aging.

As Philip C. Kolin contends, Albee's one-act plays, including *The Sandbox*, "called America to be self-reflexive" in a turbulent decade in which "the Kennedy and Martin Luther King assassinations, the Watts riots in Los Angeles, the Vietnam War, and the Stonewall protests of gays and bisexuals would all force the nation to confront its failings" (17). Unlike other Albee plays of the sixties, *The Sandbox*, however, focuses on a dual theme that was rather unvoiced in the American plays of the sixties: aging and death. Interestingly, the same theme of aging and death also appears in William's play written three years after Albee's, *The Milktrain Doesn't Stop Here Anymore*. Williams had, according to Christopher W. E. Bigsby, a "romantic fascination with extreme situations, with the imagination's power to challenge facticity, with the capacity of language to reshape experience" (32) in a manner that no playwright had before him, especially in regard to the dying and old characters. Indeed, considering his famous characters, especially those "whose lives have reached their apogee and can look forward only to a decline," there is only one play about an old dying actress written in the sixties when the playwright himself was "on the very verge of his vertiginous plunge into the drink and drugs which came close to annihilating his personality" (65, 67).

In my reading of these two plays, I am following the approach to aging and identity as described by cultural critic Margaret Morganroth Gullette, who was among the first to call for a distinctive age or aging studies in the 1990s (qtd. in Bouson 6). Gullette followed immunologist Élie/Ilya Metchnikoff's ideas on aging and longevity in *The Prolongation of Life: Optimistic Studies* (1908/2004) as well as Simone de Beauvoir's notions in her quintessential but largely neglected book *The Coming of Age* (1970) by challenging the so-called "regimes of decline" or narratives of decline (Gullette, *Agewise* 5) and the strategies of ageism. The term "ageism" was invented in 1969, a year after the term "sexism" appeared. According to Gullette, ageism should be used in the plural form as "ageisms" (*Ending Ageism* xviii) rather than the singular (a term coined by Robert Butler, the first director of the American National Institute of Aging in 1969), because it is, in Palmore Erdman's formulation, "the ultimate prejudice, the last discrimination, the cruelest rejection" of old people (3), related to "any prejudice or discrimination against or in favor of any age group" (4). Furthermore, Gullette claims that

> naming and shaming go together. Use of the term "racism" disparages and drives out hate speech, housing and job exclusions, and other racializations. Calling out "homophobia" changes LGBTQ lives. Naming discrimination against people with disabilities as "ableism" changes the status and identity of people with disabilities. Targeting "ageism" instead of our own "aging" does heavy lifting on behalf of everyone alive, and positions old people to enjoy the accomplishment of making it so far so well. (*Ending Ageism* 202)

Gullette also states that Americans in the twentieth century, especially the so-called Boomers, "generally didn't pay serious attention to ageism or even notice its precocious spawn, middle-ageism"; moreover, most Americans thought "there never can be a 'golden age' for older people," but, as the cultural critic continues, despite this grim context, "aging-into-the-middle-years, or aging-into-old-age, or even aging-past-youth, can be better or worse depending on social context" (*Agewise* 5). Furthermore, Gullette claims that "whatever happens in the body, and even if nothing happens in the body, aging is a narrative. Each of us tells her own story. But most of us lack an adequate back story," which she calls "age autobiography" (5). Age autobiography thus becomes a new genre of life storytelling that is endowed with critical revelatory characteristics.

In Albee's and Williams's dramas that deal with the imminent presence of death and dying, it is possible to trace an age autobiography by following subsequent markers of identity in the case of Grandma and Flora Goforth, who enact an agewise strategy that helps them encounter the grand finale. "Agewise," an umbrella term coined by Gullette, is a series of attitudes and strategies that confront "trends and symptomatic events in this new expanded US ageism that have been concealed or misrepresented or underreported even though they do increasing violence to essential aspects of well-being" (*Agewise* 8). An agewise attitude, therefore, is a certain constructive self-awareness that develops in later stages of life. The two dramas I chose for analysis are eloquent artistic examples of how several forms of ageisms work in the western, youth-oriented culture pertaining to women of advanced age arriving at the end of their lives, and how these women fight against societal prejudices applying various strategies. Albee's Grandma in *The Sandbox* and Williams's Flora Goforth in *Milktrain* are characters who best represent such modes of agewise journeys empowered by their final creative potential.

Aging, ageility, and death in Edward Albee's *The Sandbox*

The Sandbox: A Brief Play, in Memory of My Grandmother, which had its debut on April 15, 1960, in the Jazz Gallery, New York City, was inspired, along with *The American Dream* (1961), by the playwright's childhood experiences with his parents and his grandmother (Gussow 152). *The Sandbox* was one of Albee's favorites; it is a piece he called "an absolutely beautiful, lovely, perfect play," which was written

> for (and about) his grandmother, Grandma Cotter, his closest relative, the one member of the family with whom he had formed a lasting attachment. A crotchety and very amusing woman, she considerably brightened Albee's childhood and was a natural ally against his mother (her daughter)—and everyone else. When he left home, his one regret was having

to leave Grandma Cotter behind. She died in 1959 at the age of eighty-three before her grandson's first play was produced in New York. Still estranged from him, his parents did not tell him of his grandmother's death, and he missed her funeral. He found out later, from "spies in the house of love, so to speak," that is, from a secretary in his father's office. (135)

The Sandbox grew out of a reconceived play, *The Dispossessed* (1959-60), which was initially titled *The American Dream.* The text of this drama was partially ready when Gian Carlo Menotti requested a "short piece for the Festival of Two Worlds" in Spoleto, Italy; so Albee "took the characters of Mommy, Daddy, and Grandma from *The American Dream*, turned the Young Man into a kind of Angel of Death, put them on a beach, and presto, *The Sandbox*" (Gussow 135). A year later, *The Sandbox*'s twin play, *The American Dream* (1961), premiered in New York. This "outlandish cartoon" portrayed, similarly to *The Dispossessed* and *The Sandbox*, a dysfunctional American family, with Grandma, the oldest member of the cast as a "devilish, daft" figure and as a "constant source of amusement" and wit (Albee qtd. in Gussow 139). In the "Preface" to *The American Dream*, Albee sets the parameters of this drama by claiming that "the play is an examination of the American Scene, an attack on the substitution of artificial for real values in our society, a condemnation of complacency, cruelty, emasculation and vacuity; it is a stand against the fiction that everything in this slipping land of ours is peachy-keen." Moreover, he added that the play "is a picture of our time—as I see it, of course. Every honest work is a personal, private yowl, a statement of one individual's pleasure or pain; but I hope that *The American Dream* is something more than that. I hope that it transcends the personal and the private, and has something to do with the anguish of us all" (21-22).

The Sandbox adheres to all the above criteria but unlike *The American Dream*'s consumerist opulence, it was conceived to be played on a minimal, "bare" stage with two simple chairs set side by side and a "large child's sandbox with a toy pail and shovel;" its background "is the sky, which alters from brightest day to deepest night" (Albee, *The Sandbox* 8), prefiguring someone's long day's journey into eternal night. The characters of the play include a glacial Daddy and a callous Mommy—portraying the playwright's mother, Frances Albee, who was a model for characters featuring in *The American Dream*, *A Delicate Balance* (1966), and *Three Tall Women* (1991). The couple escort Grandma to her last act into a grave-like sandpit, with the Musician and the Young Man assisting in the process. Daddy (aged 60) is described as a small, gray, thin man; his wife, Mommy (aged 55), is a well-dressed, imposing woman (8). Their names, according to the descriptions in the script, are "empty of affection," pointing to the "pre-senility and vacuity of their characters" (8), whose implicit ageism is imminent in their own fear of the end. According to Kolin, the play encapsulates "familiar Albee targets as anti-Momism, hollow rituals, failure to communicate, sterile couplehood, complacency, and hypocrisy" (26). Among these quasi-hollow characters, Grandma (aged 86) stands out: she is the play's protagonist and Mommy's mother, a "tiny, wizened woman with bright eyes" (8), actually the most dynamic of all characters. The play also features the Young Man (aged 25), nicknamed the Angel of Death, who is a "good-looking, well-built boy in a bathing suit" (8) doing calisthenics that suggest the "beating and fluttering of wings" (9) along with the

Musician, whose nondescript age suggests also a young man. It is these two who show real affection and true care for Grandma in a sterile, consumerist world devoid of sentiments and burdened with meaningless regulations.

At the beginning of *The Sandbox*, Mommy and Daddy arrive at an unremarkable beach that seems for them to be the perfect location to place Grandma to rest. "There's sand there—and the water beyond" (9), Mommy says. The play's sandy beach setting has a double denotation: it stands for a playground and a burial ground and connotes the infantilization of Grandma, who is taken there to die. Similarly to a disobedient child, the elderly woman is, as the stage directions run, *"borne in by their hands under her armpits; she is quite rigid; her legs are drawn up; her feet do not touch the ground; the expression on her ancient face is that of puzzlement and fear"* (10-11). Their condescending, ageist attitude suggests that the couple act against Grandma's wishes as she is unable to touch ground anymore. In a dehumanizing act, Mommy and Daddy discard their disabled parent by putting her into a sandbox to shovel sand on herself; by this they push the responsibility of dying to her alone. Realizing what is happening to her, Grandma decides not to communicate with them more than a baby does: she screams and groans "Ahhhhhh! Ah-haaaaaa! Graaaaaa!" (12). Her onomatopoeias sound like a *"cross between a baby's laugh and cry"* (12), indicating the tragicomic nature of her dead-end situation. This lack of communication provides the generative moment of the plot: terminally disabled, Grandma realizes that the end of her day(s) has arrived, but her productive subjectivity manages to make the experience less uncanny by playing a trick on the others present.

Motionless and distant, Mommy and Daddy watch Grandma's agony and wait patiently for her to stop moving; as foreseen by Albee, their communication is empty of meaning and lacks any ceremonial traits. The couple's attitude suggests that this is yet another mundane act devoid of any ritual content. Resisting sentimentality and knowing that she will not get any reaction from her family members, the protagonist suddenly undercuts theatrical illusion, breaks the fourth wall, and starts to talk directly to the audience (Kolin 27), complaining about how Mommy and Daddy treat(ed) her. By this metadramatic turn, she adopts her audience making them instant relatives and participants in her play(ground). Moreover, with a keen awareness of her situation, Grandma makes herself not only visible (by shoveling sand) but also heard (by screaming and groaning) and understood by all, when she finally speaks out, summarizing her life in terms of familial relationships that reflect the lack of respect towards the old:

> GRANDMA. Ah-haaaaaa! (*Looks for reaction; gets none. Now . . . directly to the audience*) Honestly! What a way to treat an old woman! Drag her out of the house . . . stick her in a car . . . bring her out here from the city . . . dump her in a pile of sand . . . and leave her here to set. I'm eighty-six years old! I was married when I was seventeen. To a farmer. He died when I was thirty . . . I'm a feeble old woman . . . how do you expect anybody to hear me over that peep! Peep! Peep! (*To herself*) There is no respect around here. (*To the* YOUNG MAN) There's no respect around here! (13-14)

Grandma's succinct age autobiography involves a kind of conscious ageility. The term was coined by Leni Marshall (33) in the process of writing on the convergence of disability and age studies. Conscious ageility derives from the term of "conscious aging," defined by Margaret Cruikshank in *Learning to Be Old: Gender, Culture and Aging* (2003), and from the idea of "disability" connected to it, meaning the aging-awareness of disabled people together "with an understanding of one's self-identity and social identity as variable, and with an appreciation for the possibility that the self can remain whole even as it changes" (Marshall 33). Indeed, as Marshall emphasizes, "people with disabilities mark their bodies as aging more quickly: their bodies are temporally beyond a cultural norm. In this formulation, Otherness is coded as aged-ness. Conversely, elders may try to maintain their connection to the cultural norm of able-bodied-ness in an effort to stave off the Otherness that they code as disability" (23).

The idea of old age as "Other" was brought into critical discourse by Simone de Beauvoir, who described advanced age as a "forbidden subject," a "shameful secret that it is unseemly to mention" (7, 10). In this context, ageility thus connotes a double Otherness that materializes in the ageility of Grandma caught in her near-death moment. Quickly realizing her hopeless situation, she overcomes the emotional dimensions and the limitations of her own body and age in an absurdist turn: by embodying the defensive mechanism of feigning death, she freezes. Her tonic immobility makes her folks believe she is finally dead:

(GRANDMA *plays dead.* (!) MOMMY *and* DADDY *go over to look at her; she is a little more than half buried in the sand; the toy shovel is in her hands, which are crossed on her breast.*)

MOMMY. (*Before the sandbox; shaking her head*) Lovely! It's . . . it's hard to be sad . . . she looks . . . so happy. (*With pride and conviction*) It pays to do things well. (*To the* MUSICIAN) All right, you can stop now, if you want to. I mean stay around for a swim, or something; it's all right with us. (*She sighs heavily*) Well, Daddy . . . off we go.

DADDY. Brave Mommy!

MOMMY. Brave Daddy! (*They exit, stage-left*) (20)

In this dysfunctional family there is no sense of loss, sorrow or grievance at all—as if Grandma was just another unneeded object to be safely deposited in a proper place; their congratulatory support is absurdly coined as "brave" before they leave the internment ground. After her family leaves, Grandma, however, finds herself totally paralyzed.

Robert A. Neimeyer and James L. Werth, two specialists in end-of-life psychology, claim that death triggers "despair, paralysis or defensive avoidance, on the one hand, or some form of acceptance, affirmation or even meaning on the other" (388). However, death is not there yet for Grandma, and she has enough time to think about her big move that finally makes her welcome what Tennessee Williams termed in *A Streetcar Named Desire* (1947) "the kindness of strangers." Realizing this dead-end, she agewisely accepts the Young Man's quasi-memorial service and the Musician's music (who continues to play as the curtain slowly comes down). These two thanatic interlopers reconceptualize end-of-life intimacy: they act as if they were Grandma's children and she, in return, calls them "kids," "dear," and "sweetie." They also provide Grandma with skilled nursing and with an atmosphere of trust and love; with their hospice service and palliative care they facilitate her rite of passage. This moment is similar to what psychologist Elizabeth MacKinley describes in her study on death and spirituality as a "unique, spiritual journey" (399), a "successful negotiation of a final identity that gives retrospective meaning to life and prospective meaning to death" (396). During the act of sand shoveling, Grandma recollects her life as part of her larger age autobiography and realizes her new agewise stance when she says:

> GRANDMA. I am *smart that way*. Anyhow, I had to raise . . . that over there all by my lonesome; and what's next to her there . . . that's what she married. Rich? I tell you . . . money, money, money. They took me out of the farm . . . which was real decent of them . . . and they moved me into a big town house with them . . . fixed a nice place for me under the stove . . . gave me an army blanket . . . and my own dish . . . my very own dish! (Albee, *Sandbox* 15-16, emphasis added)

The attitude of the two young men, whose accompanying "this final journey in life with the one dying is a special position," is reserved for "those privileged to be part of this journey" (MacKinley 399). Grandma's conscious ageility and her final, agewise attitude make the departure ceremony a serene voyage into afterlife, uplifting the mournful event to the elevated level of sublime love. The Young Man, an alter ego of the playwright in this short memory play, bids a final goodbye to Grandma (modeled on the playwright's beloved grandma), whose last words soothe the one left behind in an intimate, "dear" moment of shared death experience:

GRANDMA. (*After they leave; lying quite still*) It pays to do things well . . . Boy, oh boy! (*She tries to sit up*) . . . well, kids . . . (*but she finds she can't*) . . . I . . . I can't get up. I . . . I can't move . . . (*The* YOUNG MAN *stops his calisthenics, nods to the* MUSICIAN, *walks over to* GRAND-MA, *kneels down by the sandbox*)

GRANDMA. I . . . can't move . . .

YOUNG MAN. Shhhh . . . be very still . . .

GRANDMA. I . . . I can't move . . .

YOUNG MAN. Uh . . . ma'am; I . . . I have a line here.

GRANDMA. Oh, I'm sorry, sweetie; you go right ahead.

YOUNG MAN. I am . . . uh . . .

GRANDMA. Take your time, dear.

YOUNG MAN. (*Prepares; delivers the line like a real amateur*) I am the Angel of Death. I am . . . uh . . . I am come for you.

GRANDMA. What . . . wha . . . (*Then with resignation*) . . . ohhhh . . . ohhhh, I see. (The YOUNG MAN *bends over, kisses* GRANDMA *gently on the forehead*)

GRANDMA. (*Her eyes closed, her hands folded on her breast again, the shovel between her hands, a sweet smile on her face*) Well . . . that was very nice, dear . . . (19-20)

AMERICAN DRAMA

Aging, memory, and death in Tennessee Williams's *The Milktrain Doesn't Stop Here Anymore*

Similarly to a number of other plays by Williams which focus on the theme of death and dying produced in the 1960s including, for example, *The Mutilated* (1966), *Kingdom of Earth* aka *The Seven Descends of Myrtle* (1968), *In the Bar of a Tokyo Hotel* (1969), and *The Frosted Glass Coffin* (1970); *The Milktrain Doesn't Stop Here Anymore* is, in Christopher Bigsby's words, a "brutal, apocalyptic and death-centered" play with a high-camp figure as the protagonist (63). This protagonist is Flora "Sissy" Goforth, the famous aging actress, one of Williams's characters "whose lives have reached their apogee and who can look forward only to a decline whose reality they choose not to confront" yet try to "live with compromise, to soften the edges of a reality which they see as threatening" (Bigsby 66). Moreover, Mrs. Goforth is, according to Howard Taubman, a "dying woman with a flamboyant past and a bruising tongue," a "coarse and coy, wise and foolish, vulnerable and tyrannical" old woman "full of pretense, yet has reached the point of no more pretense." *Milktrain*'s stage directions do not provide any specific description of this character; however, she is briefly portrayed in *Man Bring This Up Road*, a short story Williams wrote between 1959 and 1960, which was then adapted into drama. Here, the character of Goforth (her name was left unchanged in the play) is described as a wealthy widow "edging timorously into her seventies" (347) and resembles in many respects Alexandra del Lago, also named Princess Kosmonopolis, from *Sweet Bird of Youth* (1959), which Williams wrote in the same period of time. And while Kosmonopolis continuously chases (her) youth and is still into more lively adventures, Sissy Goforth's activity is postponing death—up to a point.

NEGOTIATING AGE

Mrs. Goforth retired to her Italian estate of Divina Costiera [the Divine Coast], a metaphorical antechamber of Elysian Fields (the final resting place of the souls in Greek mythology) to write her memoirs. She is secluded but has a number of people who visit her from time to time. Her last visitor, Chris Flanders, becomes her Angel of Death, and assumes a peculiar role in the reconceptualization of her agewise transition into her end. He appears as a Young Man (he is thirty-four) bearing "a white sack over his shoulder" and "looks back as if to make sure he's no longer pursued" by Mrs. Goforth's lupos, the Cerberus-type of dogs (Williams, *Milktrain* 144). His equivalent character in the short story is Jimmy Dobyn, an "odd combination of ski instructor and poet" (Williams, *Man Bring This Up Road* 349). Chris, however, is a more complex character than Jimmy: he is a wandering artist who makes mobile decorative structures and who wrote poems published as *Meanings Known and Unknown.* Chris has the same qualities as Brick Pollitt in *Cat on a Hot Tin Roof* (1955), Val Xavier in *Orpheus Descending* (1957), and Lawrence T. Shannon in *The Night of the Iguana* (1961); they all deal "in ambivalence, the poetic, the allusive, the metaphorical" (Bigsby 41). Accordingly, he "has the opposite appearance to that which is ordinarily encountered in poets as they are popularly imagined," with his rough and weathered appearance and with his eyes "wild, haggard," Chris "has the look of a powerful, battered but still undefeated fighter" (Williams, *Milktrain* 147). Moreover, he is the embodiment of the ultimate usher, a 1960s beatnik-faced Thanatos, whose job is to escort old, dying people to their final journey, easing their passage to afterlife. Chris has indeed a distressing demeanor but his presence is at the same time soothing for Mrs. Goforth; as a result, she is unable to send him away, despite the fact that even Marquesa Constance

Ridgeway-Condotti, nicknamed the Witch of Capri, bluntly warns her about the hazards of her visitor's company:

> THE WITCH. Chris, poor Chris Flanders, he has the habit of coming to call on a lady just a step or two ahead of the undertaker. [*She sits.*] Last summer at Portofino he stayed with some Texas oil people and at supper one night that wicked old Duke of Parma, you know the one that we call the Parma Violet, he emptied a champagne bottle on Christopher's head and he said, I christen thee, Christopher Flanders, the 'Angel of Death.' The name has stuck to him, Sissy. Why, some people in our age bracket, we're senior citizens, Sissy, would set their dogs on him if he entered their grounds, but since you are not superstitious. (170).

Mrs. Goforth believes the story, yet lets the Trojan Horse Guest remain in her palace. Hostile to him at the beginning, Mrs. Goforth realizes she needs to learn how to "go forth" in this last period of her life and by challenging her own fate, she lets Chris stay to help her facing agewise the inexorable exit. Nonetheless, she accommodates him in the "Oubliette," a little Polynesian grass hut reminding one of a vault or dungeon, where people were put to be forgotten [from the French word *oublier* meaning "to forget"] and where "undesirables are transferred to when the villas are overcrowded" (195). Chris, however, cannot be made invisible or suspended as a mobile being in the wind. Therefore, the hostess, after rightly perceiving her ageility in what J. Brooks Bouson called the "embodied shame" of a terminal illness alongside "the dreadful secret of gendered ageism" (v), starts talking to him and brings up the tabooed issue of passing away in one of their in-depth discussions. She is almost ready to openly acknowledge her situation and prepare for her final departure as her "last career" move but needs a final touch, of which Chris is fully aware.

CHRIS. *[who has come down to her]* Mrs. Goforth, are you still afraid of— *[He hesitates.]*

MRS. GOFORTH. Death—never even think of it. *[She takes his arm and they move down to a bench and sit.]*

CHRIS. Death is one moment and life is so many of them.

MRS. GOFORTH. A million billion of them if you think in terms of a lifetime as rich as mine's been, Chris.

CHRIS. Yes, life is something, death's nothing . . .

MRS. GOFORTH. Nothing, nothing, but nothing— I've had to refer to many deaths in my memoirs,—Oh, I don't think I'm immortal. I still go to sleep every night wondering if I'll— wake up the next day . . . (198-99)

For Mrs. Goforth the next day is another chance to finish not only her memoirs but also her age autobiography, a story that goes beyond the usual life-account, which she dictates to her secretary, Blackie.

Although Flora Goforth claims that her life has to be recorded because of a book contract, it is obvious she needs this oral history therapy in her quickly deteriorating physical state to keep the illusion of life going on. As MacKinley contends, storytelling is a "vital part of the process of dying," "important for the person coming to the end of their life" because "as the person's life is completed for the first time their whole life can be told and perhaps meanings can be seen in context for the first time" (398). Moreover, the act of remembering stories resonates—as Elena Bendien observed following Michel Foucault's ideas on memory—with the contemplation of self-care and the preparation for old age as "specific tactics to maintain identities in later life" (93). Mrs. Goforth's memoir is an earnest attempt to reaffirm her existence and maintain her agewise identity during times of death anxiety and distress; moreover, in the retelling of her life she tries to find meaning in the process of dying. The more amazing the narrative is, the less fear of ending she has:

> MRS. GOFORTH. A legend in my own lifetime, yes, I reckon I am. Well, I had certain advantages, endowments to start with, a face people naturally noticed and a figure that was not just sensational, but very durable, too . . . . Hell, I was born between a swamp and the wrong side of the tracks in One Street, Georgia, but not even that could stop me in my tracks, wrong side or right side or no side. Hit show-biz at fifteen when a carnival show, I mean the manager of it, saw me and dug me

on that one Street in One Street, Georgia. I was billed as the Dixie Doxey, was just supposed to move my anatomy but was smart enough to keep my tongue moving, too, and the verbal comments I made on my anatomical motions while in motion were a public delight. So I breezed through show-biz like a tornado, rising from one-week "gigs" in the sticks to star-billings in "The Follies" while still in m'teens, ho, ho ... and I was still in my teens when I married Harlon Goforth, a marriage into the Social Register and Dun-and-Bradstreet's, both. Was barely out of my teens when I became his widow. Scared to make out a will, he died intestate so everything went to me.

CHRIS. Marvelous. Amazing.

MRS. GOFORTH. That's right, all my life was and still is except here lately I'm a little run-down, like a race-horse that's been entered in just one race too many, even for me ... (184)

The protagonist of *Milktrain* was once herself the one who accompanied other people, namely her husbands, on their end-journey. And now, towards the end of her life, deploying an agewise attitude she recognizes that Chris has the same potential she used to have, but she denies this companionship by trying to postpone, once again, something that could not be withheld for long:

> MRS. GOFORTH. —Well, I've escorted four husbands to the eternal threshold and come back alone without them, just with the loot of three of them . . . It's my turn, now to go forth, and I've no choice but to do it. But I'll do it alone. I don't want to be escorted, I want to go forth alone. But you, you counted on touching my heart because you'd heard I was dying and old dying people are your speciality, your vocation. But you miscalculated with this one. This milk train does not stop here anymore. (222)

The metaphor of the milktrain, the central trope of the play, is revealing at this point: with multi-stop milk runs milktrains used to run between the 1930s and the 1960s in the USA and the UK before the pasteurization process was introduced in the food-processing industry. If these vehicles did not stop in a place it meant the territory was empty, deserted, or dead. In this drama, similar to a milktrain, Chris stops for Flora Goforth so that she can stop living; she has to die in order to finally "complete her memoirs." This is her own deadline.

Mrs. Goforth's age autobiography, a memoir of dying, is written through the daily routine of resisting death through remembering, chronicling, and storytelling. Blackie, the *secretary*, writes down the oral history Sissy dictates as well as records on tapes, so she knows all secrets present in the nascent volume of *Facts and a Figure* reminding the reader of the voluntary and involuntary memories of Marcel Proust's unfinished *In Search of a Lost Time* aka *Remembrance of Things Past* (1913-22). These secrets come to book-life when Mrs. Goforth passes away because, as Paul Kalanithi wrote in *When Breath Becomes Air* (2016), words have a longevity that people do not have. Age autobiography comprising the stories she lived and relived by remembering them in a book serve a subversive basis for Sissy's developing sense of ageility: she is incapable of finishing the book—unless she dies in the midst of writing it. By the time Chris, the crossover escort between a "saint" (Williams, *Milktrain* 172) and a "graveyard sexton" (160) with "his best bet in strangers" (222) arrives, these recollections help her recognize the mysteries of aging by finding meaning in the process of dying. And with Chris's help, Mrs. Goforth has the final say—in the form of an ultimate, unfinished sentence from her age autobiography, which is completed by her peaceful departure into the realm of the dead.

> MRS. GOFORTH. . . . Before you go, help me into my bedroom, I can't make it alone . . . and the bed . . . was the bed of Countess Walewska, Napoleon's Polish mistress, it's a famous old bed, for a famous old body . . .
>
> CHRIS. Yes, it looks like the catafalque of an empress. [*He lifts her on the bed, and draws a cover over her.*]
>
> MRS. GOFORTH. Don' leave me alone till—
>
> CHRIS. I never leave till the end. [*She stretches out her blind, jeweled hand. He takes it.*] (223)

Agewise end

Albee's *The Sandbox* and Williams's *Milktrain* convey images of advanced age that challenge ageist perspectives in a decade when few art forms dared to venture into discussing the tabooed and controversial subject of aging and death. The two plays illustrate the ways in which two dramatic characters who reached end-life experience and their own, personal understanding of ageility exit according to their newly acquired knowledge. In discussing William Faulkner's *Intruder in the Dust* (1948), Ellen Matlok-Ziemann claims that "old age and frailty can be conceived of as a harmonious part of being in the world" (260). These two American dramas on the apprehension of mortality written in the sixties fully subscribe to this idea because they portray a surprising harmony achieved by the protagonists' serene, agewise attitude before they leave the stage of their lives.

In Albee's play, Grandma realizes her inability to move—or simply just to do anything more in life—and confines herself to the absurdist *play*ground she was placed in by her family members. She participates in a quasi-ceremonial farewell staged by two strangers, a Young Man and the Musician, who faithfully accompany Grandma on her last day till the end of her last syllables. In Williams's drama, Mrs. Goforth, who rehearses her own death each day by remembering her past, comes to a halt in her storytelling and closes off her memoir. In addition, with a newly contextualized sense of ageility she becomes more empowered by the presence of Chris Flanders, her Angel of Death, who brings the "flag-lowering ceremony on the late Mrs. Goforth's mountain" (232). The characters who escort these two elderly women on their last journey on Earth reconceptualize the sense of intimacy between people: they are strangers but stand closer to the dying ones than their kin. The dialogic potential of their empathy, care, and unconditional support during the end-game of the protagonists accommodates difference in various contexts by blurring the boundary between the old and the young, between men and women, because death has neither age nor gender. These intergenerational exchanges help elder characters' agewise enterprises into the unknown gain a cathartic sense of freedom.

On their deathbed, both Albee's and Williams's protagonists are reconnecting with their past in idiosyncratic ways. They build up a conscious age autobiography (Grandma's recollection of her upbringing, youth, marriage, early widowhood, parenthood, and old days; Mrs. Goforth's memory of her teenage adventures into showbiz, her marriages and life of glamour and fame) in an inventory of events and feelings assessing a complete(d) life and achieve an agewise identity that comes full circle in the very moment of grace. Grandma's lost autonomy puts her in a farcical situation that questions the idea of self-reliance and individual independence by subscribing to the decline narratives of old age; while Mrs. Goforth, who subverts usual stereotypical constructions of old age, remains autonomous and in a status that Linn Sandberg calls an "affirmative old age" (11) by emphasizing her sexual nature in telling the stories of her loves. Although quite different in their death plots, both protagonists seek, in Sandberg's words, a "conceptualization and acceptance of old age in all its diversity" (35). Although Grandma and Mrs. Goforth seem to be at the opposing ends of the diversity spectrum, their handling of aging and death from different perspectives contribute to the complex representation of transgressive images of aging and to the critical thinking about end-of-life stages in the literary field and beyond.

Works Cited

Albee, Edward. *The American Dream. New American Drama.* Intro. Charles Marowitz. Bristol: Penguin, 1966. 19-60.

---. *The Sandbox. Two Plays by Edward Albee: The Sandbox and The Death of Bessie Smith (with Fam and Yam).* New York: Signet, 1963. 8-21.

Bendien, Elena. "KwikFit versus Varying Speeds of Aging." Kriebernegg et al. 80-100.

Bigsby, C. W. E. *Modern American Drama 1945-2000.* Cambridge: Cambridge University Press, 2000.

Bouson, J. Brooks. *Shame and the Aging Woman: Confronting and Resisting Ageism in Contemporary Women's Writings.* New York: Palgrave Macmillan, 2016.

Cruikshank, Margaret. *Learning to Be Old: Gender, Culture and Aging.* Lanham, MD: Rowan and Littlefield, 2003.

de Beauvoir, Simone. *The Coming of Age.* Trans. Patrick O'Brian. New York: Putnam, 1972.

Gullette, Margaret Morganroth. *Agewise: Fighting the New Ageism in America.* Chicago: University of Chicago Press, 2011.

---. *Ending Ageism, or How Not to Shoot Old People.* New Brunswick: Rutgers University Press, 2017.

Gussow, Mel. *Edward Albee: A Singular Journey.* London: Oberon, 1999.

Johnson, Malcolm L., Vern L. Bengtson, Peter G. Coleman, and Thomas B. L. Kirkwood, eds. *The Cambridge Handbook of Age and Ageing.* Cambridge: Cambridge University Press, 2005.

Kolin, Philip C. "Albee's Early One-Act Plays: A New American Playwright from Whom Much Is to Be Expected." *The Cambridge Companion to Edward Albee.* Ed. Stephen Bottoms. Cambridge: Cambridge University Press, 2005. 16-36.

Kriebernegg, Ulla, Roberta Maierhofer, and Barbara Ratzenböck, eds. *Alive and Kicking at All Ages: Cultural Constructions of Health and Life Course Identity.* Bielefeld: Transcript Verlag, 2014.

MacKinley, Elizabeth. "Death and Spirituality." Johnson et al. 394-400.

Matlok-Ziemann, Ellen. "'Old Woman that Will Not Be Kept Away': Undermining Ageist Discourse with Invisibility and Performance." Kriebernegg et al. 259-73.

Marshall, Leni. "Ageility Studies: The Interplay of Critical Approaches in Age Studies and Disability Studies." Kriebernegg et al. 21-40.

Neimeyer, Robert A., and James L. Werth. "The Psychology of Death." Johnson et al. 386-94.

Palmore, Erdman B. *Ageism: Negative and Positive.* New York: Springer, 1999.

Sandberg, Linn. "Affirmative Old Age: The Ageing Body and Feminist Theories on Difference." *International Journal of Ageing and Later Life* 8.1 (2013): 11-40.

Taubman, Howard. "Theater: Tennessee Williams's 'Milk Train.'" *The New York Times* 15 Jan. 1963. Web. 28 Dec. 2018.

Williams, Tennessee. "Man Bring This Up Road." *Collected Stories.* Intro. Gore Vidal. London: Vintage, 1999. 347-58.

---. *The Milktrain Doesn't Stop Here Anymore, Cat on a Hot Tin Roof and Other Plays.* Harmondsworth: Penguin. 1976. 133-225.

10.2478/9788367405423-012

"No Country for Old Men": A Poignant Portrayal of Aging and Ageism in Arthur Miller's *Mr. Peters' Connections*

Ambika Singh

Arthur Miller's late play *Mr. Peters' Connections* (1998) is a moving portrayal of what it is like to grow old in modern times and experience a loss of vital connections. It also offers a significant commentary on how the disconnectedness experienced by older adults is a direct consequence of a predominantly ageist atmosphere. On the face of it, however, the play is a massive muddle of mundane conversation with many voices focused on individual agendas, stuck amongst whom is Mr. Harry Peters, the play's central character, making desperate attempts to catch hold of the "subject." Peters embodies the constant "otherness" older adults must face in a world where aging is viewed more as a kind of "virus," a terminal disease rather than a natural course of human existence.

From the moment Peters appears onstage, there is a feeling of the show already being over. Caught somewhere between "life and death" (Abbotson 249), between "waking and sleeping" (Miller and Gussow 185), he happens to wander into an *"old abandoned nightclub in New York City,"* where around a *"dusty upright piano"* some furniture lies *"upended"* (Miller, *Collected Plays* 401). He came to this neighborhood to buy himself a pair of extra narrow shoes that he finds only at a local store owned by Larry and then happened to venture into the surreal space of the nightclub to wait for his wife, Charlotte, whose name he keeps blocking out until towards the end when she finally joins him. A former Pan Am pilot, having once "flown into hundreds of gorgeous sunsets" (420), Peters is now at that stage of life where the future appears vague and the past rather distant. *"Undirected to anyone,"* he says, "deep down I always seem on the verge of weeping. God knows why, when I have everything" (401).

In Peters one encounters both a desperate need for death and its fear. Indeed, it is both his quest for meaning and his feeling of meaninglessness that have brought him to this bizarre nightclub, where he may have his chance to reflect upon his long life—and perhaps decipher its meaning, its "subject." It is here that he would meet his "connections," the people who once meant something to him, but now, looking back, all of them appear as perfect strangers he has to make an effort to know again; only he is too tired now. In his preface for the play's 1998 edition, Miller defines it as a play "taking place inside Mr. Peters' mind, or at least on its threshold, from where it is still possible to glance back toward daylight life or forward into the misty depths" (Preface viii). The playwright mentions that Mr. Peters's "connections," some alive and some dead, are the main characters of the drama of his life and that the entire action of the play "is the procession of Mr. Peters' moods," each of them beckoning up the next (viii). All of Peters's dispositions embody his anxieties and fears. His dialogue throughout the play points again and again to a state of weariness, fatigue, numbness, and a feeling of complete resignation. He feels so utterly exhausted that at three different points in his conversations with other characters, he clarifies that "conflict" and "suspense" are not his game anymore (Miller, *Collected* 402); he is too old for "sad stories" (409) and too old to face "reality" (407)—just too old for the world. He feels he has lived enough and that now he must look "forward to a warm oblivion" (431). Just a few pages into the play Harry Peters appears as a terribly hopeless, aging man.

An inability to grasp the "subject," feeling meaningless and reduced—all seemingly "normal" aspects of aging—are thus depicted as intrinsically connected with the problem of ageism in Miller's portrayal. Robert Scanlan calls *Mr. Peters' Connections* "a theatrical summation" of all of Miller's plays that precede it (187), and Susan Abbotson suggests it can be broadly understood as a study of the lives of older adults (246). Yet, despite the play's apparent merit and the concerns it accentuates, like most other late pieces in the Miller canon, *Mr. Peters' Connections* lies largely unexplored by both scholars and audiences. The essay looks at the play through the lens of critical gerontology and analyzes how in the course of Miller's narration Peters emerges as a moving representation of scores of American seniors for whom the present is appalling and the future offers little hope. Without making it a loud agenda, the playwright shows us how an ageist environment contributes to older adults' dilemmas. Miller portrays this predicament and argues the case for older adults in a society that could not care less for them. The perplexed, wake-sleep state of the play's titular character is a symbolic representation of how older adults feel unanchored amidst the mammoth changes taking place around them, as Miller imaginatively underlines the utter helplessness, isolation, and agony of growing old.

The perils of aging in an ageist society: Persecution through prejudices and stereotypes

Miller himself referred to *Mr. Peters' Connections* as an "outrageous piece of work," a "funny play" (Miller and Gussow 185), which moves forward in such a way that, unguided by Miller's preface, it becomes impossible to even decode who among its characters is dead and who is still alive. Yet, despite the complete disarray that this play appears to be, the dilapidated nightclub emerges as a symbol for society at large—a world full of "living dead" and "known strangers." The whole process of understanding Peters's feelings of isolation and purposelessness can be "a numbing experience" for the audience as the playwright creatively draws "parallels" between the life of a worn-out, aging man nearing the end of his life and the "spiritual weariness" of the fatigued nation he lives in (Brantley). It is an apt depiction of the existential dilemma commonly experienced by older adults in the contemporary environment, where no one has any spare time to pay heed to another's quest for meaning. Not pointing at one specific problem of older adults, Miller subtly draws attention to several. Notably, the playwright manages to do this without ever mentioning the term "ageism" anywhere in the play's text. Only meanderingly does Miller comment on how casual, often unintended ageist remarks and prejudices kill the contentment of growing old and how, similarly to "race" and "gender," "age" is a significant marker of discrimination in many societies.

Simone de Beauvoir, who is mostly acclaimed for her feminist manifesto rather than for her annotations on old age, brings into light the common frustrations and isolation experienced by older adults in *La Vieillesse* [The Coming of Age], pointing to the myriad factors that render older adults lonely, inadequate, and mostly useless. De Beauvoir discusses how a "long tradition" of viewing old age negatively has loaded the word "old" with "pejorative connotations" (288). In her view, ageist prejudices engulf many modern societies to such an extent that numerous older adults attempt to be perceived as very "old," even before they have reached that state— because, oftentimes, it is "less tiring to let oneself go than to fight" (286). In their essay "Acting Your Age," Sarit A. Golub et al. discuss how the tag "old" or "elderly," in agreement with the generally established stereotype, implies "incompetent" (289). Ashton Applewhite, a leading anti-ageism activist and the author of *This Chair Rocks: A Manifesto Against Ageism*, discusses how negative social conditioning teaches us to loathe the whole process of aging, seeing it only as a "trauma" (44-45). Ageist stereotypes internalized since childhood may "interfere with the value that the elderly place on their own lives" (Golub et al. 291), which is why many older adults themselves turn into the "worst ageists" and avoid activities they do not find "age appropriate" (Applewhite 43). Ursula A. Falk and Gerard Falk state that assumed stereotypes also force older adults to act befuddled and "mindless" (27), which is again a direct outcome of internalizing "stereotypes of olders as useless and debilitated" (Applewhite 44). Harry Peters, too, is a product of an ageist culture that inhibits his enthusiasm for life. In a youth-worshipping world "we're supposed to deny being old" (Showalter xi), yet we see Peters making a concerted effort to be identified as an "old man." Peters constantly exaggerates how old and tired he feels while there are other characters telling him that he does not look "all that old" (*Collected Plays* 403).

> CALVIN. You've been around.
> PETERS. And around again, yes—Pan Am captain twenty-six years. I'm really much older than I look. If you planted an apple tree when I was born you'd be cutting it down for firewood by now.
> CALVIN. I was going to say, you don't look all that old.
> PETERS, *a chuckle*. I am older than everyone I ever knew. All my dogs are dead. Half a dozen cats, parakeets . . . all gone. Every pilot I ever flew with. Probably every woman I ever slept with,

> too, except my wife. . . . Or maybe death is
> polite, and we must open the door to let him
> in or he'll just hang around out there on the
> porch. (403)

Notably, even the remark "you don't look all that old," often
perceived as a compliment, bears ageist connotations. De
Beauvoir believes the trauma and prejudice related to old age
can fill one with so much resentment that sometimes older
adults "take their revenge upon the outside world by
exaggerating their infirmity" (303), which is strongly evident
in Peters's case. He feels that even his "low cholesterol" is
reason enough to die (*Collected Plays* 405).

By placing at the play's center a befuddled aging man,
Miller highlights the ways in which Peters's reaction to his
"age" and his impatience with the idea of staying longer are not
exclusively his own. Falk and Falk state that "American seniors
as well as people of all ages conduct themselves in a manner
expected of them by the culture which includes ageism and its
attendant impositions of disability, dysfunction, and
disengagement" (38). *Mr. Peters' Connections* depicts how
unconcernedly ageism is practiced every day in modern
societies, because of which older adults' victimization is often
not even recognized as oppressive or harmful. To exemplify the
same, we can consider the playwright's own case. A cursory
look at some of the performance reviews of *Mr. Peters'
Connections* will possibly be enough to substantiate how people
are ageist in the most casual sense, without ever realizing what
their words may end up doing to the self-esteem of an older
adult. Stephen Fay refers to it as "the sort of play authors write
when they're in their 80s" (n. pag.), and Matt Wolf calls Miller
a playwright "loath to come to rest" (n. pag.). The language

used in these reviews may not at all sound offensive to most people, but it is ageist and derogatory, nonetheless. If these reviews were not products of an ageist culture, they would have employed a relatively more positive vocabulary to express the same opinions, which would read something like: "it is always necessary to ask how old a writer is who is reporting his impressions of a social phenomenon as like the varying depth of a lens, the mind bends the light passing through it differently according to age" (Miller, *Collected Essays* 348), or "as playwrights and their audiences age, their dramatic subjects reflect their shifting concerns" (Switzky 140). Unfortunately, others do not use such positive language to describe the creative attempts of aging playwrights and view their works through an ageist lens. In fact, most theater reviews on *Mr. Peters' Connections* make it appear as if an octogenarian playwright has a natural duty to write about aging—because he is essentially expected to be talking about his own life.

Some of Miller's late plays do indeed address his anxieties related to aging and ageism and showcase senior men and women as their main protagonists. Among the playwright's late plays, *Elegy for a Lady*, the first part of the double bill *Two-Way Mirror* (1984), is a dialogue between Man and Proprietress, the owner of a gift shop. The subject of the conversation is that Man, a businessman, wishes to buy a farewell gift for his many years younger, dying girl-friend. Soon the talk branches out to other subjects, most importantly to Man's anxiety about his age and its effect on the relationship: "I love her. But I am forbidden to by my commitments, by my age, by my aching joints . . . I can't bear the sight of my face in the mirror—I am shaving my father every morning!" (*Two-Way Mirror* 18-19). As Mária Kurdi comments, "the Man, who can be regarded as an Everyman figure in modern times, . . . sees himself as an old man for whom it is no longer possible to indulge in self-forgetting activities" (269). Likewise, Miller's 1987 double bill *Danger: Memory* stages older adults grappling with memories, looking back on life, and feeling stranded—demonstrating how both excessive forgetting and remembering can prove fatal to human existence. The anxieties Miller obliquely touches upon in *Elegy for a Lady* and *Danger: Memory* receive a fuller expression in *Mr. Peters' Connections* since Peters comes across as a more comprehensive exploration of what Leonora expresses in *I Can't Remember Anything* about feeling "imaginary" (*Collected Plays* 7). [1] Nevertheless, a playwright need not be an "octogenarian" to write about aging, ageism, or memories in general. Miller was just seventeen when he wrote the initial story of his magnum opus, *Death of a Salesman*, and still in his early thirties when the play was first produced on Broadway (Bigsby 100). The fact that he could create Willy Loman at such a young age validates how one does not have to be nearing death to understand or portray the conflicts of much older adults. Loman's story, like Mr. Peters's, is, at its heart, that of an American senior who fails to find any meaning for himself and a purpose to go on. Legend has it that so profound was the impact of *Salesman* on American business mogul Bernard Gimbel, the owner of the chain of departmental stores bearing his name, that the day after the play's opening night, the senior entrepreneur issued a notice to all his stores against firing employees based on their being "overage" (Eyre 10).

---

1 One of the two one-act plays from *Danger: Memory* features Leo and Leonora, two older adults who have been lifelong friends to each other. The main action of this play comprises only their conversation that takes place in Leo's "*living-room kitchen in a nondescript wooden house on a country backroad*" (Miller, *CP* 3).

The lack of connectedness Peters and Loman feel can be attributed to America's ageist milieu that callously rejects the old and rugged in favor of the young and new. It is in Linda Loman's plea in *Salesman* where we find Miller's concern most clearly reflected: "he's not to be allowed to fall into his grave like an old dog. Attention, attention must be finally paid to such a person" (40); and this concern is recurrent throughout Miller's career: the angst against the forces of American capitalism that render older adults such as Willy Loman and Harry Peters completely bereft of "life-force," of enthusiasm to go on and not die "like an old dog." Willy Loman's cry of anguish in the play, "they don't know me any more" (61), and his wish to be perceived of as the most "well-liked" salesman there ever was evidently correspond with Peters's desire to be recognized as the most efficient Pan Am pilot. Both Loman and Peters feel frustrated at how quickly the world forgets and discards old people.

Disconnect, isolation, and those perpetual longings for the "good old times"

In de Beauvoir's view, the kind of sadness and sense of loss older adults experience are often not caused by any specific misfortune but by being forced to live in a society that only offers them "boredom," a "humiliating sense of uselessness," "loneliness," and "indifference" (464). In *Mr. Peters' Connections*, Arthur Miller emphasizes how after a certain age, older adults begin to look at themselves from an external, almost detached viewpoint. They experience a sense of disconnection with the world around them and also with their own lived experiences that force them to be sometimes shocked and sometimes surprised by their current situation in society. In the second part of *La Vieillesse*, subtitled "The Being-in-the-World," de

Beauvoir insists upon looking at an elderly individual as a "subject"—as someone who is inwardly aware of his state and "reacts" to it. She states that even though "old age" is what naturally happens to every living being, most people are rather "dumbfounded" when they reach this stage of life (283), and that this realization can fill them with a sense of "profound indignation" (292). Hunting frantically for a "subject," Peters himself is also the "subject" here. In its entirety, the play is all about Peters's "reaction" to his situation—his aging decay and the approaching of death. A rhythm is maintained in the dramaturgy: he recurrently loses track of his hunt for the "subject" and each time he somehow manages to get back to it. Almost fifteen times in the play, his fundamental question about the "subject" is raised but he fails to receive or find an answer. At one point, he exclaims exasperated, "there is no subject anymore" (*Collected Plays* 414). At yet another point, he says that he is just trying to find some "connection" with "continuity" with his past, which is why he must know the "subject." At the same time, he adds, "but I'm exhausted . . ." (419).

Peters's feelings of disconnect and detachment dominate his life to an extent that he is known for not speaking a single word for "eight hours at a time"; therefore, he is amazed at how fluent he feels in this ramshackle nightclub (403). This change draws attention to the fact that when encountered by memories of the past, Peters is able to talk, express, and wrestle once again with the "subject." He meets and strikes up conversations with people at the nightclub, never forgetting to pose his question about the "subject." He first converses with Calvin, whom he later recognizes as his long dead brother, and then with others such as the shoe-store man, Larry Tedesco, who comes looking for his wife. Later Leonard and Rose, a young couple, also enter. Rose is expecting and the man with her is not the father of her child. In the fashion of absurdist plays such as Samuel Beckett's *Waiting for Godot*, where characters indulge in conversation that keeps spiraling, leading to nothing, characters in Miller's play keep arguing, competing, venting, and generally digressing. Language in *Mr. Peters' Connections* reflects the irrationality and amorphousness of life itself. Peters and other characters talk, yet none of them seems to be expressing themselves, and, as a result, meaningless dialogues comprised of repetition and absolute nothings carry on throughout the play.

Language thus mirrors the separation and isolation that Peters perpetually experiences in his life. Instead of being an effective means of communication, dialogue in this play only appears to be a means of killing time. Peters keeps wondering why exactly he is here and Calvin keeps reminding him that he came to the nightclub to wait for his wife. "IF SHE DOESN'T COME, DOES IT MEAN I CAN'T LEAVE?! WHERE IS MY POOR GOD-DAMNED WIFE!" (423), he exclaims, tired and frustrated. Peters's anxiety forces the audience to wonder about where exactly he wishes to go from the nightclub and exactly what brought him here. There seems to be absolutely no association between the questions asked and the answers given amongst characters of the play. Thus, Peters's query about the "subject" remains unanswered. At one point, he and Calvin indulge in a completely absurd conversation about shoes:

> PETERS. . . . I decided to buy shoes. I have very narrow feet.
> CALVIN. Not as narrow as mine, betcha—triple—A.
> PETERS. Quadruple—A. *Extending a foot.* Narrow as herrings—I said I'd meet her here.

CALVIN. I used to take a quintuple—A but I don't have time to go running all over the city looking for them anymore. . . . I am busy!

PETERS. Well I'm busy too . . .

CALVIN. Not as busy as I am.

PETERS. I assure you, I am just as busy as you are. I got these in that shoe store right on the corner. (404)

In *Waiting for Godot*, Estragon's boots symbolize the struggles of daily life and his constant putting them on and pulling them off his attempts at killing time. Metaphorically, the "boots" suggest being grounded and attached to the base realities of life. This obsession with shoes in *Mr. Peters' Connections* draws attention to another of Miller's late plays, *The Ride Down Mt. Morgan*, in which the image of shoes is an "integral part of the play's ending" (Singh 188). It reflects "stability, a comfortable support and footing" of Nurse Logan's family that the central character of the play, Lyman Felt, a bigamist, wants for himself at the end when he is abandoned by his two wives (188). In Peters's story, too, shoes appear to signify "the need for a stable ground under one's feet" (187). In Abbotson's view as well, shoes imply Peters's recognition of reality and being "grounded" despite the man's constant desire for flight (249). When his wife, Charlotte comes to see him, Peters says to her: "when I woke up this morning, I did not plan for shoes" (*Collected Plays* 429). It seems to imply that Peters is not really looking for "stability or life on earth" but only an end to this meaninglessness (Singh 188).

The title of the play underlines the importance of connections in human life, about which Jan Baars and Chris Phillipson argue that

[c]onnections play a significant role in the constitution of meaning. Seeing connections and experiencing connectedness with other people, with specific regions, cultures, nations or even the world, is constitutive for the experience that our lives have meaning. However, during long lives connections may become unclear or problematic, and experiences of connectedness with "normal" adults may come under pressure because of ageist practices. (11)

When one's foundational people such as one's close group of family and friends are no longer around, older adults are bound to feel an acute sense of "bereavement" (de Beauvoir 443). Almost all the people Peters could once relate to are now long dead except for his wife. With the deaths of their family and friends, older adults suffer the "loss of a certain image of themselves," which they found only in and through those people (366). When they find nobody around them with whom they shared part of their childhood or youth—with whom they could simply sit and cherish those memories of the past, it pushes them to a kind of "existential dilemma." Peters's dead brother and his dead beloved are simply a reflection of his desire to connect to his past—to his identity. With no connections to bind life together, older adults are forced to look at death as a relatively more rewarding option (de Beauvoir 443). And even when the idea of death appears to be comforting, there remains a concurrent anxiety attached to its prospect, traumatizing the individual. Discussing "death anxiety" commonly experienced by older adults, Adrian Tomer and Grafton Eliason explain "future-related regret" as "an emotional response" to the recognition that the future years required for the attainment of planned goals are no longer accessible and this realization is accompanied by feelings of deep melancholy and discontent (348). In such a state of hopelessness, an ageist environment can prove to be even more unfavorable to one's sense of self—shrinking life to just waiting for the "end."

Gordon D. Jensen and Fredericka B. Oakley refer to ageism as a process consisting of "vicious cycles" (25). They assert that once a person is segregated in the "discriminated category," they are more likely to be avoided by younger people (25). Older adults are thus forced to stay constantly nostalgic for old times—given that they find nothing relatable in their experiences of today. This inability to experience con-nectedness is perhaps the worst aspect of growing old as it dilutes the very meaning of one's existence. A significant concern that Miller highlights is the enormous gap older adults feel when they converse with today's youngsters, whose "lingo" and content of talk they completely fail to understand. Peters's comment to Leonard, "I truly wonder whether the country could be saved if people could stay on the same subject for more than twenty seconds" (Miller, *Collected Plays* 428), highlights the frustration older adults experience in a world that jumps from subject to subject, without letting anyone have a relevant and substantial discussion on any one topic.

Another significant challenge faced by older adults that Miller highlights through Peters's situation is their problem with recollecting stories of the past, their moments of glory that can keep rekindling their desire to live. Even though people of all age groups need some amount of validation every now and then, in old age this need can be amplified, yet, sadly, in today's fast-moving world listeners can be hard to come by. The lack of interest of the youth in maintaining meaningful communication with older adults leads to an acute crisis in the lives of the latter as it does not let them have their chance at "life review," which facilitates "existential validation" (Falk and

Falk 96). Tomer and Eliason also agree that "life review" is integral to one's sense of self as it fulfills "different functions at different stages of the life span" (354). The process of reminiscing about and reviewing life events and episodes can "foster the integration of past conflicts" and is therefore extremely essential for those who have lived most of their life span and are aware of their "time and place in the seasons of life" (353). In de Beauvoir's view, frequently turning to memories of the past can be viewed as older adults' mechanism to survive in their current situation—past those glorious times when they felt like "first class individuals" (435).

"If you forget me—who . . . who the hell am I!" (Miller, *Collected Plays* 434), Peters says while searching for a "subject." His desperation to experience "connectedness" reflects his intense need to list and celebrate his life's achievements and the hurdles he crossed to come so far. Falk and Falk emphasize the importance of "life review" underlining older adults' need to feel they did not live "in vain," that they contributed to others and to their society—and that they indeed "made a difference" (96). To explain, they cite the example of Coleridge's Ancient Mariner, who feels an intense need to narrate the same story again and again (96). By catching hold of "willing and unwilling listeners," the Mariner reviews his life, thus alleviating his uncertainties and anxieties (96). Peters also appears to be looking for listeners who will appreciate the achievements of a sixteen-year-old who once washed airplanes yet still managed to learn to fly, marking as his greatest success to have served as a respectable Pan Am pilot for twenty-six years.

Exclusion galore: Alienating ageist practices in personal and public domains

Discussing growing old and the vulnerability of older adults in America, Elinor Langer contends that for American citizens this last phase of their lives is imaginably the "worst" (471). Various developments in medical science have controlled several life-threatening human diseases, because of which more men and women today live longer but the older adults of America are usually completely "bored and alienated" (471). The alienation experienced by older adults in America is a natural part of a culture where "old" is a "dirty word" (Falk and Falk 26). Yet, speaking strictly about parts of the world that are either western or westernizing, it is imperative to take note of the fact that ageism is not typically an American problem. In most modern nations, social antipathy towards senior generations has only increased in recent years, because instead of helping older adults defy their "biological fate," modern societies choose to chuck them aside—while they are still living, while they could still accomplish so much more in the years that remain (de Beauvoir 380).

In *Mr. Peters' Connections*, Miller touches upon the theme of alienation and feelings of worthlessness experienced by older adults as a result of prevalent ageism in various personal and public domains. He imperceptibly shows us how being above a certain age naturally means purposelessness in modern societies. The playwright sheds light on how ageism is a natural byproduct of socio-economic structures that render men and women mere numbers. Harry Peters has had a professionally productive life but now he feels acute worthlessness as he has no projects to pursue. He is expected to be "retired and resting" perennially until he is finally taken by death. The play focuses on how depression in old age can also be a consequence of this state of joblessness. De Beauvoir also argues how being completely bereft of "projects" can make older adults become so passive and aimless that they begin to look at death as "acceptable" (443); yet, the challenge lies in the fact that "death" by nature is tentative. "Death is neither near nor far: it *is* not" (442). Unfortunately, people usually fail to understand how one's "job," whether "drudgery" or a "source of interest," is an essential factor binding a person to the social environment, which is why being retired often gives one a feeling of "rejection" (263). Echoing this, Jensen and Oakley also claim that in "post-industrial societies" older adults are rendered useless and are often left to "suffer an irreparable loss of status and care" (22). They assert that the "human potential of the older person in America is not fully realized" as they do not occupy "positions of value and are unable to exercise their skill and knowledge because of exclusion from participation in their previous roles" (20, 21). Even though Peters's story offers a narrative about the situation of older Americans, yet it also reflects the state of all societies that are living in the aftermath of massive capitalism and industrialization, where people's value is determined essentially by their economic/material contribution.

Miller addresses the theme of how ageist practices at the workplace lead to resentment among older adults as they are often forced to retire according to the customary retirement age. Jensen and Oakley view "mandatory retirement" as one of the "most significant manifestations of ageism in America" (23). Peters's sense of low self-worth directly connects to his sense of purposelessness: the loss of his passion, the joy of flying planes. Like many other older adults of America, Peters does not know what to do with his time. Oftentimes, if not completely retired, older adults are forced to take up jobs that do not make full use of their potential and skills, as it happens with Mr. Peters. He has not been able to come to terms with how he was prematurely thrown out of a profession that he considered his "calling":

> CALVIN. Look, you're not flying anywhere, are you?
> PETERS, *sitting up*. Flying! They haven't let me into a cockpit for eighteen years! I had at least five years of flying left in me when they dumped me like a bag of shit! And the Democrats are no better! (*Collected Plays* 411)

Peters was forced to take up the job of professor at Princeton; the frustration of ending up explaining to a class "which war you were in" is what he equates with talking "futility" (413). His bitterness pushes him to pinpoint "humiliation" as the "subject" of life (413). Although the exploitation of older adults in the labor force is a common practice in modern nations, it is especially so in purely profit-driven consumerist societies, where older employees are mainly seen as enemies of the younger workforce (de Beauvoir 225). When companies are downscaling, older adults are those most likely to be shunted off to the side and this rejection ends up taking a toll on both their personal and professional lives (Applewhite 150).

Since people's "biological" and "chronological" ages do not always coincide, fixing the same age of retirement for every worker is conceivably the most unfair workplace policy practiced across the world (de Beauvoir 263). In fact, one's "chronological age is an increasingly unreliable benchmark of pretty much anything about a person" (Applewhite 47). Miller's play emphasizes how it is not only the lack of professional representation that adversely affects older adults' lives but also feelings of exclusion and otherness experienced in every other public and personal sphere. The signboard that constantly reminds us that "youth is valued" is hard to overlook (Kite and Wagner 129). Whether it is interpersonal social communication or finding representation in mainstream media, older adults just seem to be experiencing estrangement at every possible level. For instance, each time only young bodies are showcased as desirable, it gives older adults another reason to feel sorry for themselves. Ironically, in times when every other cosmetic procedure is aimed at the replenishment and retention of youth, we expect older adults to feel comfortable in their own "skin." Conspicuously, "social gerontophobia" is so widespread that older adults are often forced to "temporarily" escape the "penalties imposed for old age" by way of cosmetic surgery and other such treatments (Falk and Falk 7). Peters is traumatized encountering this trend of body-worshipping. It is difficult for him to accept a world where people spend large sums of money on cosmetic procedures such as "breast augmentation," money that looks big enough to have bought a house in the old times (*Collected Plays* 414).

Along with pinpointing the trend of body worshipping, Miller throws light on how health and basic living have been made such complicated issues in today's world. A bizarre conversation about the importance of eating bananas highlights the same:

> ROSE.   Maybe you're low on potassium. You should eat bananas. . . . You only have enough bananas when one more would make you want to throw up. I know about such things, I'm a dancer, dancers need trace elements for the knees.
>
> PETERS, *nods with a certain alarm.* Trace elements for

the knees? You see, this is what I mean; when
I was young no human being from one end of
the United States to the other would have
uttered that sentence. For example, my father
and grandfather—I don't recall them ever in
the presence of a banana. And they lived into
their nineties. (*Collected Plays* 418) [2]

The obsession with finding one's panacea against aging does
not stop here; from attaching excessive value to "trace
elements" to buying anti-aging lotions and potions for a
wrinkle-free face, it travels to the fields of medical science and
surgery. Selling people "the dream of eternal youth" is the most
lucrative business of the pharmaceutical industry (Falk and
Falk 40). It is money-spinning because while "our ageist society
pathologizes natural transitions," its capitalist forces try to loot
us by offering us medicines and therapies to "fix" them
(Applewhite 74).

The character of Harry Peters embodies the sense of
disgust men and women feel with their own bodies because of
an environment that promotes "anti-aging." It also conveys
how older adults are also often shamed into being "asexual." [3]

---

2 The obsession with bananas naturally draws attention to Samuel Beckett's
Krapp's Last Tape, which features an aging character reliving his past through
a diary tape. Beckett shows him eating bananas and uses the banana motif
throughout the play. The presence of bananas in the play has been interpreted
variously, but prominent among the varied interpretations is the reference to
Krapp's desire for phallic pleasures, his overindulgence in bodily needs. In fact,
the primary theme of *Krapp's Last Tape* is that of living in the shadow of past
regret and unfulfilled goals set for oneself in youth, which can hamper one's
emotional balance in old age. The conversation about bananas in *Mr. Peters'
Connections* can also be interpreted as pointing at the overindulgence and
excessiveness of modern youth, which takes Peters by shock.

3 Little is written about Miller's connection with Agnes Barley, an abstract
painter he forged a close relationship with after his third wife, Inge Morath,

In de Beauvoir's words, "disgust at one's own body takes various forms among men and women; but in neither, age may provoke it, and if this happens they will refuse to make their body exist for another" (320). For most older men and women, suppressing sexual needs and desires appears to be a better option than coming across as "a lecherous old man" or "a shameless old woman" (320). Cathy May, Peters's dead beloved, keeps appearing and disappearing in the play and is often seen as a representation of Miller's second wife, Marilyn Monroe. [4] In her first appearance, Peters sees her nude, only wearing a pair of heels. It can be viewed as symbolic of his unconscious desires—both sexual and emotional. Cathy's glamorous, nude image fills Peters with excitement, sadness, and guilt. He is ashamed of himself, his body, and his desire for anything that is sexual by nature:

> PETERS. An old man talking about a . . . a woman's powder room—?— it's obscene! Look at the veins in the back of my hands?—shall these warped fingers stroke a breast, cup an ass . . . ? And you call life fair? No . . . no-no . . . *Fumbling*. Why don't I just sit here acting my age, quietly reading my paper till my wife comes? Tell you the truth, I've just had lunch and it makes me drowsy . . . (407)

passed away. Their brief affair before Miller's death attained controversial status as Agnes was fifty-five years Miller's junior. A particular article published in *The Telegraph* referred to their relationship as "not sexual" but "very intense" (Leonard). Relationships that involve only younger people are seldom scrutinized in the same way.

4 Cathy is also often compared to the Monroe figures in Miller's other plays: Maggie in *After the Fall* and Kitty in *Finishing the Picture*.

Sadly, "sex among the old is a laughing matter in America" and since both religious groups and people in general are so averse to the idea of sex in old age, there is a "very high degree of gerontophobia in this area" (Falk and Falk 127). Applewhite also opines that "nowhere is ageism more sexist, and vicious, than in the domain of sexuality," which is perhaps why most Americans believe that sex is the business of the young and older adults are not sexually active (122). Even though "the right to intimacy is lifelong," older adults are constantly denied their rights (Applewhite 123). Everywhere around us, we only see younger bodies being portrayed as the ideal sexual beings; "examples of older people, let alone sexually active ones, are few and far between" (124).

This brutal exclusion from mainstream representation forces older adults to feel guilty for their sexual desires, which is Peters's feeling too. His rebuke to himself "why don't I just sit here acting my age" (*Collected Plays* 407) reflects how older adults are trained to feel incapable. The caution "act your age" that means fulfilling "expectations of industry, gravity, and the acceptance of responsibility" for young children has a completely "burdensome connotation" for older adults (Golub et al. 278). It is chiefly based on the assumption that older adults are just like children, who need to be told and continually reminded of how they should act. This expectation that older adults must "act like old people" can often become "oppressive" as it proposes that one's individual behavior, irrespective of how one actually feels, must be "determined by a chronology over which the individual has no control" (278). Peters's age-reminders to himself express his surrender of "a degree of agency, responsibility, and control" over his own body and mind (278).

An unexpected finale: When the "subject" meets Peters

About the ambiguous nature of Miller's late plays (with special reference to his double-bill, *Two-Way Mirror*), Christopher Bigsby highlights how Miller's writing career that began with "certainties," in which "character and plot were means to an end," and "agencies of social, political, economic circumstance," turned into a different direction later (360). His drama opened up to the realms of "ambiguity," where he appeared captivated by "means by which we invent not only ourselves but others, by a past that is not fixed in time and space but invoked by need and deformed by memory" (360). *Mr. Peters' Connections* is conceivably a prime example of this acceptance of vagueness of life and the playwright's fascination with the human potential to rebuild the past as per need and circumstance. The audience is constantly left to do the guessing game as this former pilot finds himself in a cryptic time and place and tries to reconnect with his past—fiddling with many questions. In his "narcoticized twilight state between semi-wakefulness and a presumably eternal sleep" (Brantley), Harry Peters plunges through his memoirs, giving us but debris of an era and a life gone by. Though vague and distorted, his memories take us through his life's journey. There are moments in the play when it gets difficult to even conclude if Peters is actually reliving these memories or simply constructing them. He appears to be bringing all his experiences of different times together to give himself and his life some kind of coherence, some meaning—some substantial "subject." Reflecting on the character of Mr. Peters, Miller said in an interview: "it's tough to be near death and have to think that there's no definition to your life" (Bigsby 405), which sums up the main challenge of growing old and becoming aware of approaching death. Like the dilapidated nightclub, Peters's life has also seen many transitions to reach this state. There is regret related to past love, unfulfilled dreams and promises along with desperation to connect once more, and the ensuing frustration about how he cannot. He has lived a life full of varied experiences and yet the "subject" remains blurred.

In Miller's theatrical oeuvre, *Mr. Peters' Connections* can scarcely be viewed as a play "well made," which is exactly what the playwright pinpoints about the nature of human life. It is the randomness of life that is reflected also in the way the play ends. The drama that began with confusion leaves us in a state of absolute ambiguity. Placing the ending of *Mr. Peters' Connections* alongside those in some of Miller's other late plays such as *Broken Glass, The Ride Down Mt. Morgan, The Last Yankee,* and *Resurrection Blues,* Miller's emphasis on ambiguity and hope becomes quite clear. All of these plays reinstate the playwright's belief in establishing connection, in accepting life with its myriad uncertainties, in finding hope despite disarray and seeming defeat. Throughout *Mr. Peters' Connections,* we see characters digress, forget names and events, and talk endlessly in spirals about mundane things such as bananas, mahogany toilets, laundry methods, and vacuum cleaners. In the midst of this zigzag of many voices, Peters keeps struggling with his search for the "subject." He does not give up and towards the end he urges all other characters around him at the nightclub to think of the "subject":

> PETERS. Rest now. All rest. Quietly, please. Quietly rest. While we think of the subject. While breath comes blessedly clear. While we learn to be brave.
> (ROSE *and* LEONARD *sit on either side of* PETERS. *Farther upstage, frozen in time, Larry is looking into the empty shopping bag,* CHARLOTTE *is working her*

calculator, CALVIN *is staring into space,* ADELE *is examining her face in the mirror . . .*) (*Complete Plays* 436)

In the midst of this last scene, to the surprise of both Peters and the audience, Rose suddenly calls him "Papa":

ROSE.   Papa?
PETERS (*opens his eyes, listens*). Yes?
ROSE.   Please stay.
PETERS (*straight ahead*). I'm trying!
ROSE.   I love you, Papa.
PETERS. I'm trying as hard as I can. I love you, darling. I wonder . . . could that be the subject! (436)

Whether Rose is actually Peters's daughter or someone who finds him a father-like figure remains uncertain but what emerges as crystal clear is that the "subject" Mr. Peters was looking for is "love" (Abbotson 249). In Bigsby's view, in his "dream world," Peters encounters his daughter, Rose, also as a perfect stranger because at this stage in his life, even she is a "representative of a younger generation, more evidence of a broken continuity than anything else, though it is continuity he seeks." (412). Nonetheless, in his association with Charlotte and Rose, Peters is finally able to find a "connection." The play ends with Mrs. Charlotte Peters planning to renovate the ramshackle nightclub into something new and innovative, which can be interpreted to be symbolically suggesting how life can always be refashioned despite much wear and tear. With Rose being pregnant and the warmth of family unity felt at the end of the play, the audience is left with both anticipation and uncertainty. Miller's play thus exemplifies how the human pursuit for meaning is meant to prevail despite anxieties related to death. In being connected Mr. Peters finally comes to find his purpose to stay. Thus, with its own innate serendipitous movement, with a narration that refuses to directly tell us whether it is Peters's "contemplation of life itself" or a "confrontation with death" or both (Bigsby 406), *Mr. Peters' Connections* explicitly validates how "a pattern can be born in the formlessness of life that reveals no inherent order or purpose" (Centola, "Chaos" 28). It also authenticates how "change" that naturally accompanies the process of aging does not necessarily mean "decay." Harry Peters's story highlights connectedness and love as essential to battle against all modern-day evils, whether that is "ageism" or any other -ism for that matter.

Works Cited

Abbotson, Susan C. W. *Critical Companion to Arthur Miller: A Literary Reference to His Life and Work.* New York: Facts on File, 2007.

Applewhite, Ashton. *This Chair Rocks: A Manifesto Against Ageism.* Networked Books, 2016.

Baars, Jan, and Chris Phillipson. "Connecting Meaning with Social Structure: Theoretical Foundations." *Ageing, Meaning and Social Structure: Connecting Critical and Humanistic Gerontology.* Ed. Joseph Dohmen and Jan Baars. Bristol: Policy, 2013. 11-30.

Bigsby Christopher. *Arthur Miller: A Critical Study.* New York: Cambridge University Press, 2005.

Brantley, Ben. "Theater Review: Peter Falk's Search for Meaning." *The New York Times* 18 May 1998. Web. 14 July 2018.

Centola, Steven R. "'Pattern Born Amid Formlessness': The Law of Chaos in the Plays of Arthur Miller." *The Arthur*

Miller Journal 1.1 (2006): 19-29.

de Beauvoir, Simone. *The Coming of Age.* Trans. Patrick O'Brian. New York: Putnam's Sons, 1972.

Eyre, Richard. "Foreword." Miller and Gussow 9-14.

Falk, Ursula A., and Gerhard Falk. *Ageism, the Aged, and Aging in America: On Being Old in an Alienated Society.* Springfield, IL: Thomas, 1997.

Fay, Stephen. "Miller's Short Tale about the Meaning of Life." *The Independent.* Independent Digital News and Media, 22 Oct. 2011. Web. 25 Sept. 2019.

Golub, Sarit A, et al. "Acting Your Age." Nelson, *Ageism* 277-94.

Jensen, Gordon D., and Fredericka B. Oakley. "Ageism Across Cultures and in Perspective of Sociobiologic and Psychodynamic Theories." *The International Journal of Aging and Human Development* 15.1 (1982-83): 17-25.

Kite, Mary E., and Lisa Smith Wagner. "Attitudes Toward Older Adults." Nelson, *Ageism* 129-62.

Kurdi, Mária. "The Deceptive Nature of Reality in Arthur Miller's *Two-Way Mirror.*" *Cross-Cultural Studies: American, Canadian and European Literatures: 1945-1985.* Ed. Mirko Jurak. The English Department, University of Ljubljana, 1988. 267-71.

Langer, Elinor. "Growing Old in America: Frauds, Quackery, Swindle the Aged and Compound Their Troubles." *Science* 140.3566 (1963): 470-72.

Leonard, Tom. "Miller's Fiancée Quits His Home after Ultimatum from Family." *The Telegraph* 18 Feb. 2005. Web. 25 Sept. 2019.

Miller, Arthur. *Collected Plays (1987-2004).* Ed. Tony Kushner. New York: Library of America, 2015.

---. *The Collected Essays of Arthur Miller.* Ed. Matthew Charles Roudané. New York: Bloomsbury, 2015.

---. *Death of a Salesman: Certain Private Conversations in Two Acts and a Requiem*. New York: Penguin, 1998.

---. Preface. *Mr. Peters' Connections*. New York: Penguin, 1998. viii.

---. *Two-Way Mirror*. London: Methuen, 1984.

---, and Mel Gussow. *Conversations with Miller*. Centenary Ed. London: Nick Hern, 2015.

Nelson, Todd D. "Preface." Nelson, *Ageism* ix-xiv.

---, ed. *Ageism: Stereotyping and Prejudice Against Older Persons*. Cambridge: MIT Press, 2002.

Ng, Sik Hung. "Will Families Support Their Elders? Answers From Across Cultures." Nelson, *Ageism* 295-310.

Scanlan, Robert. "The Late Plays of Arthur Miller." *Arthur Miller's America: Theater and Culture in a Time of Change*. Ed. Enoch Brater. Ann Arbor: University of Michigan Press, 2008. 180-90.

Showalter, Elaine. "Introduction." *Out of Time: The Pleasures and the Perils of Ageing*. By Lynne Segal. London: Verso, 2014. xi-xviii.

Singh, Ambika. "Individual and Social Paralysis in the Later Plays of Arthur Miller." Diss. MNIT Jaipur, 2019.

Switzky, Lawrence. "Introduction: Modern Drama, Aging, and the Life Course." *Modern Drama* 59.2 (2016): 135-42.

Tomer, Adrian, and Grafton Eliason. "Toward a Comprehensive Model of Death Anxiety." *Death Studies* 20.4 (1996): 343-65.

Wolf, Matt. "Review of *Mr. Peters' Connections*." *Variety*. 7 Aug. 2000. Web. 25 Sept. 2019.

10.2478/9788367405423-013

Part IV
Fiction

"No country, this, for old men": A View of the Aging Artist through Intertexts in J. M. Coetzee's *Disgrace*
Angelika Reichmann

At fifty-two, a scholar of Romantic poetry and the writer of an opera about Byron, David Lurie, the protagonist of J. M. Coetzee's *Disgrace* (1999), clearly qualifies as an aging artist figure. Indeed, in the study that most sharply focuses on aging in *Disgrace* up to date, Robert Scott Stewart and Michael Manson argue that it is a novel about aging at two levels: it is a story about the rather "stereotypical" personal crisis of "a middle aged white man" (169, 175), and it is an "obliquely" political narrative about the capability of the post-apartheid South African state to age gracefully (169). Key to both, they propose, is a need for a "radical shift from a European based liberal conception of the self to one that is more community based and relational" (169-70). Such a shift, they argue, might enable Lurie to overcome his central failure: his inability to sympathize with others and treat them not as abstractions (176-77) but as subjects, to recognize them as the other (170). Limited as Lurie's development in this respect is, Margot Beard demonstrates—in contrast with Stewart and Manson—the centrality of the European literary tradition to it: in her reading, the trajectory of Lurie's *Bildung* leads from misreading to understanding Wordsworth and Byron, Lurie's "dead masters," and particularly the "empathetic imagination" crucial to the Romantic vision of morality and creativity (63-73). In this context, Beard also draws attention to the fact that Lurie broadens his conception of disgrace to mean "a state of

NEGOTIATING AGE

being" (Coetzee, *Disgrace* 172), thus evidencing a Wordsworthian reading of the term, since the Romantic poet thought that "the state of being without grace is the condition of us all and the beneficence of grace is a gift rarely bestowed and never guaranteed" (66).

In my view, Beard's reading exposes a third level of interpretation for the disgrace of aging in Coetzee's text which both Stewart and Manson and she herself ignore: *Disgrace* in many ways is about death, and not only does it represent aging as a problem of middle-aged men but also uses it as the image of the shared human condition—it meditates on whether life, the time allotted to humans in general, is anything else but the disgraceful ante-room of death. And that meditation—owing largely to the inherently ageist discourse of the unreliable focalizer—ends on a much less optimistic note than readings focused on Lurie's development would suggest. While those interpretations highlight Lurie's empathy to the euthanized dogs, which is evidenced, for instance, in the last chapter, and the Wordsworthian overtones of his last scene with Lucy, his ageism surfaces in the proliferation of negative stereotypes in his vision of himself and in his evocation of a set of intertexts from outside Romanticism. [1] These, on the one hand, deny a

---

1 The abundance of intertexts in *Disgrace* can be explained as a general feature of Coetzee's novelistic art and as a feature brought to the fore here because the main character is a professor of English literature. As for the former aspect, Coetzee's often-quoted artistic credo, itself formulated in the intertextual context of Daniel Defoe's *Robinson Crusoe*—hence the image of cannibalism for imitation and plagiarism—runs as follows: "For it seems to him now that there are but a handful of stories in the world; and if the young are to be forbidden to prey upon the old then they must sit for ever in silence" (Coetzee, "He and His Man"). In Coetzee's art, however, systematic rewritings of seminal European texts—*Robinson* in *Foe* (1986) and Dostoevsky's *Devils* in *The Master of Petersburg* (1994)—in hindsight seem to form rare exceptions, which he produced at the heyday of postmodernism and which largely comply with its poetics of virtuoso playful intertextuality (see Hutcheon 124-40). As Ottilia

lasting nature to any insight within the novel's fictional world by unmasking the inherently subversive chiastic operations of Lurie's consciousness. On the other hand, besides effectively undermining the narrative's Romantic discourse, they also demonstrate the cultural codedness, even social entrenchment of negative stereotypes about the aged, which explains why literature in the novel seems to be unable to provide Lurie with a lasting, protective worldview in the face of his own approaching death. Lurie's unreliable perspective of the aging artist, shaped by the often contradictory Romantic and modernist legacies together, largely contributes to a bleak and at the same time perplexing image of post-apartheid South Africa, an effect further intensified by intertextually coded suggestions of cyclical repetition.

Lurie as unreliable focalizer: Ageism

Coetzee's vision of his mother country is, indeed, perplexing: although *Disgrace* was awarded the Booker Prize, it has received a mixed reception owing to charges that the novel paints an extremely negative image of post-apartheid South Africa which proliferates racial stereotypes and does harm to the evolving new state (Attridge 105). Set in Cape Town and the Eastern Cape, presumably in the years preceding its 1999 publication, *Disgrace* features Professor Lurie's forced

Veres demonstrates in her study of mythical allusions in Coetzee's four early novels (*Dusklands, Foe, Waiting for the Barbarians,* and *The Life and Times of Michael K*), fragmentary—and often implicit—intertextual references form a typical aspect of his art that, nevertheless, deserve close scrutiny. Veres's analysis calls attention to intertextual fragments in Coetzee's art which establish continuity among a number of his novels. Notwithstanding their brief and impressionistic nature, they can provide a major insight into the discussion of his central themes, among which Veres focuses on "colonial encounters" (19-24). Indeed, my reading of similarly fragmentary and, in Beckett's case, implicit literary allusions in *Disgrace* relies on the same fundamental assumptions.

resignation from his university position following charges of sexual harassment, an event which is juxtaposed to the gang-rape of his lesbian daughter by three black intruders later on. Most difficult of all is to accept at face value Lucy's resignation to the consequences—as her father understands—in the name of white guilt and historical justice. That is, she decides to give birth to her child conceived from rape and to accept the marriage proposal of his tenant-neighbor Petrus, which will entail the loss of her land in exchange for the protection of the black man. This alleged accep tance of Lucy's rape is what Athol Fugard called "a load of bloody bullshit" (qtd. in Mardorossian 73). [2] Fugard's comment might be only a more outspoken version of the main character David Lurie's and many lay readers' sentiments. And the two opinions, as Carine M. Mardorossian also highlights, are inseparable from each other (73), because *Disgrace* uses Coetzee's trademark narrative technique (a story told in the present simple tense through the main character as the focalizer) and is thus limited to Lurie's perspective and narrative consciousness.

One explanation for the novel's bleak but compelling vision of post-apartheid South Africa might be the fact that, as Mardorossian and Mike Marais both point out, Lurie as a focalizer is unreliable because his perspective is defined by a sexist and racist ideology; nonetheless, it is still difficult to establish the necessary critical distance from his views. [3]

---

2 In somewhat more sophisticated terms, many scholars contend that "the novel is implicated in the very economy it seeks to criticize" and thus "reproduces and perpetuates stereotypical representations of black and white relationships in South Africa" (Mardorossian 73).

3 Central to Mardorossian's argument is the juxtaposition of the representations of the two instances of rape in *Disgrace*—Lurie's "affair" with Melanie and Lucy's gang rape (76-80). That is, through Lurie's perspective readers are encouraged to see Lucy's rape (black on white sexual violence) as a horrible

Importantly, Lurie's opinions also speak of his internalized ageism, which largely contributes to the novel's apparently pessimistic vision of the future almost in terms of a blind street leading to inevitable destruction, while making his assessment of his situation extremely difficult to refute. Ageism in the narrower sense means a "stereotypical construction of older people, aging and old age" (Ayalon and Tesch-Römer, "Introduction" 1), and in *Disgrace* that construction is a negative one right from the start. [4] The very first sentence suggests an ageist perspective by posing sex as an age-related problem and thereby confirming "key myths"— ageist stereotypes, in other words—of "older people's sexuality" (Gewirtz-Meydan et al. 150): "For a man of his age,

crime that goes unpunished, while Lurie's "not rape, not quite that" of Melanie (25) is represented in the light of an excessively and unjustly punished, almost innocent, affair. Key to this effect is the fact that "authorial complicity moves in and out without clearly allowing readers to discern where it begins and ends" (78). Although from the very beginning of the novel "Coetzee is encouraging readers to distance themselves from his protagonist," they still find themselves easily identifying with his views on events, because "the safe distance between the authorial narrator and the character constantly vanishes" (77). Thus, Lurie's racial and gender bias remains oblique and largely unnoticed, as if his white male perspective was a neutral one and the norm (79). Mardorossian concludes that it is "impossible not to participate in his way of thinking" (79)— at least not until his reaction to Lucy's rape reveals how deeply biased his opinions are (80). Similarly to Mardorossian, Mike Marais also repeatedly calls attention to the difficulty of keeping a critical distance from the perspective of the novel's unreliable focalizer, which is grounded in the discourse of race ("J. M. Coetzee's *Disgrace*" 83-85; "Violence" 102).

4 Ageism has both positive and negative forms (Ayalon and Tesch-Römer 2). Stereotypes may vary from society to society and usually include both positive and negative traits. Thus, Hummert's 2011 research "yielded seven general stereotypes, four negative and three positive, shared by people of all ages about older adults: Severely Impaired; Despondent; Shrew/Curmudgeon; Recluse; Golden Ager; Perfect Grandparent; and John Wayne Conservative" (qtd. in Shiovitz-Ezra et al. 136), while Cuddy and Fiske's surveys suggest that older people are generally believed to have "lower competence" and to emanate more "warmth," and are thus often approached with "pity and sympathy" (qtd. in Shiovitz-Ezra et al. 136).

fifty-two, divorced, he has, to his mind, solved the problem of sex rather well" (Coetzee, *Disgrace* 1). There is another stereotype implied by this overture which is related, but certainly not limited, to the issue of sex: Lurie's opening statement also points to the stereotype of old-age loneliness (Shiovitz-Ezra et al. 139). That threatens Lurie not only because of his two failed marriages, but more importantly because the literature professor, as Derek Attridge highlights, has "a deeper sense of being unfit for the times in which he lives" (110) and an "immense distaste [for] a new global age of performance indicators and outcomes measurement, of benchmarking and quality assurance, of a widespread prurience that's also an unfeeling puritanism" (105-06). In short, he feels alienated in a "post-Christian, posthistorical, postliterate" world (Coetzee, *Disgrace* 32). Stereotypical as Lurie's self-conception as a lonely old man might be, loneliness is a matter of subjective experience not to be confused with, but potentially rooted in social isolation (Shiovitz-Ezra et al. 131), and his experience of that is hard to discredit.

In the light of the negative feedback Lurie receives about himself from his environment, it is understandable that his ageism seems to be directed predominantly against himself in the solipsistic world of *Disgrace*. In the new, highly utilitarian world he can have a special course on Romantic poetry only because it is held "good for morale" in his department (Coetzee, *Disgrace* 3), and most of his presumably non-white students find it difficult to relate to the monuments of European patriarchal culture he defends. A telling demonstration of this is Melanie's "involvement" in contemporary (non-white) women's writing—Adrienne Rich (1929-2012), Toni Morrison (1931-2019), and Alice Walker (1944-)—as opposed to her lack of interest in Wordsworth and her inability to remember the

German title of a work she claims to have actually liked (12-13). Although Lurie's contempt for the new world modeled in the utilitarian reorganization of his university is obvious, he cannot dissociate himself from the negative implications of the changes with regard to his self-conception: as a white male humanist intellectual, he finds himself powerless, a prematurely obsolete and marginalized remnant of pre-globalization apartheid South Africa. His manifold falls from power have occurred in the novel's prehistory and are only aptly allegorized post-factum in his dismissal from his university position. In that sense, his evocation of Romantic representations of the fallen angel (32-34) is both a reflection of past trauma and a foreshadowing of his future: identifying himself with the magnanimous but demonic figure of Lara/Lucifer through the image of the snake/serpent (2-3, 16), Lurie clearly outlines a downward trajectory for both his past and future career. Such a negative stereotypical self-perception which emerges through people's "internalizing the negative representations of old age that are prevalent in society" is described in reference literature as "self-ageism" (Kite et al. qtd. in Lev et al. 62). The resultant image of an aging man of intellect, a character associated with art and humanities, who feels redundant in the new South Africa, might give rise to empathy rather than distancing audiences. Regardless of its veiled but nonetheless morally unacceptable sexist and racist foundations, Lurie's clearly stereotypical dark vision of aging is difficult to discard as simply the biased view of an unreliable focalizer.

Readers might also find themselves unwittingly complicit in Lurie's views because the ageist discourse they are enveloped in highlights a universal fear of passing away, which probably strikes a sensitive cord with many. This is spectacularly evidenced in Lurie's mental treatment of the already mentioned "problem of sex," which almost predestines his affair with Melanie to confirm his darkest fears. From the start, Lurie seems preoccupied with "the physical unattractiveness and undesirability of older people" and "the idea that it is shameful and perverse for older people to engage in sexual activity" (Hafford-Letchfeld qtd. in Gewirtz-Meydan et al. 150). Both of these convictions are obstacles in his attempts to establish a sexual relationship with the—typically much younger—women he desires. That is, he envisions (incidentally evoking a Kafkaesque metaphor) young women who feel only disgust at the thought of his body: "They [prostitutes] tell stories, they laugh, but they shudder too, as one shudders at a cockroach in a washbasin in the middle of the night. Soon, daintily, maliciously, he will be shuddered over. It is a fate he cannot escape" (Coetzee, *Disgrace* 8). Because of that disgust, the idea of subjecting a young woman to sexual intercourse with an older man is perceived to be as good as perverse. In response to his ex-wife's reminders of that idea ("Do you think a young girl finds any pleasure in going to bed with a man of that age? Do you think she finds it good to watch you in the middle of your. . . ?" [44].) Lurie feels compelled to concede that "[p]erhaps it is the right of the young to be protected from the sight of their elders in the throes of passion. That is what whores are for, after all: to put up with the ecstasies of the unlovely" (44). Consequently, through Lurie's own perspective his own image is established as that of a—not only metaphorically—near-castrated, powerless, undesirable old man, who is unable to accept the inevitable facts of his own aging and death, which he can interpret only in terms of disgrace: "He ought to give up, retire from the game. At what age, he wonders, did Origen castrate himself? Not the most graceful of solutions, but then aging is not a graceful business. A clearing of the decks, at least, so that one can turn one's mind to the proper business of the old: preparing to die" (9). A major irony of this negative self-image is that, strictly speaking, Lurie might certainly be aging but not old at all: middle-aged at worst. [5] Indeed, at the individual level it is especially middle-aged people whose ageism is most often rooted, as Lurie's train of thought suggests, in "the threat of death, the threat of animality, and the threat of insignificance" (Martens qtd. in Lev et al. 57), of which the old are constant reminders. Cruel as Lurie's stereotypical and ageist view of himself is, it partly originates in a fact that is impossible to explain away—the universal fear of one's own inevitable mortality—which blissfully hides its more specifically South African roots in post-apartheid history: Lurie's loss of the privileges that he as a white male humanist intellectual held before.

Anti-Bildung through intertexts I: Dostoevsky's *Devils* and chiastic thought

It is not so much Lurie's fear that might establish a distance between his ageist self-perception and readers but rather the premature and extremely bleak nature of his views: he is at an age when typically people are still able to "unconsciously sustain faith in cultural worldviews, which enable them to portray human life as meaningful, important, and enduring" (Lev et al. 55). The quoted readings of *Disgrace* suggest that the prime candidate for such a protective discourse, as far as Lurie is concerned, is literature/art in general and Romanticism in particular. Nonetheless, much of

---

5 That category is defined in gerontology as including adults "from 35-40 to 59-65 years" (Lev et al. 54).

the literary tradition with which Lurie is familiar is nothing but the promoter of the negative stereotypical vision of sexuality in old age, which is his major concern. This is what Lurie's hindsight, his mental comment on the perception of his own affair with Melanie as "unnatural" (Coetzee, *Disgrace* 190), reveals:

> On trial for his way of life. For unnatural acts: for broadcasting old seed, tired seed, seed that does not quicken, *contra naturam*. If the old men hog the young women, what will be the future of the species? . . . Half of literature is about it: young women struggling to escape from under the weight of old men, for the sake of the species. (190)

Lurie's scandal with Melanie proves Romanticism—at least in the version Lurie endorses at the beginning of the narrative— to be inadequate as a protective worldview against the terror of aging and death. By implication, it fails to provide Lurie with a paradigm for finding meaning in his remaining life in a globalized, post-apartheid South Africa. Beard's optimistic reading implies that Lurie's reinterpretation of the Romantic legacy brings about a fundamental change in both these respects. Let me argue, however, that the opposite scenario seems to be coded from the start in Lurie's utterly negative view of aging itself and himself as an aging man, [6] as do his references to modernist literary texts focusing on the same.

The non-Romantic intertexts in *Disgrace* which address aging directly or indirectly seem to bracket, as is demonstrated below, those relatively optimistic readings of the novel based

---

6 Since ageism often works as "a self-fulfilling prophecy" in real life (Ayalon and Tesch-Römer 2), it can hinder subjects from developing effective short- and long-term strategies for coping with aging such as "successful" or "active ageing" and acceptance of the inevitable (in later life) (Lev et al. 65-67).

on Lurie's development—however limited it might be—and his concomitant changing perspective. A closer look at those intertexts apparently confirms Mike Marais's more pessimistic interpretation. In "J. M. Coetzee's *Disgrace* and the Task of the Imagination," Marais indirectly questions Beard's optimistic reading in terms of Lurie developing a true understanding of empathetic imagination. Marais points out that "there is much evidence in *Disgrace* to support the claim that Coetzee has furnished *Disgrace* with the structure of an anti-*Bildungsroman*, a novel which involves the forfeiture rather than consolidation of the protagonist's self" (79). While apparently the plot of *Disgrace* follows an "ethical trajectory" leading from "selfish egotism to cathartic altruism," in his view this movement proves to be "chiastic," "doubling back on itself" to "dispute . . . what it seems to assert even as it is asserted" (79). Key to understanding this paradoxical nature of Lurie's plot line is the realization that he faces the "impossible task" of "infinite sympathy"—one that would be based on an "uncommitted non-position . . . outside of language and the positions that it inscribes in culture"—which would thereby enable him to feel sympathy even "despite himself," even for Pollux, one of the rapists (81-82). [7] Taking my clue from Marais, let me add that

---

7 Lurie's inability to do so—his violent assault on the "disturbed child," Marais argues in "Violence, Postcolonial Fiction, and the Limits of Sympathy"—is a "failure of sympathy" (103) and a "failure of imagination" ("J. M. Coetzee's *Disgrace*" 80). Both surface in Lurie's inability to look at Lucy as if she was a stranger, from a position outside history and culture, and thus his inability to fully sympathize with her and not to misread her (81-83). Marais, however, goes on to emphasize that while the novel "denies the reader direct access to Lucy" (84), it also encourages readers to supplement *Disgrace* with a reading of her that is left "unsaid" in the novel (85-87)—to do "what cannot be done" (87). This is what he elsewhere interprets as Coetzee's strategy to counter what Slavoj Žižek calls "symbolic violence" (qtd. in Marais, "Violence" 94) "in an attempt to secure unlimited sympathy through limiting the degree to which the text and reader's situatedness in culture limit sympathy" (99).

the "impossible task" of "infinite sympathy" would also involve Lurie's taking up an "uncommitted non-position . . . outside of language" and approaching his own present (aging, therefore emasculated and powerless) and future (dead) self from it. His sustained references to intertexts outside Romanticism point towards a failure—or rather a "chiastic" back and forth movement—in that respect, too. Readers, however, might find it rather complicated to dissociate themselves from the subtle intricacies of Lurie's approach to his own death, even though it is shaped by a markedly white and male intellectual's perspective in post-apartheid South Africa. If anything, his allusions highlight the shared quality and the cultural embeddedness of his stereotypical views, just as well as the paradoxical nature of the discourses transcending the limitations of those, and Lurie's own inability to commit himself ultimately to any saving paradigm.

This chiastic movement of Lurie's consciousness—and thus perspective—is clearly indicated by one of the novel's intertexts from outside Romanticism: Dostoevsky's *Devils* (1872). At the same time, the Russian novel links chiastic habits of thought to the problematic nature of established discourses especially in the context of addressing the ultimate questions of human existence. The intertextual connection of the two novels is predicated on the similarity of the crimes Dostoevsky's Stavrogin and Lurie commit, which calls attention to less obvious but highly significant parallels between the two central characters. [8] The importance of this Dostoevsky novel in Coetzee's oeuvre and, in particular, in his

---

8 Since Coetzee's reception rather mentions than interprets them (Kossew, "The Politics of Shame and Redemption" 156-59; Marais, *Secretary of the Invisible* 168), they seem to call for further critical attention. Their detailed discussion falls beyond the scope of this study, but see Reichmann.

addressing the political crisis that surrounded the birth of post-apartheid South Africa can hardly be overestimated: Dostoevsky's seminal, tragic vision of terrorism at a moment of political crisis is the fundamental intertext behind *The Master of Petersburg* (1994). The book is technically Coetzee's first post-apartheid novel, a text overtly concerned with artistic dilemmas in the face of death and anarchy. It appears to be just logical that faint echoes of the same narrative should reverberate in *Disgrace*, as if reinforcing the relevance of Dostoevsky's artistic vision when it comes to representing intellectual crisis at the time of a major historical/political turnover.

In the present context, the Russian novel's sharp critique of Romanticism aside, Stavrogin and his disciples' obsession with utopian thoughts of bringing (historical) time to an end (see Kroó) seems to be the novel's most relevant aspect, since it is directly connected, if not to aging in *Disgrace*, then to the political allegory centered on it: to the potentially graceful aging of post-apartheid South Africa. Specifically, Stavrogin's desire for a completely new discourse of spiritual and political rebirth is, as Katalin Kroó demonstrates, directly linked to two central tropes of *Devils*: the image of demonic possession by "old philosophical clichés" (250) (старые философские места [Достоевский 148]) is countered there with images of exorcism (Кроо 227-61)—a chasing out of devils. The "old philosophical clichés" in *Devils* are nothing but the established discourses addressing the ultimate questions of human existence, which fail to provide acceptable answers for those who are—like Dostoevsky's Stavrogin and Coetzee's Lurie— "not cold but not hot" with respect to faith (Coetzee, *Disgrace*

195). [9] It is this Dostoevskian context, evoked through the tropes of old thoughts and exorcism in *Disgrace*, which not only qualifies some of Lurie's established ideas as obsolete and based on stereotypical preconceptions, but also widens their scope way beyond their direct reference to Lurie's sexual tastes: "He does not like women who make no effort to be attractive. . . . Nothing to be proud of: a prejudice that has settled in his mind, settled down. His mind has become a refuge for old thoughts, ... He ought to chase them out, sweep the premises clean. But he does not care to do so, or does not care enough" (72). The drift of Lurie's thoughts suggests a generalizing tendency; therefore, the final call for the dismissal of his earlier convictions and a clean start comes to involve all his ideas in its scope—whether they pertain to sex, race, life, and death, or art and literature. At the same time, Lurie's similarity to Stavrogin, specifically his inability to ultimately commit himself to any discourse of truth, provides a rather bleak prognosis for the potential outcome of his attempt to introduce a new one. Stavrogin, also a character rooted in Romanticism, commits suicide after his failed attempts at spiritual rebirth—a plot element which distinctly echoes in Lurie's professional "suicide," that is, his refusal to defend himself during the disciplinary action, and his final stasis-like waiting.

The context of *Devils* also suggests that the two allusions in *Disgrace* between them describe Lurie's thought processes as chiastic while they also perform such a chiastic movement. Both have rich metatextual implications with regard to interpreting Lurie and therefore the entire text of *Disgrace* narrated

---

9 See the Biblical quote characterizing those unable to commit themselves either to faith or to disbelief, which both Stavrogin and the Elder Tikhon know by heart: "So because thou art lukewarm, and neither cold nor hot, I will spue thee out of my mouth" (Dostoevsky 458).

through his consciousness. As to representing Lurie's thought processes, "not cold but not hot" suggests a state of permanent doubt, a fundamentally subversive attitude, which Coetzee associates elsewhere with Dostoevsky in general: "The outrage felt by many of Freud's first readers—that he was subverting their moral world—was therefore misplaced. This is, I trust, a Dostoevskian point" (*Doubling the Point* 244). Lurie's doubtful, subversive attitude is confirmed by the paradoxical contrast between his self-description through the metaphor of "refuge for old thoughts" and his immediate call to get rid of those very thoughts. The working of subversion as chiasmus, in turn, is exemplified by the same call to leave behind well-established discourses (assertion) and by Lurie's immediate recognition of his inability to do so (doubling back). Nonetheless, if "refuge for old thoughts" is read as an ironic comment on the "post-Christian, posthistorical, postliterate" world surrounding Lurie, it reveals itself to be a hidden assertion that he should indeed maintain an asylum in his mind for discarded ideas and thereby resist the dominant tendencies of his era. That would mean another, implicit doubling back on the explicit assertion—the call for change—in his train of thought. This performance of chiastic movement can also be read as a metatextual comment on the consciousness of the focalizer, which suggests an intertextual approach to *Disgrace* only to discard it immediately. That is, "refuge of old thoughts" first asserts the relevance of the novel's intertextual reading by being as it is, an allusion, and suggesting that *Disgrace* can be understood by tracking down intertextual references in Lurie's thoughts. But allusions—old thoughts in the sense of being by definition pre-existing texts, ideas formulated prior to the context in which they are evoked—are also subject to the purifying urge behind "sweeping the premises clean," which metatextually discredits all the insights that Lurie and his readers supposedly derive from literary texts (including the present ones suggested by *Devils*). This might concern all conclusions based on pre-existing discourses, which may all be ill-fitting paradigms for post-apartheid South Africa.

Anti-*Bildung* through intertexts II: Eliot, Yeats, and Beckett

In the light of the Dostoevskian revelations about Lurie's habits of thought, it might come as no surprise that Disgrace evokes fundamentally contradictory intertexts with reference to aging and the trope of the aging man. On the one hand, there are Lurie's attempts to find meaning in the remainder of his life through a Romantically based reinterpretation of empathy and thus to create a renewed protective discourse against the disgrace of death, which is also reflected in the Wordsworthian representation of the novel's closing scenes. On the other hand, Disgrace also refers to major modernist intertexts which counter that optimism by corroborating stereotypical views of old men, especially in terms of "the problem of sex" and the decline of (artistic) creativity. If anything, they highlight the inadequacy of available discourses for addressing the issue of one's own demise.

The first of these allusions to appear in the novel is a sequence which evokes T. S. Eliot's "The Love Song of J. Alfred Prufrock" (1917), through its rhythm and music rather than through exact quotation: "He is mildly smitten with her [Melanie]. It is no great matter" (Coetzee, *Disgrace* 11). Possibly, one of the parallel places in Eliot's text is the weighty " [t]hough I have seen my head (grown slightly bald) brought in upon a platter, / I am no prophet—and here's no great matter," a straightforward denial of the speaker's own significance and a disassociation of the aging artist figure, shown as ridiculous ("I have seen the eternal Footman hold my coat, and snicker"), from the Romantic mediators of transcendental truth. The other potential candidate for the source of this allusion is Prufrock's imaginary evocation of a failed attempt to connect with a woman. It reinforces the connotations above and combines them with an ambiguous reference to a failure to satisfy (women's) expectations and to the inappropriateness of both nonverbal ("bitten off the matter with a smile") and verbal ("That is not what I meant at all") expression, thus underpinning Lurie's inability—or the general impossibility—of finding an adequate discourse to address his situation. The reference to "Prufrock" in its entirety calls for a figurative reading of Lurie's aging, since it also evokes the artist Eliot in his twenties, who prematurely created the persona of the aging Prufrock as a mask. Prufrock, who sees "the spiritual impotence" surrounding him but is "powerless to act upon" his "longings to unite the physical and spiritual realms" (Manganaro 85), clearly parallels not only the Lurie who is unable to defend his daughter from her assailants, but also the one whose action is finally limited to profound inertia in waiting. Even Lurie's chiastic thought processes find their equivalent in Prufrock's vain attempts to comfort himself for his inaction with the mantra-like "there will be time," only to find that reversals—chiastic movement, if you like—are immanent to his concept of time: "In a minute there is time / For decisions and revisions which a minute will reverse." As opposed to Romanticism, here the artistic imagination offers as much of an escape from this ostensible action of moving back and forth as it poses a threat: "We have lingered in the chambers of the sea / By sea-girls wreathed with seaweed red and brown / Till human voices wake us, and we drown." The

Eliot allusion—just like the Dostoevskian—undermines the very idea of Lurie's commitment to a final credo, with the added bonus of targeting Romantic notions of art and the artist with shattering irony, while highlighting how central negative stereotypes of old age are to the European literary tradition.

Apparently, Coetzee's allusion to another definitive figure of modernism, W. B. Yeats, embodies a strong counterpoint to the implications of the "Prufrock" reference. That is, Stewart and Manson, who anchor their comparative analysis of Cormac McCarthy's *No Country for Old Men* and *Disgrace* in the two novels' shared Yeatsian intertext, "Sailing to Byzantium" (1927), start out from the premise that the poem is an element and continuation of the Romantic tradition. Thus they equate reaching Byzantium with achieving transcendence in the Romantic context (160-62). [10] Ultimately, they recognize Lurie's changed purpose with his opera rather than its contents as an indication that he might still be able to develop. They argue that abandoning the idea of using his opera for a triumphant return to society (177-79), just like his evolving

---

10 Stewart and Manson emphasize the parallel between the artist-speaker of Yeats's poem and Lurie, the writer of an opera about Byron, though they argue that his "connection to Yeats's speaker is mostly ironic, since David's art is a failure, at least in the traditional terms" (161). Nonetheless, in their reading Lurie does change and the critics directly connect his limited development with the Yeatsian allusion: they interpret *lösung* as the (Freudian) sublimation of the self (and desire) in art and identify it with achieving transcendence as artistic re-creation of the self in Byzantium (180). See: "What is being asked for is, in fact, Lösung (German always to hand with an appropriately blank abstraction): sublimation, as alcohol is sublimed from water, leaving no residue, no aftertaste" (Coetzee, *Disgrace* 142). The term translates into English as "solution," both as in the Nazis' Final Solution (Endlösung), to which *Disgrace* clearly alludes apropos of the killing of sick, old, unneeded dogs, and as in dissolving solid material in liquid. It is this second meaning that Lurie rephrases as sublimation, to pun on both Freudian terminology and a notion central to Romanticism.

empathy for the euthanized dogs (180), signifies a potential to move beyond thinking and acting only in terms of the self and thereby "to begin to overcome his disgrace and to begin the difficult task of aging gracefully" (181). That is, the quotation towards the end of the narrative "The young in one another's arms, heedless, engrossed in the sensual music. No country, this, for old men" (190) [11] can be read as the clue to the final word in *Disgrace* about Lurie's moderately successful *Bildung*, yet again rooted in the Romantic tradition through "Sailing to Byzantium." The very fact, however, that in chronological terms this reading presupposes a major step backwards to Romantic solutions from the modernist anxieties and skepticism implied by the allusions to "Prufrock" and *Devils*, which would be yet another blatant example of Lurie's thoughts doubling back on themselves, should raise at least some suspicions. So should the context of the allusion: it directly follows Lurie's meditations—quoted previously at some length—on the uniform negative literary images of old men's sexuality (Coetzee, *Disgrace* 190), which have been shown to be stereotypical and of which the Yeatsian representation, by implication, can be exemplary.

Upon closer inspection, the Yeatsian intertext as a Romantic final word to Lurie's dilemma and a key text of his development proves to be an odd choice, indeed. As the context of the almost verbatim quote suggests, the poem—instead of moving away from them—to a large extent reiterates those views on old age that determine Lurie's self-image right from the start: it generalizes that "[a]n aged man is but a paltry thing, / A tattered coat upon a stick" and envisions a speaker desperate to be liberated from his body, which is seen as

---

11 See "That is no country for old men. The young / In one another's arms, . . . Caught in that sensual music" (Yeats).

animalistic and as the cause of his approaching demise (compare "the threat of animality" mentioned among the root causes of ageism in middle-aged people): "Consume my heart away; sick with desire / And fastened to a dying animal / It knows not what it is." As far as the poem offers art as a solution to that problem, the art the speaker prefers is not necessarily associated either with transcendence or with Romanticism. Some readings of the poem suggest that the world of "transcendent order" is "rejected" by the speaker in preference for the "golden bird"—"a worldly artefact of time"—in a culture that keeps the sacred and the profane in an "aesthetic balance" (Vendler 82-83). The bird itself has been linked with "Modernist toys" due to its automatic quality (Albright 72), rather than the heritage of Romanticism. The straightforward identification of Byzantium (and art) with transcendence is also undermined by the companion poem, "Byzantium" (1932). There again, as Helen Vendler argues, the speaker turns his back on a disembodied existence and "the poem ends in an eternal standoff" (93) as a result of the speaker's rejection of a final choice. This seems to be consistent with Margaret Mills Harper's characterization of Yeats, the poet as "a continually moving figure, perhaps turning or spinning rather than moving in a single direction, to indicate that movement is not necessarily progress" (145). The contradictory readings of "Sailing to Byzantium" suggest that instead of following a trajectory of development—either within the context of Romanticism or taking Lurie from Romanticism to Modernism—Lurie's career is associated with ambiguities, doubts, indecisions, and going through the motions of progress, yet not achieving it.

Such an implication of indeterminacy is also confirmed by another, though this time vague, Yeatsian allusion in *Disgrace*:

the repeated evocations of "Leda and the Swan" (1923). [12] In Yeats's poem the word "shudder" signifies Zeus's definitive sexual act, a beginning which coincides with the end in this mythic vision and brings about the momentary collapse of time ("A shudder in the loins engenders there / The broken wall, the burning roof and tower / And Agamemnon dead"). In *Disgrace* shudder appears—apart from the previously quoted excerpt, which forms a heavily ironic contrast with the later instances, though also links it to a sexual context—twice with reference to Lurie's desire for Melanie: "on the pillion, [she] sits with knees wide apart, pelvis arched. A quick shudder of lust tugs him" (35) and "[a]gain it runs through him: a light shudder of voluptuousness" (78). The second occurrence is triggered by a memory only, resulting in a collapse of time in this text, as well: the fateful beginning, Lurie's desire for Melanie, lives on in the present. Though it has brought Lurie's career to an end, the sensual experience itself is not willing to pass into oblivion.

---

12 The relevance of the mythic narrative to the discussion of *Disgrace* is beyond doubt, see the passage where "they [Lurie's students] might as well have been hatched from eggs yesterday" (Coetzee, *Disgrace* 32) and a dialogue between Lurie and his daughter which calls readers' attention to the unusual name one of the rapists bears: "'Not Mncedisi? Not Nqabayakhe? Nothing unpronounceable, just Pollux?'—'P-O-L-L-U-X. And David, can we have some relief from that terrible irony of yours?'" (200). These excerpts clearly evoke one of the most archetypal rape narratives in European culture as an interpretative context of the rape narratives in *Disgrace*. In contrast, evidence for the presence of the Yeatsian version seems to be rather circumstantial. One might argue that between them the emphatic allusions to the myth and Yeats—though not to "Leda and the Swan"—indirectly recall the memorable sonnet, as well. Given the fact that the other allusions discussed here testify to the generally fragmentary nature of Coetzee's quotations, which are almost never exact ones, any trace of the Yeatsian "Leda and the Swan" in *Disgrace* can suffice to evoke the poem. In my reading, the relatively rarely used word "shudder," appearing in a distinctly sexual context, is such a trace. The number of repetitions and the similar contexts do not only establish the significance of this motif, but also point towards the Yeatsian sonnet as its potential source.

Thus, this Yeatsian intertext brings into relief a collapse of binaries, which results in the impossibility of providing unambiguous solutions for the dilemmas proposed. This is also underpinned by the poem's open ending, the rhetorical question closing Yeats's famously ambiguous sonnet on history, colonization, and also poetic creation. Strengthening the implications detailed above, "Leda and the Swan" also explicitly introduces into Coetzee's narrative the cyclicality of mythic time and thus overtly raises the possibility of a repetitive plot structure.

Repetition, or rather eternal return, is a key element to the (post)modernist intertext of *Disgrace*, which again challenges the discourse of art in general as "saving grace," evoking Samuel Beckett's *Waiting for Godot* (1953). [13] In "Sailing to Byzantium," Yeats does represent art as the way out from the impasse of inevitable aging and death, and *Disgrace* repeats the same gesture. As Attridge highlights in his interpretation of an often-quoted excerpt of the novel's closing chapter, the text associates a potentially adequate discourse to address the issue with a moment of grace through art (113):

His hopes must be more temperate: that somewhere amidst the welter of sound there will dart up, like a bird, a single authentic note of immortal longing. As for recognizing it, he

---

13 Samuel Beckett's profound influence on Coetzee is a matter of critical consensus, the details of which would exceed the limitations of a footnote— or of an article, for that matter. See, for example, Kannemeyer 149-52. Let it suffice to recall that for Coetzee Beckett "was an artist possessed by a vision of life without consolation or dignity or promise of grace, in the face of which our only duty—inexplicable and futile of attainment, but a duty nonetheless—is not to lie to ourselves" (qtd. in Kannemeyer 572). Beckettian waiting is a most prominent motif, for example, in *Waiting for the Barbarians*, but elements of a desolate scenery and futile, repetitive human action also associate other Coetzee texts with *Waiting for Godot*, notably *Foe*.

will leave that to the scholars of the future, if there are still scholars by then. For he will not hear the note himself, when it comes, if it comes—he knows too much about art and the ways of art to expect that. (Coetzee, *Disgrace* 214)

Nonetheless, the passage immediately brackets this possibility by displacing that moment (of grace) into an indefinite future beyond the scope of one's own lifetime and consciousness. In that sense, Lurie seems to hope against hope, clinging to a promise like Beckett's Everyman-like characters in *Godot.* Indeed, Lurie's final fate of waiting in a desolate courtyard for the birth of his grandchild, the faint promise of a (better) future and a new relationship with his daughter, and his whiling away time with music on a childish banjo might in themselves remind readers of Beckettian waiting on an almost barren stage. Especially so, because *Disgrace* has earlier evoked a vision of life as infinite waiting (for a child) through Lucy's words, which first refer to finding out whether she is pregnant but then trail off into a seemingly irrational comment on eternal waiting: "Science has not yet put a limit on how long one has to wait. For ever, maybe" (125). [14] Lurie has called his life in the provinces and helping out in the animal clinic a punishment of indefinite end, a "disgrace without term" (172), which also amplifies the Beckettian resonances of his final state. This indirect evocation of *Waiting for Godot* is actually also the culmination and combination of the earlier references to Eliot and Yeats. Not only can the bird be conclusively interpreted as

---

14 Seeing life as infinite waiting is not alien to the Yeatsian paradigm, either. See his proverbial observation that "life is a long preparation for something that never happens," which actually appears in *Reveries over Childhood and Youth* as "all life weighed in the scales of my own life seems to me a preparation for something that never happens" (XXXIII). I wish to express my appreciation to Mária Kurdi for drawing my attention to this parallel.

a version of Yeats's golden bird, but also the descriptions of the kind of music Lurie is writing at the end of the novel evoke both Yeats and Eliot as well as the chiastic movement of their "decisions and revisions." The "music itself . . . , the voice that strains to soar away from the ludicrous instrument but is continually reined back, like a fish on the line" (184-85), on the one hand, recalls Yeats's "[t]he salmon-falls, the mackerel-crowded seas, / Fish, flesh, or fowl" in "Sailing to Byzantium." On the other hand, because of its strange back and forth movement it is described as forming a "crablike motif" (Coetzee, *Disgrace* 186), which is loosely reminiscent of the crab motif in the "Love Song," that is, of Prufrock's desperate cry: "I should have been a pair of ragged claws / Scuttling across the floors of silent seas." It is in a skeptical spirit inspired by both Romanticism and his modernist masters that Lurie is "trying to accept disgrace" as his "state of being" (Coetzee, *Disgrace* 172).

He is trying, but does he accept it? Or does he accept it unconditionally? True to the metatextual implications of its Dostoevskian intertext, *Disgrace* ends, in my opinion, with a gesture that in yet another modernist context doubles back on the above-quoted humble acceptance of aging and death, confirms an ongoing preoccupation with the finite nature of allotted human life-time, and rejects the vision of patient infinite waiting as a version of "aging gracefully." The novel's ending, where Lurie symbolically gives up a young dog for *lösung*—one that he feels particularly attached to and could probably keep alive for one more week—has invited various interpretations in Coetzee criticism. So far, however, to the best of my knowledge, no special significance has been attached to the facts that the dog is number twenty-four on the list of those to be exterminated that day, and the closing chapter bears the same number. Taken as a banal reference to the twenty-four hours of the day, the number can be seen as an almost redundant confirmation of the finite nature of the text—of its inevitable ending, together with the dog's life and through that, metaphorically, Lurie's own. [15] This strong emphasis on the limitations of time contradicts the acceptance of infinite waiting, indeterminate disgrace and expresses a preference for putting an end to it even as an act of mercy, rather than prolonging suffering indefinitely. The gesture can be interpreted as a rebellion which—by this time not really surprisingly—takes the reader back to the beginning of the novel and Lurie's self-image as a Romantic figure. This time, however, it appears in the context of the modernist novelistic tradition: modernism is associated with the one-day novel, with the condensation of subjective life-experience ostensibly into the objective timespan of one single day. This is what the

---

15 Through the leitmotif of disgrace, Coetzee builds up a consistent parallel between rejected, victimized dogs and marginalized humans—Lurie and his daughter—in the new South Africa. That culminates in Lucy's final comparison of her condition and status to a dog's: "'Yes, I agree, it is humiliating. But perhaps that is a good point to start from again. Perhaps that is what I must learn to accept. To start at ground level. With nothing. . . . No cards, no weapons, no property, no rights, no dignity.' [David:] 'Like a dog.' [Lucy:] 'Yes, like a dog'" (*Disgrace* 203). Lucy's final description of dispossession could just as well apply to her father, whose empathy for disowned and later euthanized dogs thus has a somewhat narcissistic aspect to it: he feels for them, among others, because they suffer a fate similar to his. The parallel seems to be more apt in Lurie's case because of his strong sense of being redundant and useless and his pessimistic view of having only one thing to look forward to: death. Consequently, offering up the music-loving dog for *lösung* gives a reading of the dog metaphor diametrically opposed to Lucy's in its tone and attitudes. Lucy's words, at the same time, widen the scope of the dog metaphor and thus the scope of disgrace, whether it refers to being victimized, aging, or dying. In the narrower sense, the trope includes all white South Africans, regardless of their physical age, sex, or sexual orientation, while in the wider sense her words call for an acceptance of the disgrace of aging and dying as the general human condition.

twenty-four "hours" of the chapters also evoke: they might make up only one day, after which another one begins, equally rich in "decisions and revisions" in an endless (mythic?) cycle of repetitions. Indeed, after the allusion to cyclical time through Yeats and the day as a reference unit in repetitive structures through Beckett's play, [16] the twenty-four chapters are only one among the multiple indications that Lurie's narrative is conceivable in terms of returns rather than progress.

Conclusion

A closer look at the non-Romantic intertexts of *Disgrace* can inform the novel's interpretation in two closely intertwined ways and thereby confirm readings which—instead of an optimistic, humanist narrative of development and progress— emphasize Coetzee's tendency of "doubling the point," a phrase rich in Dostoevskian overtones. [17] That is, tracing down those

---

16 Apart from the well-known structure of *Waiting for Godot*, *Endgame* and Clov's particular "definition" for yesterday—and therefore all days—might also be relevant here: "HAMM. 'Yesterday! What does that mean? Yesterday!' / CLOV. 'That means that bloody awful day, long ago, before this bloody awful day'" (Beckett 28). I wish to express my appreciation to Mária Kurdi for bringing this similarity to my attention.

17 Coetzee's *Doubling the Point: Essays and Interviews* includes his insightful reading of *Devils* in "Confession and Double Thoughts: Tolstoy, Rousseau, Dostoevsky." He borrows the title of that essay from Dostoevsky's *The Idiot* and identifies double thoughts with a "*doubling back* of thought" (222, emphasis in the original). It is in the context of this mechanism that he interprets the thought processes of major Dostoevskian characters, including Stavrogin— and his confession—in *Devils*. Most importantly, he sees Dostoevsky as associating "true confession" or "self-truth" with "faith and grace" (230-31). Interpreting Coetzee's essay in the light of his later comments, Rachel Lawlan comes to the conclusion that Coetzee's contrast of two kinds of representations of confession (Tolstoy's vs. Dostoevsky's) embodies two conflicting voices and desires in Coetzee himself: those of "cynicism and grace." In her view, Coetzee "affiliates" himself to Dostoevsky because he is also "obsessed with the possibility of transcendence over self-doubt and the infinite regress of double thought" (140-41).

allusions first of all strengthens an aspect of the focalizer's unreliability, which is especially hard to overcome: the stereotypical, ageist nature of his discourse, which draws on established (literary) discourses. Directed largely against himself, this bias is something readers might find extremely difficult to distance themselves from, because it is fed by the fear of one's own inevitable death, against which the focalizer, or rather the novel, does not—cannot—offer any unquestionable "cultural worldviews" as protection. The Romantic solution, countering the fear of death by finding transcendence and grace through art, is compromised by the non-Romantic allusions, which, in their turn, can offer a much more skeptical vision. This results at the close of *Disgrace* in the parallel presence of Romantic visions and the skeptical solution of placing the moment of grace beyond the limits of one's own lifetime and consciousness. Lurie's stereotypical conception of himself and his depressing vision of post-apartheid South Africa are thus enveloped in a highly intellectual discourse which partly masks its own roots in the self-same historical context by redirecting attention to universal and ultimate issues of passing time and mortality. It provokes empathy from readers regardless of the narrative's implicit sexist and racist biases and can foster their acceptance of Lurie's various judgments at face value. Furthermore, the intertexts from outside Romanticism (predominantly from Dostoevsky and Eliot) highlight the chiastic thought processes associated with the narrative consciousness, which discredit all of Lurie's attempts to find meaning or solace for what he is facing—be it old age or life in post-apartheid South Africa—in already existing discourses. That does not mean, to return to Attridge's point, that *Disgrace* does not represent the proposed and at the same time rejected solutions—in this case, art in a

Yeatsian context—as bearers of "value" (109). Nevertheless, the simultaneous presence of various contradictory literary legacies largely contributes to the hardly resistible bleakness of the aging artist's vision in *Disgrace*. They concurrently suggest Lurie's constantly shifting allegiances within a circle of views marked out by pre-existent discourses, a process of endless Beckettian repetitions, in which glimpses of a final solution, impressions of Lurie's finding a place for himself in "this country," can always prove to be momentary.

Note

The research was funded by the EFOP-3.6.1-16-2016-00001 grant ("Complex improvement of research capacities and services at Eszterházy Károly University").

Works Cited

Albright, Daniel. "Yeats and Modernism." Howes and Kelly 59-76.

Attridge, Derek. "Age of Bronze, State of Grace: Music and Dogs in Coetzee's *Disgrace.*" *Novel* 34.1 (Autumn 2000): 98-121. *JSTOR.* Web. 30 Apr. 2018.

Ayalon, Liat, and Clemens Tesch-Römer. "Introduction to the Section: Ageism-Concept and Origins." Ayalon and Tesch-Römer 1-10.

---, ed. *Contemporary Perspectives on Ageism.* Cham: Springer Open, 2018.

Beard, Margot. "Lessons from the Dead Masters: Wordsworth and Byron in J. M. Coetzee's *Disgrace.*" *English in Africa* 34.1 (May 2007): 59-77. *JSTOR.* Web. 30 Apr. 2018.

Beckett, Samuel. *Endgame.* London: Faber and Faber, 2009.

Chinitz, David E., ed. *A Companion to T. S. Eliot.* Chichester: Wiley-Blackwell, 2009.

FICTION

Coetzee, J. M. "Confession and Double Thoughts: Tolstoy, Rousseau, Dostoevsky." *Comparative Literature* 37.3 (1985): 193-232. *JSTOR*. 30 Apr. 2018.

---. *Disgrace*. London: Vintage, 1999.

---. *Doubling the Point: Essays and Interviews*. Ed. David Atwell. Cambridge, MA: Harvard University Press, 1992.

---. "He and His Man." Nobel Lecture. 2003. *NobelPrize.org*. Nobel Media AB 2019. Web. 7 Apr. 2019.

Dostoevsky, F. M. *Devils*. Trans. M. R. Katz. Oxford: Oxford University Press. 1958.

Eliot, T. S. *Prufrock and Other Observations: Poems*. New York: A. A. Knopf, 1920. *Bartleby.com*. Web. 30 Apr. 2018.

Gewirtz-Meydan, Ateret, Trish Hafford-Letchfeld, Yael Benyamini, Amanda Phelan, Jeanne Jackson, and Liat Ayalon. "Ageism and Sexuality." Ayalon and Tesch-Römer 149-62.

Howes, Marjorie, and John Kelly, ed. *The Cambridge Companion to W. B. Yeats*. Cambridge: Cambridge University Press, 2006.

Hutcheon, Linda. *A Poetics of Postmodernism*. 1988. New York: Routledge, 2004. Taylor and Francis e-Library edition. Ebook.

Kannemeyer, J. C. *J. M. Coetzee: A Life in Writing*. Trans. Michiel Heyns. London: Scribe, 2013.

Kossew, S. "The Politics of Shame and Redemption in J. M. Coetzee's *Disgrace*." *Research in African Literatures* 34.2 (2003): 155-62. *EBSCO*. Web. 30 Apr. 2018.

Kroó, Katalin. "From Plato's Myth of the Golden Age in *Statesman* to Dostoevsky's *Devils*." *Russian Text (19th Century) and Antiquity*. Ed. Katalin Kroó and Peter Torop. Budapest: L'Harmattan, 2008. 355-91.

Lawlan, Rachel. *"The Master of Petersburg*: Confession and

Double Thoughts in Coetzee and Dostoevsky." *ARIEL: A Review of International English Literature* 29.2 (1998): 131-57. Web. 30 Apr. 2018.

Lev, Sagit, Susanne Wurm, and Liat Ayalon. "Origins of Ageism at the Individual Level." Ayalon and Tesch-Römer 51-72.

Manganaro, Marc. "Mind, Myth, and Culture: Eliot and Anthropology." Chinitz 79-90.

Marais, Mike. "J. M. Coetzee's *Disgrace* and the Task of the Imagination." *Journal of Modern Literature* 29.2 (Winter 2006): 75-93. *JSTOR*. Web. 30 Apr. 2018.

Mardorossian, Carine M. "Rape and the Violence of Representation in J. M. Coetzee's *Disgrace*." *Research in African Literatures* 42.4 (Winter 2011): 72-83. *JSTOR*. Web. 30 Apr. 2018.

---. *Secretary of the Invisible*. Amsterdam: Rodopi, 2009.

---. "Violence, Postcolonial Fiction, and the Limits of Sympathy." *Studies in the Novel* 43.1 (Spring 2011): 94-114. *JSTOR*. Web. 30 Apr. 2018.

Mills Harper, Margaret. "Yeats and the Occult." Howes and Kelly 144-167.

Reichmann, Angelika. "Stavrogin's Crime and Punishment Revisited: Dostoevskian Intertexts in J. M. Coetzee's *Disgrace* (1999)." *Mundo Eslavo* 16 (2017): 207-15. Web. 30 Apr. 2018.

Shiovitz-Ezra, Sharon, Jonathan Shemesh, and Mary McDonnell/Naughton. "Pathways from Ageism to Loneliness." Ayalon and Tesch-Römer 131-47.

Stewart, Robert Scott, and Michael Manson. "Misplaced Men: Aging and Change in Coetzee's *Disgrace* and McCarthy's *No Country for Old Men*." *Janus Head* 14.2 (Winter 2015): 159-83. Web. 30 Apr. 2018.

Vendler, Helen. "The Later Poetry." Howes and Kelly 77-100.

Veres, Ottilia. Colonial Encounters in J. M. Coetzee's Early Fiction: Two Tropes of Intersubjectivity. Dissertation. University of Debrecen, 2017. *Debreceni Egyetem Elektronikus Archívum.* Web. 7 Apr. 2018.

Yeats, W. B. *Reveries over Childhood and Youth: The Collected Works of W. B. Yeats.* Vol. 3. Ed. William O'Donnell and Douglas Archibald. New York: Scribner, 1999. Ebook.

---. "Sailing to Byzantium." *The Poems of W. B. Yeats: A New Edition.* Ed. Richard J. Finneran. London: Macmillan, 1933. *The Poetry Foundation.* Web. 27 May 2019.

Достоевский, Ф. М. *Бесы-Роман в трех частях. Бесы-Антология русской критики* [Devils—Novel in Three Parts. Devils—Anthology of Russian Literary Criticism]. Ed. Л. И. Сараскина. Москва: Согласие, 1996. 5-434.

Кроо, Каталин. *«Творческое слово» Ф. М. Достоевского: Герой, текст, интертекст* [F. M. Dostoevsky's "Creative Word": Hero, Text, Intertext]. Москва: Академический Проект, 2005.

10.2478/9788367405423-014

"Life Is a Terminal Illness": The War against Time and Aging in David Mitchell's *The Bone Clocks*
Noémi Albert

David Mitchell's *The Bone Clocks* (2014) encompasses an extended web of interconnected, carefully balanced topics, all converging on the central theme of aging with a focus on the main character, Holly Sykes, who brings together the novel's six separate chapters and their individual narrators. The chapters follow Holly from adolescence into old age in chronological order, revealing a fairly traditional life cycle invigorated with love, disappointment, betrayal, partnership, loss, children, and, finally, grandchildren. Two distinct plotlines, however, also become intertwined with the traditional one: namely, a fantastic story of two warring factions of quasi-immortals and the narrative of climate change that ultimately leads to "Endarkenment," an Apocalypse that occurs during the life of Holly Sykes.

The novel begins with scenes introducing the adolescent Holly, who decides to move in with her much older lover. After her plans have fallen through (she catches her lover in bed with her best friend), Holly decides to run away. The very act of her escape will later prove to be essential for several reasons: first, her schoolmate Ed Brubeck, who helps her through those few homeless days, later becomes a famous war correspondent and the father of Holly's daughter. Second, during her time away, her younger brother Jacko disappears mysteriously, which, she believes, happens because she abandoned him. Third, during her wanderings Holly meets a small old lady, Esther Little, who seeks asylum in exchange for some tea. All these events are enveloped in mystery, and at first no connection can be discerned among them. The connecting thread gradually develops through the introduction of the fantastic world of atemporal beings, who are almost immortal creatures forming two factions. The Horologists (like Esther Little and Jacko), through their centuries-long existence, save young lives by inhabiting them at death and thus preserving their identities. The Anchorites, by contrast, resort to murder in order to extract the souls of human beings, which help them keep their youth. One of the novel's main plotlines follows these two warring groups, with Holly Sykes assuming a central role, since she will be the one to win the war for the Horologists.

The constant war between the Horologists and the Anchorites and, most importantly, their very adverse relationship with humans—who are symbolically called "bone clocks"—present a complex picture about contemporary society's relation to old age. The central concept—namely eternal life—through either continuous rebirth or feasting on extraordinary souls, reflects on humanity's fight against aging. The issue Mitchell raises here pertains to the age-old question whether eternal life is attainable and, if it is, what it would be like. Furthermore, the name given to human beings has a rather pejorative connotation, underlining the superiority of the pseudo-immortal creatures. The joining of the images of bones and clocks emphasizes the mortality of humankind and its constant race against time.

The six distinct chapters focus on separate years, following a chronological order that encompasses the life of Holly Sykes. Thus the process of growing up and getting older is captured through small leaps throughout the decades subtly leading not only to Holly's aging self as a wrinkled old lady, but also to the Apocalypse. As time goes by in the various subplots gradually unfolding in the novel, not only is Holly getting old, but so is all of humankind, ultimately leading to "Endarkenment," an age where all previous commodities become unattainable and humanity is on the brink of extinction. This subplot of the Apocalypse gives a new twist to the issue of aging, expanding the personal story into a universal one.

The novel's first and last chapters, "A Hot Spell, 1984" and "Sheep's Head, 2043" feature Holly Sykes as their narrator, with the first one presenting her as a runaway teenager and the last one as a grandmother struggling to save her grandchildren in the era of "Endarkenment." The second part, "Myrrh Is Mine, Its Bitter Perfume, 1991" is narrated by a Cambridge undergraduate, Hugo Lamb, spending Christmas with his parents and New Year's Eve with some friends at a Swiss ski resort (1991-92). Part three, titled "The Wedding Bash, 2004," is recounted from the perspective of war correspondent Ed Brubeck, Holly's partner. The next part ("Crispin Hershey's Lonely Planet, 2015") features a novelist previously proclaimed the *enfant terrible* of British literature, who gradually gets immersed into the both mundane and fantastic life of Holly Sykes. Finally, part five, "An Horologist's Labyrinth, 2025" relates in detail the war going on between the two immortal factions, drawing in both Holly and her brother, the latter believed to be missing throughout the novel. The six disparate chapters offer a complex view on the life of the protagonist and her mortality, which stands in contrast to the immortality of the atemporal creatures.

The novel introduces three distinct but tightly connected issues, the aging self, the plot of the quasi-immortal factions, and the process of Endarkenment (which marks the aging of civilization), to probe the aging process itself and society's reaction and relation to it, that is, ageism. Mitchell's novel—blending realism with the fantastic—is an intricate statement about one of the most crucial questions concerning humankind, that of aging.

Time and mortality

The field of psychological aging may be characterized as "focusing on manifest changes or transformations that occur in human and animal behaviour related to length of life" (Birren and Schroots 3) and Mitchell's novel builds upon a meticulous investigation of one life, through depicting its "changes, transformations, and transitions" (Dixon 7), pitted against other lives.

All the different threads converge on the human preoccupation with temporality and mortality. The novel balances both death and the prospect of eternal life, ultimately becoming, as Bill Ott remarks, "a meditation on mortality, of course, but also on the hazards of immortality and the perils of power" (25). Temporality itself gradually becomes a quasi-character, providing an insight into mortal lives, primarily into the life of Holly Sykes. The passing of time captures the duality of change (through Holly) and immutability (through the atemporals).

Patrick O'Donnell emphasizes Holly's preoccupation with temporality: "A complex network of stories that circulate around Holly's involvement with larger historical, temporal, and cosmological forces, the novel alternates between fantasy and realism in projecting chronoscapes where the future of the planet is at stake" (3). Indeed, the subplot, centering on the aforementioned "invisible war" between two immortal factions, not only focuses on the prospects of immortality, but also sheds a new light on humanity and mortality as we know them.

The two distinct atemporal factions embody contrasting aspects of temporality. Horologists transmigrate, they die but after forty-nine days wake up in the body of a sick child, whom they actually resurrect through entering. This act entails members of the group changing appearance every few decades. The abandonment of a body, however, does not result in erasure, since each Horologist preserves the personality, memories, and the soul of their former hosts. Consequently, as Mitchell remarks in an interview, "their viewpoint is time's viewpoint" (Naimon 53); that is, they encompass the duality of change and immutability that characterizes the concept of time in the novel.

The Horologists have a rather benevolent relation to mortals, while the Anchorites need to make actual sacrifices in order to keep their youth. They never change their bodies, their strength lies in keeping themselves eternally young and powerful with the help of special human souls that they "decant" into black wine, which they drink ritualistically. I agree with Joseph Metz, who contends that the two groups are "allegories of two modes or models of dealing with time, history, and memory" (123), or, ultimately, "two theories of the archive" (123). The Horologists function as archivists preserving the memory of and every human trait connected to the person they inhabit, thus fulfilling the work of a historian, whereas the Anchorites are "anti-historians" (Metz 123), since they incorporate the decanted souls just like a black hole that engulfs everything. Thus the war is fought between two views on history as well as on identity: one faction celebrates multiplicity, an amalgam of different genders, races, social classes, whereas the other fights for the preservation of a singular identity by and through the destruction of human beings. In an interview conducted by Paul A. Harris, Mitchell emphasizes that in the novel the two immortal factions and their confrontation symbolize the ambiguous nature of time itself. As he states, time is both "the great enabler of being" and "a slow-burning 'decay bomb'" (8), or: "what stops everything happening all at once" as well as "what allows everything to happen" (9). Ultimately it is both our ally and enemy (Harris 9), enabling and hindering individuals at the same time. Conversely, the subject's relation to time in the novel is multifarious, emphasizing the inherently paradoxical nature of human life and mortality itself.

The novel's highly metaphoric title is a testament to the central view just outlined. "The Bone Clocks," on the first level of interpretation, comes from the atemporals' rather ironic and disdainful appellation for mortal beings. Nevertheless, the title also bears hints of melancholy and even a certain sense of futility, since the bones imply the fast approach of death, underlined by the image of the clocks. In the last chapter of the novel, the title's metaphoric field further expands with the image of an Apocalypse, with decaying bodies, the disappearance of civilization, the spread of diseases and death across the globe, human beings "ticking towards death from starvation, Ebola, widespread violence, ecological catastrophe or suicide pills" (Harris-Birtill 134).

Although Carol T. Christ claims that the novel's fantasy framework "sits uncomfortably with its human drama" (157), I would argue that there is a conscious and informed choice behind the dualism employed throughout the novel, which is to provide a more complex perspective on both aging and agelessness, on the one hand, and on the dying individual and the dying world, on the other. The three types of beings who inhabit the novel's complex world stand for three different temporalities: the first one is a rather short timespan that mortal beings are allowed to spend in the world; the second temporality is represented by the Anchorites, who follow the philosophy of "live indefinitely as long as you can find the prey"; and finally the Horologists, who, as Mitchell says, have a "Serial Repeater" timescale (Harris 14). Accordingly, the time structure of the novel is always tripartite, providing intermingling temporalities that continuously exert their power over each other.

For instance, a future Anchorite (at this point still a mortal) formulates his theory of aging while witnessing old age from close up. "You'd think old age was a criminal offense, not a destination we're all heading to" (119), claims a disappointed nurse who works in the nursing home where Hugo Lamb, the narrator of the second part, occasionally visits. Her disappointment stems from her witnessing the conscious abandonment of the elderly by their children. The seemingly amiable and good-natured young student, however, does not share the nurse's opinion. On the contrary, he divulges to readers that "our culture's coping strategy towards death is to bury it under consumerism and Samsara, that the Riverside Villas of the world are screens that enable this self-deception, and that the elderly *are* guilty: guilty of proving to us that our willful myopia about death is exactly that" (119). His words succinctly capture twenty-first-century society's general relation to the elderly and to the process of aging itself, which, although it should be seen as natural, is met with restraint and contempt.

The character of Hugo Lamb illustrates why *The Bone Clocks* might be identified as a sort of "midlife crisis book" (Morgan). His ideas about old age go beyond society's general fear of aging and point towards (and at the same time explain) his subsequent choice to join the Anchorites of the Dusk Chapel of the Blind Cathar of the Thomasite Monastery of Sidelhorn Pass. Mitchell describes what the Anchorites can offer as a "Faustian pact," which ultimately serves to bring to our notice the "need to come to a working accommodation with aging" (Morgan), since Hugo purports to deal with aging differently than through fear and loathing. In an interview, Mitchell claims that the reason for focusing on this issue was not philosophical, but rather connected to his becoming middle-aged: "My relationship to mortality needs a reboot. . . . Mortality is no longer an abstract thing over the horizon anymore. It's in your kneecaps, it's in your back, it's in your lungs" (Naimon 54). Hugo Lamb is approached by Imaculée Constantin, an Anchorite, while contemplating Rubens's *Adoration of the Magi*, a scene that has fascinated numerous great artists throughout time, since it evokes the birth of Jesus, who is surrounded by the old kings coming to worship him. The clash between generations is visible in all renderings; Rubens captured it through a grey-bearded king leaning towards the newborn, while baby Jesus is above him, holding out his hands towards the old man. The painting not only represents Jesus's role as mankind's Prince, but it also pinpoints the natural cycle of life, children taking the place of their elders.

Imaculée Constantin's tentative efforts to persuade Hugo Lamb to join the Anchorites are all the more suggestive and powerful as they are standing in front of this masterpiece. Facing mortality captured in paint, Ms. Constantin offers the young student "a form of power that allows one to defer death in perpetuity" (99). She also indicates that those possessing this power can keep their youth intact. She further intensifies his human fears of mortality, claiming that death "is inscribed in your cellular structure" (99), and it needs to be fought like an illness. The power Constantin describes lies in the preservation of "the singularity of the individual," to use O'Donnell's words

(164), with the act of preservation countervailing the passing of time. This moment serves as a reminder of humankind's inherent fears and conceptions about aging, to dismantle them gradually. The novel utilizes numerous methods to approach humankind's relation to mortality, and religion seems to be one of them. There is a rich composite of religious symbols and fantasy interwoven into the narrative. With allusions such as Cross, Lamb, and Bishop for names, Allhallows-on-Sea, St. Mary Hoo, and Eastchurch for place names, as Pico Iyer argues, "we're in the realm of hyper-realism and half-religious allegory all at once." These two distinct modes are constantly juxtaposed, sometimes through disturbing images, such as the following: "I find my lover's crucifix among her boingy curls. I hold the Son of God in my mouth, and imagine him dissolving on my tongue" (123). Lamb's train of thought immediately leads him to contemplate sex and immortality, reaching the conclusion that "[s]ex may be the antidote to death but it offers life everlasting only to the species, not the individual" (123). Consequently, sex is not satisfactory for the egotistical young man; his sole dream is the preservation of his own youth and personality, no matter the cost.

The relationship between religion and the Anchorites' way of preserving themselves, also evident in this example, is explained by Mitchell in the interview given to Paul Harris where he presents religion as one of four distinct methods usually employed by human beings to somehow deal with the approach of death. Mitchell responds: "Most sects of most of the world's religions issue passports to an afterlife in return for an unwavering faith in that sect's precepts" ("Laboratory" 12). This view provides solace for believers who then do not have to fear the demise of their selves, or souls.

O'Donnell recognizes in "the scandalous address to Mariangela's crucifix . . . the corporeal basis of Christianity to which Mitchell draws our attention throughout his novels" (8)—pointing to the corporeality that underlies each aspect of *The Bone Clocks*, most accentuated in the duality of the atemporal factions. The maddening struggle to maintain one's perfect looks and youth stands in contrast to the quasi-immortal beings that every couple of decades die just to come back in the body of different persons, thus enriching the row of faces, but at the same time that of selves, too.

"Life is a terminal illness" (167), Hugo concludes upon witnessing the elderly in the nursing home. Throughout his narrative the reader encounters explicit and rather disturbing descriptions of deaths happening around Hugo as a child and later as a young boy, such as the death of his dog, Twix, when he was seven, all brought side by side in his mind by the death of his grandfather, about which all he says is: "Who is spared love is spared grief" (152). Thus it seems that Hugo is like a sociopath incapable of feeling grief. Death and mortality interest him in a different way: "Wouldn't it be freaky if we saw the dead in the chairs opposite?" (155), he asks Holly Sykes while sitting in ski chairs. He is fascinated with death and convinced that old age is something one should fight against.

Memory as an archive

Hugo Lamb finally manages to reconcile his fears of his own aging, with the help of the Anchorites.

> They cured me of a terrible wasting disease called mortality. There's a lot of it about. The young hold out for a time, but eventually even the hardiest patient gets reduced to a desiccated embryo, a Strudlebug . . . a veined, scrawny,

dribbling . . . bone clock, whose face betrays how very, very little time they have left. (516)

This statement joins the two central and recurring metaphors in the novel of the desiccated embryo and the bone clock that have the effect of associatively connecting disparate moments and, at the same time, highlighting the exaggeration and fear seeping through his words.

An Anchorite as described by one character "was a girl who lived like a hermit in a cell, but in the wall of a church. A living human sacrifice, in a way" (431). In the novel the Anchorites, as one of them claims, exist selfishly "to ensure the indefinite survival of the group by inducting its members into the Psychosoterica of the Shaded Way" (194). In contrast, the Horologists, whose name denotes the study and measurement of time or the making of clocks and watches, are tightly connected to time, its measurement, and different temporalities. They function as living archives by incorporating several disparate identities. As Joseph Metz contends, the Horologists "preserve the histories, memories, and identities of the various bodies they become or inhabit" (123).

Although memory and the archive are traditionally conceived of as quasi-opposites (see, for instance, Boulter), Mitchell's novel presents them as facilitating and complementing each other. Pierre Nora's definition of the archive sheds light on the interplay between the two, since he considers the archive to be the "storehouse of a material stock of what it would be impossible for us to remember" (13). However, the archives appearing in the novel go beyond the imagery of a storehouse, which would imply an outside, distant collection: they themselves function both as preservers and living entities taking part in the events, in the world that they inhabit. For the subject as archive Jonathan Boulter's consideration of Freud's and Derrida's theories provides a possible approach. The central notion of their theory is loss: a phenomenon inherent in the concept of the archive. Derrida recognizes, in Boulter's words, that the subject is "always already inhabited by its own loss" and thus it "becomes an archive, a site, where loss is maintained and nourished" (1). His recognition is crucial because it identifies the subject, the self, as the center bringing past, present, and future together, so the subject becomes the archive that preserves the event.

The notion of loss that Freud and Derrida recognize to be the central element of the archive points towards the inherent duality, possibly even the paradox of preservation and loss. A similar dynamic has been recognized between memory and forgetting by Paul Ricoeur: "forgetting is lamented in the same way as aging and death: it is one of the figures of the inevitable, the irremediable. And yet forgetting is bound up with memory" and it "can be so closely tied to memory that it can be considered one of the conditions for it" (426). I agree with Boulter's conclusion that the archive becomes the subject (5) and claim that this recognition provides a key to understanding how memory works in the novel. Boulter defines the subject "[a]s crypt, as archive ventrilocated by history, the subject begins to offer itself as a site to be heard, to be read, to be interpreted" (7). Holly Sykes is a representative of the dynamic relationship between remembrance and forgetting through her humanity, whereas the Horologists reconcile preservation and loss.

As opposed to the Anchorites, who are all for destruction and concerned with their own survival, the Horologists carry on numerous lives in themselves through time. Esther Little proves to be the richest identity-possessor of them all, having already lived through several millennia and having a name that brings together all her previous identities: "a sort of Bayeux Tapestry that bound myth with loves, births, deaths; hunts, battles, journeys; . . . and the names of every host within whose body Moombaki [her other name] had sojourned" (Mitchell 436). Harris remarks that "this passage has an epic quality; it links human lifetimes to cultural histories to geological eons" ("Fractal" 152). Esther embodies "collective memory" (Mitchell 433), which encompasses all previous selves. This may be interpreted as a direct reference to Halbwachs's theory of collective memory: "The collective memory, for its part, encompasses the individual memories while remaining distinct from them. It evolves according to its own laws, and any individual remembrances that may penetrate are transformed within a totality having no personal consciousness" (51). Esther, this age-old woman chooses the novel's protagonist, Holly Sykes, to ask for asylum, to shelter her for decades from the warring faction. Thus, by sheltering Esther inside herself, Holly also becomes an archivist of sorts.

The novel's third part ("The Wedding Bash") is narrated by Holly Sykes's partner, Ed Brubeck, a journalist documenting the Iraq war, who proves an archivist in his own right. His greatest goal in life is "to make a tiny dent in the world's memory" (208), an image that captures the traumatic nature of the *visible* war Brubeck has experienced and shown to the world. His narrative constantly changes between two contrastive stories of familial bliss and the war zone, or civilization and its collapse. He believes that "the survival of a narrative, a report, or an accounting of the past, no matter how minor, is essential to any chance for change in the future" (O'Donnell 168).

On the other side of the archivists are the writers, with Crispin Hershey as the narrator of "Crispin Hershey's Lonely Planet." His *Desiccated Embryos* gradually turns into an allegory that runs through the entire work, like a ghost which is constantly mentioned and hinted at but never explicitly represented. The title also serves as another metaphor for the "bone clocks," or the aging body in general.

Human lives, human fates follow each other through the decades witnessed and lived through by Holly Sykes, surrounded by atemporals for whom human life takes barely a second. Great emphasis is laid on these transient lives, and ultimately the novel evolves mainly around them rather than the fantasy subplot. Harris remarks that one function of the atemporals is to "provide a form of Anthropocene memory" ("Fractal" 152), preserving the lives of individuals over centuries and, in some cases, even millennia. Through this vast time, however, the seemingly minor events and moments are the ones that really shine through. The individuals themselves are those through whom the memories live on, and this is most pronounced when Holly reappears in the novel as an aging grandmother. When her granddaughter wishes her good-night saying "Sleep tight, Gran, don't let the bedbugs bite" (542), Holly realizes that these words have gone full circle throughout the generations, since she used to wish her daughter goodnight in the same way. Her conclusion is: "We live on, as long as there are people to live on in" (542).

Apocalypse and remembrance

Holly Sykes as a teenager tries to come to terms with life itself, with its transitoriness:

"What if . . . what if heaven *is* real, but only in moments?
Like a glass of water on a hot day when you're *dying* of
thirst, or when someone's nice to you for no reason, or . . . "
Mam's pancakes with Mars Bar sauce; Dad dashing up from
the bar just to tell me, "Sleep tight don't let the bedbugs bite"
. . . . "S'pose heaven's not like a painting that's just hanging
there forever, but more like . . . like the best song anyone ever
wrote, but a song you only catch in snatches, while you're
alive, from passing cars, or . . . upstairs windows when you're
lost . . . ." (34, compare 542)

These words coming from a very young person will guide her
through her entire life until finally much later she learns what
is really valuable and thus finds heaven not in an unattainable,
distant utopia, but in moments. This image of heaven contrasts
that of the Anchorites and most prominently of Hugo Lamb
himself. Both characters, Hugo and Holly, have been
approached by Imaculée Constantin, preying on human vanity
and fears. However, only Hugo, whose alter ego is named
Anyder ("the principal river on the island of Utopia" [194]),
joins the group. The heaven they project is utopian indeed: they
promise eternal beauty and youth, a life without aging, without
withering away.

These two contrastive images of heaven, represented by
Hugo and Holly, stand at the core of the two distinct fates of
the characters. In the war that is played out between the two
atemporal factions, with Holly in the center, a powerful Biblical
symbol, a golden apple, as the fruit from the Tree of Life, will
become the savior of Horology. This symbol reverses the
Biblical story of eternal damnation, since, contrary to the
consequences of eating the apple from the Garden of Eden,
this fruit brings victory to humans and further deepens the

FICTION

view that the bliss all the characters are looking for is ultimately to be found on earth, in their own selves.

Humanity is saved from the war of the atemporals. But what happens when the Earth seems to be on the brink of collapse? The last chapter, set in the year 2043, when Holly is 74 years old, presents a dystopian vision of our world—that of an imminent and unavoidable Apocalypse: a "present dwelling inside, rather than fearful anticipation of a potent new intimacy between people and their worlds" (Buell 265). As Elizabeth Callaway explains, the signs of the approaching "Endarkenment" (Mitchell 533) pervade the entire novel, starting from the first chapter, "A Hot Spell," whose title implies climate change and approaching disaster. As Holly's comments on humankind's responsibility for such climate change emphasize,

> It's grief for the regions we deadlanded, the ice caps we melted, the Gulf Stream we redirected, the rivers we drained, the coasts we flooded, the lakes we choked with crap, the seas we killed, the species we drove to extinction, the pollinators we wiped out, the oil we squandered, the drugs we rendered impotent, the comforting liars we voted into office—all so we didn't have to change our cozy lifestyles. (649-50)

These words, like the last chapter, bring a new focus in the novel. The book could have ended with "An Horologist's Labyrinth," with the story of the war fought between Horologists and Anchorites, but instead it suddenly shifts emphasis. The last part introduces a pastoral setting in Sheep's Head, Ireland, featuring some elderly women and children fighting for survival, struggling from one day to the next. To a certain extent this image eradicates the one of the supernatural war, which humanity never noticed and from which they had been saved by Holly Sykes.

An entirely human-made Apocalypse offers a third distinct approach to the issue of aging. Holly, now an old woman, faces a world that is also old, rapidly degrading, and dying. The Apocalypse presented through her is "quotidian and prosaic," existing "in the everyday" (Callaway 9). Contrary to the grandiosity of the atemporals' war, Endarkenment is never shown in large proportions, but always through day-to-day struggles of one elderly woman, her family, and friends. Ultimately everything boils down to memory being the greatest element of one's identity, one's life itself, and, furthermore, the possibility of life itself. As Aleida Assmann and Linda Shortt observe, "memory is not only susceptible to changes, it is itself *a powerful agent of change*" (4, emphasis in the original). Indeed, memory brings together the individual and the entire society, and, adversely, its lack, its disappearance signifies the end of civilization.

Forgetting has become one of the greatest diseases of the entire world and attendant to aging. When Holly fails to remember more and more details, she remarks: "at my age, it's like the beginning of a slow-motion death sentence. If you can't trust your mind anymore, you're mentally homeless" (572). Although one can sense resignation in these words, they express a certain degree of willingness to forget as well. As Holly explains it to her grandson, "Change is sort of hardwired into the world" (578), and, she realizes, even photographs, the objects meant to capture separate moments and to keep them fixed, change and fade (578). Photography theorist Damian Sutton claims that "life exists as absolute change, a duration defined only by the interaction of objects and perceptions," and the subject is meant to continuously strive for "making sense of experiences of the present, our memories of the past, and our awareness of the oncoming future. This situation is full of tumult and paradox, and perhaps this is why the photograph— with its own paradoxes—always seems to reflect it" (34). Thus, according to Sutton, the photograph is capable of mirroring this "absolute change"; its very existence is as a testament to the inherent paradox of duration and change.

The photograph has symbolic significance in the course of remembrance across Mitchell's novel. The photo of Holly's daughter, Aoife, and her husband functions as a remnant of their selves; however, it is shown as already in the process of fading, of withering away. Holly, upon realizing that it has become impossible for her to reprint it, since the computers barely function, concludes that "my feckless generation trusted our memories to the Net, so the '39 Crash was like a collective stroke" (548). This '39 Crash points towards a certain cyclicality in the novel's time conception, since it rhymes with the actual Wall Street Crash of 1929 that shook the entire world. Hence, there is a sense that decline is a returning motif, capturing at once the ephemerality of human fate and the eternity of humankind's struggles. Conversely, the literal fading of Aoife and Örvar's photograph is a palpable manifestation of the complexity of the mode in which the photograph captures time and the individual's relation to it.

"Civilisation's like the economy, or Tinkerbell: if people stop believing it's real, it dies," remarks Holly (572). In the final part of the novel, civilization collapses and death is everywhere. As Rose Harris-Birtill contends, "the mortals left behind are reduced to the 'bone clocks' of the book's title" (133), and the possibility of any sort of future seems scarce, with only Iceland as an exception. At the end Holly's two grandchildren are taken there, while she accepts her own doomed fate: "Incoming waves erase all traces of the vanishing boat, and I'm feeling erased myself, fading away into an invisible woman. For a voyage to begin, another one must end, sort of" (Mitchell 624).

Conclusion

Holly Sykes's concluding thought encompasses the philosophy underlying not only *The Bone Clocks*, but possibly all of Mitchell's oeuvre, since he is preoccupied with the constant war against aging, death, and oblivion. In his most famous novel to date, *Cloud Atlas*, souls wander, they live on, and they can easily travel through numerous generations, bodies, even ages. Whereas the thread is subtle in *Cloud Atlas*, the novel of six separate stories, six separate timelines and people, linked together through history and a birthmark, *The Bone Clocks* largely revolves around the intensifying complexity of the idea of living on. The characters capture different possibilities and aspects of this issue: the Horologists utilize the art of "psychosoterica," Ed Brubeck accomplishes it in war journalism, and Crispin Hershey does so through his novels. Beyond these archiving methods, however, Mitchell's novel concludes that one's life, one's soul is preserved in the memories of one's children and grandchildren.

Like Callaway, I contend, contrary to other interpretations, that the novel's final section remains the key to understanding the entire novel. As the thematic core of the novel, all the storylines circle around the issue of time: "How could you not be interested in time?" asks Mitchell. "It's like being a fish and not being interested in the sea. It's where we live. . . . We live in it. We live through it. It ages us. It changes us" (Naimon 48). Consequently, the novel becomes a work that "not only spans time but contemplates it" (48) and centers on both the individual and humanity facing Time. The last chapter reveals that the fantasy plot offers a distinct perspective upon one life, Holly Sykes's, coupled with envisioning the fate of a rapidly dissolving world. In contrast, Hugo Lamb's vision of life and aging is a nightmare from which he manages to awaken:

> Wrinkles spread like mildew over our peachy sheen; beat-by-beat-by-beat-by-beat-by-beat-by-beat, varicose veins worm through plucked calves; torsos and breasts fatten and sag; . . . DNA frays like wool, and down we tumble; a fall on the stairs, a heart attack, a stroke; not dancing but twitching. This is Club Walpurgis. They knew it in the Middle Ages. Life is a terminal illness. (167)

Through the novel, however, this image of the aging body is reversed as the reader traverses the intricate layers, timelines, and the characters' stories. Hugo and his quasi-immortal faction are defeated, and in the end it is Holly, a representative of the "bone clock," the mortal human being, who lives on in her grandchildren. Despite the apocalyptic vision of Endarkenment, there is still a remnant of hope materialized in the young generation that is taken to Iceland.

The separate levels and sub-worlds of *The Bone Clocks* alternately bring to the fore and conceal the novel's different emphases. It is ultimately a contemplation of time achieved not through the fantastic world of immortal beings, not through wars fought in Iraq or on a mountain in the Dusk Chapel of the Blind Cathar of the Thomasite Monastery of Sidelhorn Pass, but through one human life, that of Holly Sykes. This one particular life captured in all its intensity, with all its changes and transformations, points towards a possible new understanding of the process of aging and Time.

Works Cited

Assmann, Aleida, and Linda Shortt. *Memory and Political Change*. Basingstoke: Palgrave Macmillan, 2012.

Birren, J. E., and J. J. F. Schroots. "The History of Geropsychology." *Handbook of the Psychology of Aging.* 5th ed. Ed. J. E. Birren and K. W. Schaie. San Diego: Academic Press, 2001. 3-28.

Boulter, Jonathan. *Melancholy and the Archive: Trauma, Memory, and History in the Contemporary Novel.* London: Continuum, 2011.

Buell, Frederick. "Global Warming as Literary Narrative." *Philological Quarterly* 93 (2014): 261.

Callaway, Elizabeth. "Seeing What's Right in Front of Us: *The Bone Clocks*, Climate Change, and Human Attention." *Humanities* 7.11 (2018). Web. 20 June 2018.

Christ, Carol T. "Back to the Future." *The Hudson Review* (Spring 2015): 151-57.

Coupland, Douglas. "Convergences: 'Gods Without Men' by Hari Kunzru." *The New York Times* 8 March 2012. Web. 15 May 2018.

Dixon, Roger A. "Enduring Theoretical Themes in Psychological Aging: Derivation, Functions, Perspectives, and Opportunities." *Handbook of the Psychology of Aging.* 7th ed. Ed. K. Warner Schaie and Sherry L. Willis. Amsterdam: Elsevier, 2011. 3-24.

Halbwachs, Maurice. *The Collective Memory.* Trans. Francis J. Ditter, Jr. New York: Harper, 1980.

Harris-Birtill, Rose. "David Mitchell, *The Bone Clocks*." *Foundation: The International Review of Science Fiction* 44.1 (2015): 131-34.

Harris, Paul. "David Mitchell's Fractal Imagination: *The Bone Clocks*." *SubStance* 44.1 (2015): 148-53.

FICTION

---. "David Mitchell in the Laboratory of Time." *SubStance* 44.1 (2015): 8-17.

Iyer, Pico. "Juggling Worlds." *The New York Times* 28 Aug. 2014. Web. 1 June 2018.

Metz, Joseph. "Genre Beside Itself: David Mitchell's *The Bone Clocks*, Pulp Intrusions, and the Cosmic Historians' War." *Critique: Studies in Contemporary Fiction* 58.2 (2017): 121-28.

Mitchell, David. *The Bone Clocks*. London: Sceptre, 2014.

---. *The Cloud Atlas*. London: Sceptre, 2004.

Morgan, Glyn. "War in Pieces: Violence and Conflict in David Mitchell's *The Bone Clocks*." *Los Angeles Review of Books*. 2015. Web. 1 June 2018.

Naimon, David. "A Conversation with David Mitchell." *The Missouri Review* 38.2 (2015): 46-60.

Nora, Pierre. "Between Memory and History: Les Lieux de Mémoire." *Representations* 26. Special Issue: *Memory and Counter-Memory* (Spring 1989): 7-24.

O'Donnell, Patrick. *A Temporary Future: The Fiction of David Mitchell*. New York: Bloomsbury, 2015.

Ott, Bill. "Translit: New Genre Cükollapses Time and Space." *American Libraries* 28 March 2012. Web. 2 June 2018.

Ricoeur, Paul. *Memory, History, Forgetting*. Trans. Kathleen Blamey and David Pellauer. Chicago: The University of Chicago Press, 2004.

Sutton, Damian. *Photography, Cinema, Memory: The Crystal Image of Time*. Minnesota: University of Minnesota Press, 2009.

10.2478/9788367405423-015

Coda

"Who are you?" Notes on Aging and Dementia in Frank McGuinness's *The Visiting Hour* (2020)
Donald E. Morse

The Irish playwright, poet, and novelist Frank McGuinness has throughout his career created memorable elderly characters in his many plays beginning in 1985 with the monologue of the titular character in *Baglady* and then in the same year and most memorably with Piper, the only surviving member of his regiment at the Battle of the Somme in *Observe the Sons of Ulster Marching Towards the Somme*. The memories of each of them provide the substance of these plays as each tries to understand exactly what happened in the past and how it led to their present condition. After a gap of about fifteen years, McGuinness created a very different elderly person, Rima, the iron-willed matriarch of *Dolly West's Kitchen* (1999), who manages to keep household and family together and at peace through her forceful presence and strong will during "The Emergency," as neutral Ireland styled the time during World War II. With the ending of the war the lasting and far-reaching consequences of both Rima's death and the terrible toll the war takes lead inevitably to the breaking-up of her household and the beginning of new postwar lives.

In *Gates of Gold* (2002), McGuinness shifted his focus away from the power and value of the elderly to their frailty as he chronicles the last days of Micheál Mac Liammóir, who with his lifetime partner, Hilton Edwards, co-founded the Gate Theatre in 1928. The play is comic and sad by turns, filled with arguments and verbal barbs, sharp-etched dialogue and its opposite—whining. Like *Dolly West's Kitchen* it, too, resolves into a peaceful final scene of reconciliation and love with a harsh overtone of finality. This last scene of a final meal around the kitchen's table in *Dolly West's Kitchen* represents the brief calm before the family breaks apart with each sibling leaving to travel in radically different directions. In *Gates of Gold*, the final calm is not a communal meal but the lovers' final goodbye kiss before Micheál dies. However, neither the fracturing of a family nor the death of a loved one will become McGuinness's final word on the elderly. In 2015 he wrote an opera libretto for Sophocles's Theban plays—plays that he had previously translated. The complete Oedipus cycle contains one of the greatest portraits of the transformative possibilities life offers the elderly even when everything appears to have been well lost. Oedipus violates some of the deepest, most basic human relationships when he commits both parricide and incest and is justifiably ostracized from the human community condemned to wander for the rest of his life. Yet, even after these most extreme of human crimes, Sophocles dares to suggest that in the direst human violations of taboos there still remains a possibility of redemption over time. In McGuinness's opera libretto, as in Sophocles' play, Oedipus after a long travail, now old and weary of wandering, becomes in his last living moments transformed from a pariah outcast from all human society to a possible source of good fortune for the city where he will die. Summoned by Zeus he proceeds mysteriously to the underworld.

In the same decade, McGuinness also wrote two plays on dementia in the elderly, *The Hanging Gardens* (2013) and *The Visiting Hour* (2020)—a new subject for him that did not appear to offer any hope of transformation or redemption but only additional changes for the worst. *The Hanging Gardens* centers on the process a person goes through in descending into dementia, which becomes even more complicated in the play because of happening within a dysfunctional family. Sam Grant, an aging novelist, husband, and father, exhibits signs of a serious all-consuming dementia, and these signs increase incrementally throughout the play beginning with a mildly comic opening scene where Sam goes out into a rain storm in his pyjamas. As the play progresses, he will invent a fantasy child for his wife Jane, refuse to abandon his erroneous belief that his wife was a hairdresser, and, worse, violently punch her. Unable now to tell fact from fiction he, most significantly for a writer, forgets the meaning of words and finally is cast adrift without the power to speak, thus losing all language. By destroying memory Sam's dementia leads to his forgetting his past and his replacing of real memories with false ones. The rest of the family—his long-suffering wife and three adult children—are pictured as ill-equipped emotionally, mentally, and even physically to cope with their demented husband/father. This family has in effect trapped itself and each of them through a series of earlier choices that has left each individual isolated and unable to join forces with the others. At the center of their plight sits the figure of the ruined husband/father as beautifully staged in the Abbey Theatre production with Sam Grant as played by Noel Buggy seated, immobile, silent in center stage attempting unsuccessfully again and again to rise out of his chair.

The Visiting Hour

If the future of Jane and the three adult children is uniformly bleak in *The Hanging Gardens*, so is the present and any future together or apart for Father and Daughter in McGuinness's *The Visiting Hour*. Designating the characters by

CODA

their role in the family and with each other serves to emphasize the extreme nature of Father's dementia, since of all his memories and relationships of and with his daughter along with those of his late wife are the whatever should survive the longest as his brain deteriorates. Yet, all the conversations between the father and his daughter on whatever subject are at best opaque and each raises questions about what if any topic introduced by Father or even which of his verbal phrases might refer to a real event or an actual past conversation and which ones must be imaginary. His conversation with his daughter is, therefore, a mixture of truth and fantasy, of fact and blatant fiction, which is impossible for an audience to sort out having been dropped into the middle of this ongoing conversation as the curtain goes up. This dramatic situation places an audience in the position of a person visiting someone with dementia and trying to converse with them where the tendency of most such visitors will be to try and separate fact from fiction, truth from fantasy.

We in the audience simply do not know what is going on, or whom we should believe. Father? Daughter? Both? Neither? This uncertainty dominates the staging of the play where Father and Daughter are separated by the window in his nursing home room since the home does not permit visitors to hold a face-to-face meeting with a patient during the COVID19 pandemic. Instead, visitors must converse with the patient only through the glass of the window between them. This arrangement, thanks to the brilliant lighting effects of Paul Koegan on the set devised by Katie Davenport, sometimes produces the illusion of both Father and Daughter appearing as if sitting side by side, a visual image that reflects their conversation that occasionally produces the illusion of their communicating with one another.

The bleak reality, however, continues to be that of the isolated patient looking out from their bedroom window while the once-a-week visitor remains looking into the bedroom through the glass barrier from the outside as "through a glass darkly." This illusion of physical closeness proves more like one of their conversations that appears at first to focus on events that actually occurred but becomes almost impossible to follow and eventually will prove false, as in Father's repeated references to the Eurovision contest where, he claims, he came in second. The daughter's conversational asides tell us that her father's talk about his brother, like his claiming to have come in second in a Eurovision Contest or that he has lost to his arch-rival, Luxemburg, are all simply delusions. These are the false memories that dementia has created and that tragically have taken the place of his real but now lost memories. With dementia the naturally shifting memories become a museum of chimerical forms that shape-shift and/or disappear to be replaced by other false but equally shape-shifting forms.

All indications are that Father returns to and endlessly repeats various false memories during each of Daughter's visits—as will be typical of any dementia patient. A few of these repeated sequences lead to a genuine, although not a verbal rapport between father and daughter, such as in this exchange:

FATHER.   The Song Contest?
DAUGHTER. The Eurovision—got it in one, Father.
FATHER.   Was that the year I won or lost? *Silence.*
                      Maybe I came second, as usual.
DAUGHTER. Pipped at the post.
FATHER.   Gracious in defeat, I hope.
DAUGHTER. Impeccable behaviour, as always.

CODA

Father and Daughter sing from 'Are You Sure' by The
Allisons
Silence. (13)

While the father's entering the Eurovision Contest is not a real
memory but a false one to which he clings tenaciously and the
sequence must have been heard by the daughter again and again
as she visits him, the song he sings with her, "Are You Sure?"
has to be based on their singing it together probably many
times over many years and long before dementia set in—a
memory so strong that it has survived even among all the new
false ones.

It is a commonplace among psychologists and speech
therapists that spoken and sung memories and abilities, because
they are located in different parts of the brain, are, thereby,
separated from one another. Thus stutterers, for instance, can
often sing without becoming "stuck" on a particular sound, and
people suffering from a loss of memory can still recall songs
they used to sing. Here, father and daughter sing together
without difficulty or conflict. The singing is harmonious unlike
their conversation, which often reflects their frustration arising
from their inability to connect with one another and where
Daughter must either deal with or ignore the demented father's
fictitious slights and hurts, false memories and insults, and,
perhaps worst of all, his aggressive behavior and his refusal to
acknowledge their relationship or to identify her as his
daughter: "Who are you?" he asks. "Are you your sister?" (17).
On the face of it this is a blatantly absurd question, but
nevertheless one that is typical of those with dementia.
Daughter we learn has no sister as he has no brother despite
the father's assertions that each of them has such a sibling. His
question "Who are you?" is perhaps one of the most hurtful, if

frequently asked, questions a person in the grips of dementia will pose to a loved one who that demented person has failed to recognize.

Being Irish both Father and Daughter have been raised to have a song with which they identify and which identifies them. Such songs were taken for granted in families and communities as James Joyce demonstrates at the beginning of *A Portrait of the Artist as a Young Man*, where he has Stephen as an infant claim a song as his own:

> O, the wild rose blossoms
> On the little green place.
> He sang that song. "That was *his song*."
> (Joyce 176, emphasis added)

On informal as well as formal social occasions a person known to have a particular song could be often asked in company to sing it. One of the measures of how deeply Sam Grant has plunged into dementia in *The Hanging Gardens* is his inability to recognize his wife, Jane's mother's song, "The Moon Behind the Hills," which he must have heard dozens of times. Similarly, one of the measures of just how much of Father's memory has been erased by dementia in *The Visiting Hour* is revealed in his singing not his song but his daughter's song, which she rightfully views as betrayal. "Theft that's what I'd call it. Thieving, if you prefer" (25). While the father may be technically correct that the daughter is over-dramatizing this incident, it nevertheless reveals how fragile the daughter has become over the years in dealing with his ever-encroaching dementia so that this new false memory of "his" song tips the scales for her during this visit. The situation finally stabilizes only when they replay one of their "routines" from her childhood that proves to be a series of "knock knock" jokes (28),

CODA

which lead in turn to the more elaborate Easter bunny routine,
which surprisingly ends on a doubly serious note:

> FATHER. Why are we playing knock-knock at this
> stage of our lives? Is something wrong
> with us?
> DAUGHTER. Something wrong.
> FATHER. Something wrong in my head.
> DAUGHTER. Knock-knock.
> FATHER. Who's there?
> DAUGHTER. Me. I am. That's who.
> FATHER. Glad to hear it. Glad to see you. Are you
> glad to see me?
> DAUGHTER. Yes.
> FATHER. And I you.
> DAUGHTER. Who am I?
> *Silence.* (27)

The father, being baffled by her identity towards the end of her
visit, is not able to answer the daughter's seemingly simple
question "Who am I?" The momentary glimpse of the truth by
the father in "[s]omething wrong in my head" and his "[g]lad
to see you" to his daughter go as quickly as they have come to
be replaced by the omnipresent stage direction of *"Silence."*

The Visiting Hour's stage direction of *Silence* occurs over
fifty times in this 90-minute play (on average less than two
minutes elapses between one *Silence* and another *Silence*). As the
visiting hour draws to a close in the play, the silences become
more and more frequent until they come to dominate the
dialogue rather than the scraps of conversation. Such
omnipresent gaps in their verbal exchange reveal just how deep
into dementia the father has sunk and how terribly frustrating
this visit is for his daughter. She realizes that the visiting hour

tires him out but she, too, is tired and emotionally exhausted as the father asks that most terrible question of all, one that relatives of a demented person dread to hear but will hear with variations many times over, "Who are you?" and its sequel, "Are we related?" At the end of this sequence, it is also a song that brings them briefly back together. In this case the song is special because it was the mother's song, "The Waxies' Dargle." Although the father no longer remembers that he had a wife, he does recall her song and how improbable it was for her to sing it (37–39). But such recognition is fleeting at best. The distance between father and daughter widens as he returns to his false memories culminating in his singing alone "Give Me the Moonlight"—a song they never sang together and which is part of what is most probably a false memory of his being a professional singer. The two of them along with the audience are back to square one with all the uncertainty and frustration of the father having no definite clear memory of who the daughter is and what their relationship is or has been. He is now almost completely in his private world of false memories and so remains unresponsive to her last questions as well as to her offers of a football jersey or of her willingness to ask an attendant to explain why he cannot go out and so forth. Everything is now met by his *"Silence,"* including her departure.

But McGuinness does not end *The Visiting Hour* with this bleak assessment, nor does he end the play with some extraordinary event such as Oedipus's transformation in *Oedipus at Colonus*. Despite all the frustration, pain, and non-communication, Daughter will return in a week's time for her weekly visiting hour with her father. While the situation is serious, extremely frustrating, and often dire, she nevertheless accepts that this is what remains of their relationship of which

CODA

she has no intention of letting go but continues to value highly
at least in part because of her memories of their earlier loving
relationship before dementia began to destroy it. She recalls
how "[y]ou used to swing me on our garden gate. In and out,
in and out—out and in, me, on top of the gate, safe because I
was in your arms, my father's big, strong arms" (32). Although
her father does not share this beautiful memory, she clings to it
and quite possibly it lies behind her last words as she walks
away to go home, "So be it" (48). After Daughter leaves, Father
now worn out by the visiting hour and reduced to isolated
individual words nevertheless also echoes the phrase, "so be it,"
as he, too, most probably unconsciously (as he obviously
appears incapable of clear thinking or speaking at this point),
at some level affirms his and their situation and relationship
with his own "[s]o be it" (48). "So be it" is the Irish-English
translation of "amen," and, as used here and elsewhere in
McGuinness's oeuvre, it conveys a sense of acceptance of the
given situation and/or person. These words, as Hiroko Mikami
points out, are often said by characters in McGuinness's plays
including Baglady, Mary and Lizzie Burns, Peer Gynt, and by
Rosmer and Rebekka among others (160).

The importance of memory for the elderly is almost
universally acknowledged and has received careful delineation
by McGuinness in many of his plays: preeminent are *Baglady*,
Observe the Sons of Ulster, *Gates of Gold*, and the various
versions of the Oedipus myths culminating in his libretto for
Thebans. The loss of memory and its intimate relation to a
person's identity becomes a crucial part in *The Hanging Gardens*
as Sam Grant loses his identity as novelist and fiction writer,
husband and father, leaving him in wordless silence. In *The
Visiting Hour*, a similar loss has now been replaced by Father's
false memories, which threaten not only his identity but also

the daughter's, for if the father no longer recognizes his daughter, it is doubtful that she alone could sustain their relationship. As the number and size of their common memories shrink, the issue becomes not how they will, but how they *can* relate to one another at all.

Most people who suffer from dementia become notoriously self-centered, as vividly pictured in *The Visiting Hour*. This condition often arises from their being lost without any clear line of demarcation between their history with its true memories of events and people and those fantasies induced by the dementia. The demented thus lose the ability to separate fact from fiction as well as their ability to take care of themselves. Father in *The Visiting Hour* is clearly at this stage and must, therefore, be confined to a nursing home because no matter how much Daughter might wish to care for him she could not possibly manage to do so. Similarly, Sam Grant in *The Hanging Gardens*, having been enveloped by deep dementia, will from now on require professional help. Neither of McGuinness's plays holds out any real hope for resolution of either the unprepared and ill-equipped Grant family facing the insoluble dilemma of Sam's descent into black silence in *The Hanging Gardens* or of Daughter breaking through the false memories and rising incoherence of her father in *The Visiting Hour*.

Both plays also display some of the consequences of the current phenomenon of an aging Irish society, where "the number of older people aged 65 and older is expected to double . . . to over one million in 2031" (bluebirdcare.ie)—less than a decade from now. That million represents the cohort most susceptible to dementia and within it the number of the elderly actually afflicted with dementia is expected to treble to about 45,000 by 2041 (bluebirdcare.ie). Moreover, *The Visiting Hour* mirrors not just the Irish nation but also the world in the throes of a pandemic. For weeks before the time of the play, no visitors had been allowed to enter the nursing home and in the dramatic time of the play itself all visitors must remain outside, like the Daughter sitting on the bench opposite her father's window, nor are they allowed to be in physical proximity to any patient. Throughout the play visitors and patients are reminded several times during their visit through annoying announcements given over a loudspeaker system that their visit must not go beyond their allotted one hour per week. McGuinness wrote *The Visiting Hour* while Ireland was in lockdown to fight and hopefully stop the spread of COVID19. As the restrictions eased slightly the play went into rehearsal and was produced when all Irish theatres were still closed and live audiences were forbidden, and therefore the premiere had to be streamed. All of which creates a situation for visitors in the play not unlike that which most people experienced during the Irish lockdown where social distancing, surgical masks and isolation combined to stem the first wave of COVID19 at the price of atomizing society and eliminating most social occasions.

The Irish theatre has long been known for its dramatization of social issues confronting the Irish people so much so that the eminent Irish theatre scholar Christopher Murray devoted a whole critical book to showing how that theatre has been holding "a mirror up to nation." In the twentieth and twenty-first centuries the mirror, as held up by Frank McGuinness, has begun to reflect the social and political reality of an aging Irish nation from the 1980s to the present, especially the most recent plays. The result, as Andy Murray perceptively saw is that both Sam Grant in *Gardens* and the Father in *Hour* have lost their "capacity for telling stories." The stories that they tell may or may not be theirs for this "capacity" "is now suddenly out of control. In a very terrifying way, the boundaries between fact and fiction are extremely blurred" (Andy Murray). Those plays, in particular the timely and beautifully crafted *The Hanging Gardens* and *The Visiting Hour* do indeed hold a "mirror up to nation," an Irish nation that is visibly aging and increasingly afflicted with dementia in its many forms. We may hope that that Irish nation heeds the warning.

Works Cited

"Dementia Cases Set to Treble by 2041." *Bluebird Care.* Web. 25 Feb. 2020.

Joyce, James. *A Portrait of the Artist as a Young Man. The Essential James Joyce.* Ed. Harry Levin. 1948. Frogmore, Herts: Triad/Panther, 1977. 175-365.

McGuinness, Frank. *The Hanging Gardens.* London: Faber, 2013.

---. *Thebans: Opera in Three Acts.* London: Faber, 2014.

---. *The Visiting Hour.* London: Faber, 2021.

Mikami, Hiroko. *Frank McGuinness and His Theatre of Paradox.* Gerrards Cross: Colin Smythe, 2002.

Murray, Andy. "A Novel Idea for Veteran Playwright McGuinness." *Irish Examiner* 22 Oct. 2013. Web. 3 Jan. 2022.

Murray, Christopher. *Twentieth-Century Irish Drama: Mirror up to Nation.* Manchester: Manchester University Press, 1997.

10.2478/9788367405423-016

Notes on contributors

Maha Alatawi, assistant professor at Prince Sattam bin Abdulaziz University in Saudi Arabia, finished her Ph.D. in drama studies at University College Dublin, Ireland, where she also worked as a tutor. Her broad research interests are in Irish theatre, narrative theory, music and space in drama, and lately in topics on medical humanities focusing on illness and ill characters in Irish drama. She has two book articles published in *The Palgrave Handbook of Contemporary Irish Theatre and Performance* and *The Theatre and Films of Conor McPherson: Conspicuous Communities*, as well as an essay in *The Harold Pinter Review* with other journal articles accepted for publication later. She presented papers at conferences in Dublin, Galway, Madrid, London, and New York and won the award for best paper/best presentation at the International Conference in Literature and Culture, Madrid.

Noémi Albert, lecturer at the University of Pécs, earned her BA from Babeş-Bolyai University, Cluj-Napoca, Romania in 2013 and her MA and Ph.D. from the University of Pécs in 2015 and 2021, respectively. She participated in several conferences in Hungary, Spain, Romania, Croatia, Poland, and the Czech Republic. Albert published reviews, translations and scholarly papers in conference proceedings and distinguished Hungarian and international journals. She is a member of the Narratives of Culture and Identity Research Group and was the recipient of various research grants (such as Campus Mundi, Erasmus+, and ÚNKP), which allowed her to conduct research in Vienna, London, St Andrews (Scotland), and Beersheva (Israel). Currently, she is working with contemporary British novels, investigating them from the joint perspectives of spatial and memory studies.

Csilla Bertha, University of Debrecen, Hungary, is a member of the International Advisory Board of *Irish University Review*, the Editorial Board of *Hungarian Journal of English and American Studies*, a founding director of Centre for the International Study of Literatures in English, honorary chair of the Hungarian Yeats Society, has published widely in English and Hungarian on Irish drama and theatre (with particular attention to Brian Friel and Tom Murphy), interart relations, memory and sites of memory, and parallels between Irish and Hungarian literature. Her *A drámaíró Yeats* [Yeats the Playwright] (1988), was the first scholarly work on Yeats's drama published in Hungary. The volumes she co-authored and co-edited include *More Real than Reality* (1991), *The Celebration of the Fantastic* (1992), *A Small Nation's Contribution to the World* (1993), *Worlds Visible and Invisible* (1994), *Brian Friel's Dramatic Artistry* (Carysfort 2006), and several special thematic journal issues of *HJEAS* and *IUR*. She edited *Homeland in the Heights*, an anthology of modern Hungarian poetry in English translation, with Donald E. Morse co-translated Transylvanian-Hungarian plays, a volume of which, *Silenced Voices*, was published by Carysfort, Dublin in 2008. Her latest editions of Hungarian literature in English include the anthologies *Down Fell the Statue of Goliath* (2017) and *A Nation Dismembered* (2020).

David Clare, lecturer in Drama and Theatre Studies at Mary Immaculate College, University of Limerick, does research in Irish drama. His books include the monographs *Irish Anglican Literature and Drama* (Palgrave Macmillan, 2021), *Bernard*

NOTES ON CONTRIBUTORS

Shaw's Irish Outlook (Palgrave Macmillan, 2016), and the edited collections *The Golden Thread: Irish Women Playwrights, 1716-2016* (2 volumes, Liverpool University Press, 2021) and *The Gate Theatre, Dublin: Inspiration and Craft* (Carysfort/Peter Lang, 2018). He previously held two Irish Research Council-funded postdoctoral fellowships at the National University of Ireland, Galway and he is curator of the IRC-funded www.ClassicIrishPlays.com database. Dr. Clare has previously published essays on Brian Friel and Martin McDonagh in the *Irish University Review, Studies in Burke and His Time*, and *Emerging Perspectives*.

Réka M. Cristian, associate professor of American Studies, chair of the American Studies Department, Institute of English and American Studies, University of Szeged, is co-chair and founding member of the Inter-American Research Center at the same university. She is the author of *Cultural Vistas and Sites of Identity: Literature, Film and American Studies* (2011) and co-author with Zoltán Dragon of *Encounters of the Filmic Kind: Guidebook to Film Theories* (2008). She is founding editor and editor-in-chief of *AMERICANA E-Journal of American Studies in Hungary*, as well as its e-book division, *AMERICANA eBooks*. Her research areas include modern American literature, with special regard to American drama, American modernism, theories of American Studies, film theory and the American film, and cross-cultural exchanges of the Americas in American literature and film.

Kevin De Ornellas, lecturer of English Drama at Ulster University, is the author of *The Horse in Early Modern English Culture* (Fairleigh Dickinson University Press, 2014), the author of *Focus on "The Wesker Trilogy"* (Greenwich Exchange

Press, 2020), and the co-editor of the two-volume *Companion to Contemporary British and Irish Literature* (Wiley-Blackwell, 2020). His book *Beginning Modern Drama* will be published in 2024 (Manchester University Press), as will his co-edited essay collection on *Literary Evaluation* (Wiley-Blackwell) and his edition of *Eglantine* by Charlotte Nooth (Routledge). He has published refereed research essays in journals such as *Shakespeare, The Journal of Popular Television*, and *The Glencree Journal*. He has published over a dozen peer-reviewed essays in books about drama and culture and has published dozens of book reviews, a dozen play and exhibition reviews, hundreds of encyclopedia articles and has delivered a hundred conference papers. He serves on the Management Committee of the Riverside Theatre, Coleraine.

Kinga Földváry, associate professor at the Institute of English and American Studies at Pázmány Péter Catholic University, Hungary, has several research interests which include problems of genre in film adaptations of Shakespeare's plays, twentieth- and twenty-first century British literature, and theories of visual and popular culture. She is the author of *Cowboy Hamlets and Zombie Romeos: Shakespeare in Genre Film* (Manchester University Press, 2020).

Eamonn Jordan, professor in Drama Studies at the School of English, Drama and Film, University College Dublin, has published several books in the field of Irish theatre, including *The Feast of Famine: The Plays of Frank McGuinness* (1997), *Dissident Dramaturgies: Contemporary Irish Theatre* (2010), *From Leenane to LA: The Theatre and Cinema of Martin McDonagh* (2014), *The Theatre and Films of Conor McPherson: Conspicuous*

NOTES ON CONTRIBUTORS

Communities (2019), and *Justice in the Plays and Films of Martin McDonagh* (2019).

Mária Kurdi is professor emerita in the Institute of English Studies, University of Pécs, Hungary. Her main research fields are modern Irish literature, English-speaking drama, and comparative studies. Her books include *Representations of Gender and Female Subjectivity in Contemporary Irish Drama by Women* (Edwin Mellen, 2010), *Approaches to Irish Theatre through a Hungarian's Lens* (University of Pécs, 2018), and a monograph on J. M. Synge in Hungarian (Kronosz Kiadó, 2021). The volumes she edited include *Literary and Cultural Relations: Ireland, Hungary, and Central and Eastern Europe* and *Radical Contemporary Theatre Practices by Women in Ireland* (co-edited with Miriam Haughton), both published by Carysfort in 2009 and 2015, respectively. In 2022 *The Theatre of Deirdre Kinahan*, co-edited by Mária Kurdi and Lisa Fitzpatrick, was published by Peter Lang. Mária Kurdi is the author of numerous articles in English and Hungarian journals as well as in essay collections.

Dónall Mac Cathmhaoill, writer, director, and academic from Ireland, currently lectures in Creative Writing at The Open University. His Ph.D. from Ulster University examines modes of authorship in theatre for social and political advocacy. His research interests are in authorship and structures of production in theatre for social change, theatre in post-conflict societies, and LGBTQ+ theatre and identity politics in Irish theatre. He has published articles in the *Glencree Journal* on theatre for reconciliation and in the performing arts journal *Platform* on presenting trans stories in theatre. Upcoming publications include a book chapter on ethics and aesthetics in community theatre and a monograph on advocacy in post-conflict Irish theatre. His playwriting includes six plays and a classic serial for BBC Radio 4, television commissions for BBC Drama and BBC Education, and various theatre works. He was director of Irish theatre company Tinderbox in Belfast and a producer and head of education at Soho Theatre in London. Other major companies he has worked with include Bruised Sky, London; 7:84 Theatre Company, Scotland; Jagriti Theatre in Bengaluru, India; Kisi, Reykjavik; and the Irish-language company Aisling Ghéar.

Donald E. Morse, honorary professor at the University of Debrecen and emeritus professor at Oakland University, has been four times Fulbright Senior Lecturer, twice Soros Professor, and once a Rockefeller Study Fellow. He has edited or co-edited books including *The Irish Theatre in Transition*, *More Real than Reality: The Irish Fantastic* with Csilla Bertha, *A Small Nation's Contribution to the World* with Bertha and István Pálffy, and *The Dramatic Artistry of Brian Friel* with Bertha and Mária Kurdi. His monographs include *The Novels of Kurt Vonnegut* and *The Mythic Fantasy of Robert Holdstock*. His latest book, *It's Time: A Mosaic of What It Is like to Live in Time*, appeared in 2022. He translated and published several Hungarian plays with Csilla Bertha, including *Silenced Voices: Hungarian Plays from Transylvania*. He lectured widely in Europe, the US, and Asia, chaired the annual International Conference on the Fantastic in the Arts for thirty-five years, hosted Bloomsday in Detroit for twenty-five years, has edited the *Hungarian Journal of English and American Studies* since 2007, and is the chief editor of the new HJEAS Books series from Debrecen University Press.

NOTES ON CONTRIBUTORS

Christopher Murray, professor emeritus in the School of English, Drama, and Film at University College Dublin, where he taught for thirty-six years, is a former editor of *Irish University Review*. He has written extensively on Irish theatre and drama. Among his books are *Twentieth-Century Irish Drama: Mirror up to Nation* (Manchester University Press, 1997), *Seán O'Casey: Writer at Work, A Biography* (Gill and Macmillan, 2004), and *The Theatre of Brian Friel* (Bloomsbury, 2014). For Beckett's centenary he edited *Samuel Beckett: 100 Years, Centenary Essays* (New Island, 2006). In succession to Joe Dowling, he was chair of the management board of the Gaiety School of Acting (Dublin) 2010-17.

Angelika Reichmann, professor of English Literature at Eszterházy Károly Catholic University, is the author of *Desire—Identity—Narrative: Dostoevsky's* Devils *in English Modernism* (2012) and has published widely on English and Russian modernist rewrites of Dostoevsky's classic novel, on Andrey Bely, Joseph Conrad, Aldous Huxley, and John Cowper Powys, among others. Her most recent articles focus on J. M. Coetzee and Dostoevsky. Her chief academic interests also include adaptation theory, psychoanalytic literary criticism, and the female Gothic. She is a member of the Translation Studies Research Group at Eszterházy University and co-editor of the *Eger Journal of English Studies*, as well as the volume on the Victorian and Modernist periods in the Hungarian series of English literary history published in 2022. She has been the secretary of the Hungarian Society for the Study of English since 2015.

Ambika Singh, academic and independent researcher, is based in Rajasthan, India. Singh's research interests include

American theatre, feminism, race studies, trauma, and critical gerontology. Her essays have been published in the *Arthur Miller Journal* and in the *Hungarian Journal of English and American Studies*. She recently edited the Methuen Drama Student Edition of Arthur Miller's *Broken Glass*, published by Bloomsbury Publishing, United Kingdom. She has also been involved in content management at educational institutes and book companies.

Giovanna Tallone, independent scholar, graduated in Modern Languages at Università Cattolica, Milan, holds a Ph.D. in English Studies from the University of Florence. Her research interests include Irish women writers, contemporary Irish drama, and the remakes of Old Irish legends. She has published essays and critical reviews on Éilís Ní Dhuibhne, Mary Lavin, Mary O'Donnell, Clare Boylan, Lady Gregory, Brian Friel, Vincent Woods, and James Stephens. Her articles and chapters have appeared in various international journals and collections, including *ABEI Journal, Estudios Irlandeses*, and *Hungarian Journal of English and American Studies*. She is a member of the editorial board and a reviewer of *Studi Irlandesi: A Journal of Irish Studies*.

10.2478/9788367405423-017

Index

INDEX

INDEX

INDEX